WHAT ARE STOCKS REALLY WORTH?
THE SMARTVALUE FORMULA FOR BUYING LOW AND SELLING HIGH

by John B. Malloy

Published by:

ANALYTICAL BOOKS
P. O. Box 345, East Dennis, MA 02641

10 9 8 7 6 5 4 3 2 1

Printed in the United States of America

Publishers Cataloging-in-Publication Data
Malloy, John B.
What are stocks really worth?: the SmartValue formula for buying low and selling high /
John B. Malloy
  p. cm.
Includes index.
ISBN: 0-9664208-0-2
1. Stocks valuation
I. Title
HG4661.M35 1998
332.632 2   Library of Congress Catalog Card Number: 98-96295

Dedication

To my father and mother, Jack and Clara Malloy.
I am forever in their debt.

Acknowledgement

A hearty "Thank you!" to Dick Adami, Bob Burger, and Joy Van Buskirk, who played the role of an average reader using this book to learn how to value stocks. They reviewed early drafts over many cups of coffee and muffins, and identified those places where the going was difficult. Readers owe them a debt of gratitude.

Thanks also to Value Line Publishing Inc. for permission to reproduce the Value Line sheets for Cisco Systems, Coca-Cola, and Microsoft.

Contents

Contents

Contents

Contents

16. What Is Microsoft Worth? (Cont'd)

17. When Do I Sell? 227

18. Risk 241

List of Illustrations

List of Illustrations (Cont'd)

List of Tables

List of Tables (Cont'd)

Disclaimer

This book provides accurate and authoritative procedures for finding what stocks are worth. While the formulas in this book are reliable, the results they yield depend on forecasts of a firm's future performance and on the individual investor's financial situation. This book is not intended as investment advice. The forecasts of how Coca-Cola, Cisco Systems, and Microsoft might perform in the future, while reasonable, are only examples to illustrate how to apply the procedures in this book. The illustrations of how to find what these stocks are worth are not a recommendation to buy, not buy, sell, or hold those stocks. They are only examples of how one investor might apply the SmartValue formulas to find what those stocks are worth. Readers must make their own forecasts before deciding whether these stocks are attractive or not.

Readers should recognize that they will find different values for these stocks if they make more optimistic or more pessimisitc forecasts of how those firms will perform in the future. They will also find different values for these stocks if their individual financial situation differs from the examples in this book.

If you do not wish to be bound by this disclaimer, you may return the book to the publisher for a full refund.

Preface

The stock market is booming as this is written. The S&P 500 Stock Index has grown steadily at 21 percent per year for the past three years. At the same time, however, GDP measured in dollars not adjusted for inflation has grown only 5 percent per year. How can this be? How can the stock market grow 21 percent per year in an economy that is only growing 5 percent per year?

The short answer is that it can't. At least, not for long. Investors are being swept along in the euphoria about stocks. They are pushing prices through the roof. Investors seem to believe the market will go up tomorrow just because it went up today. If investors had a way to tell what stocks were really worth, they would not be so anxious to buy at today's high prices. They might even decide that now is the time to sell rather than to buy.

Investors need a way to find what stocks are really worth. The longer the present boom continues, the more urgent is their need. That is what this book is for. To help investors make intelligent investment decisions. To help them avoid paying too much for stocks. I hope this book satisifes those needs, and that investors find it an indispensable tool for guiding their investment decisions.

John B. Malloy
South Dennis, Massachusetts
February 26, 1998

Chapter 1

The Investor's Dilemma

SmartValue

Credentials

What's Ahead

How to Use This Book

"**Buy low, sell high!**" That is the classic advice for investors. It is the Golden Rule of investing. Buy a stock when its price is low. Hold on to the stock while the firm grows and the price of the stock rises. Then sell the stock at a high price. What could be easier? How can you go wrong? You are on the road to riches, right? Whoa! Not so fast! There is a serious problem. The Golden Rule is useless. Why? Because investors do not know what stocks are worth. If you do not know what a stock is worth, how can you tell if the price is low and it is time to buy? How can you tell if the price is high and it is time to sell? You could have bought Coca-Cola for $64 in 1997. But if you do not know what Coca-Cola is worth, how can you tell whether $64 is an opportunity to buy low? Or an opportunity to sell high? You can't. There is no way. You cannot make an informed judgment about investing in a stock.

That puts you as an investor in a dilemma. You are investing hard-earned money to meet a critical goal. Perhaps you are investing so you can retire comfortably, or educate your children. You know investing is risky. Wise investment decisions are essential. If the Golden Rule is useless, what do you do? Who do you turn to? Professional advisors? Columnists in magazines or TV? Your broker? Investment letters? Your brother-in-law? Turning to professional advisors is futile. They do not know what stocks are worth, either.

> "**Buy Low, Sell High**" is useless advice. Why? Because investors do not know what a stock is worth. How can they tell if the price is low and it is time to buy, or if the price is high and it is time to sell?

Look at all the professionals who manage mutual funds. Do they earn higher returns than index funds? Index funds invest blindly in the 500 stocks that make up the S&P 500 stock average. They do not use professional advisors. Wouldn't you expect professionals to beat index funds consistently? They do not. Only one out of seven fund managers beat the S&P 500 index fund in 1995. Success is random. The manager who beats the index this year is not likely to beat the index next year. Or look at the Wall Street Journal's running "Darts vs. Experts" contest. The Journal invites a group of professionals to select their best stocks. A Journal staffer then selects stocks by throwing darts at the financial page. The professionals are ahead as this is written, but only by a slim 42 to 39 margin. How far should you trust a professional advisor who beats dart throwers by such a skinny margin? If professionals cannot do any better than that, what can you expect from columnists in magazines and TV, your broker, investment letters, and your brother-in-law?

What do you have left? Tips, rumors, and hunches. The financial media inundate you with stock picks. They emphasize the firm's bright prospects. But they tend to be vague about whether the stock costs too much. By the time you hear these recommendations, other investors have bid the price so high the stock is no longer a buy. You might choose safety, and invest only in the AT&T's and Coca-Colas of this world. Solid, mature firms with proven track records. But other safety-conscious investors have already flocked to these stocks, and bid their price so high they may no longer be attractive, either.

SmartValue

You do not have to tolerate this dilemma any longer. I am going to show you how to find what any stock is really worth. I am not going to masquerade platitudes as investment advice. I am going to show you a state-of-the-art way to get solid results. Quantitative results. You will be able to analyze any stock and conclude, "This stock is worth $35 per share to me. It may be worth more to somebody else. It may be worth less. But it is only worth $35 to me". I have called my method "SmartValue". You will have no difficulty understanding SmartValue and using it. It is not difficult. I will show you how to tune the analysis to your particular situation — to the minimum rate of return you should accept, to your tax bracket, to your investment horizon, and to your tolerance for risk. Then you can find what any stock is worth to you, not to some "average" investor.

SmartValue puts you in control of a powerful and cutting-edge system for analyzing stocks. More advanced than most professional analysts use. Worksheets make the computations easy. You do not have to be a rocket scientist. Do you remember grammar-school arithmetic? Can you add? Subtract? Multiply? Divide? Can you use a hand calculator? That is all you have to know. Just follow my worksheet's easy step-by-step instructions, and you can find what any stock is really worth. You will not even need a computer. An inexpensive hand calculator will do nicely. I will illustrate SmartValue by taking you step by step through each worksheet. Not with a fictional firm like the "XYZ" corporation. We will analyze real stocks. I will show you how to use SmartValue to find what Coca-Cola, Cisco Systems and Microsoft are worth. Coca-Cola is a good example of a mature firm. Cisco Systems and Microsoft are excellent examples of hot growth stocks.

As you learn SmartValue, you will understand why stocks have value. You will learn the critical keys that tell what a stock is worth. You will know which of the myriad statistics and indices you read in the financial pages you should pay attention to, and which you can safely ignore. You will become a confident and successful investor. You will be able to apply the Golden Rule because you will know what stocks are really worth. You will be able to tell when prices are low and when they are high. Suppose SmartValue tells you a stock is worth $30 per share. If the market price is $40 per share, the stock costs too much. Do not buy it. If the stock costs only $20 per share, it is a bargain, and you should consider buying it. SmartValue will also help you make selling decisions. If the market prices that $30 stock at $40 per share, the stock is overpriced. Sell before the market corrects the price. If the market prices the stock at only $20 per share, hold on. The market will eventually raise the price to its real value

Credentials

When someone promises you the key to intelligent investing, you are right to be suspicious. You should ask, "Who is this guy? What does he know about stocks? Why should I believe what he says?" Let me give you some personal background so you can form your own judgment about how far you can trust what I am going to tell you.

I have an engineering degree from M.I.T. and an MBA from the University of Chicago. After nine years with Amoco as a research engineer, I spent the next 27 years doing a wide variety of economic studies for Amoco's chemical business. One area of my work — analyzing potential acquisitions — is really stock analysis in disguise. An economic analysis of an acquisition is actually an exhaustive analysis of buying the acquired firm's stock. Furthermore, Amoco was not interested in acquiring old firms past their prime. It was interested in young firms with a bright future. Growth stocks, in market parlance. I worked out ways to analyze growth stocks realistically by accounting for how growth gradually slows and profitability falls as growth firms mature. I will show you how to use these methods so you can value growth stocks realistically, too.

Finding what a stock is worth requires forecasting how much cash that firm is going to generate for its shareholders in the future. A period as manager of Long-Range Planning for Amoco's chemical business gave me hands-on experience forecasting the cash a firm is likely to generate. I will use that experience to suggest useful ways you can use to forecast the cash any firm will generate for you.

I will also show you a way to value stocks that is on the cutting-edge of today's technology. American firms analyzed investments in a primitive way as late as the 1970's. They simply forecast how many years it would take a new plant to pay back the money spent to build it. One project might recover its investment cost in five years, then go out of business the next day. Another might also recover its investment cost in five years, and go on generating profit another 20 years. No matter. They both have a five-year payback period. How did firms decide what payback period was acceptable? There was no objective way. An investment might have a five-year payback period. Does five years get your money back fast enough? Or is five years too long to wait? American firms made many seat-of-the-pants judgments in that era.

Payback is obsolete. Modern firms do not use payback anymore. They use discounted cash flow (DCF) analysis instead. DCF analysis overcomes payback's limitations. DCF analysis includes all the cash a project generates, not just the cash generated during the payback period. It accounts for the fact that a dollar you will not receive until some time in the future is worth less than a dollar in your hand today. It provides an objective standard — the cost of capital — for deciding whether a project is attractive. Suppose a firm is investing capital that costs 12 percent. A project that promises a 15 percent return is attractive because it promises a return higher than the cost of the capital it uses. A project that promises only a 10 percent return is not attractive; it does not return the cost of the capital it uses. Good investments promise a return higher than the cost of capital; poor investments do not. Look at stocks the same way. Insist that they earn a return higher than the cost of the money you are investing in them.

I am going to put all that experience at your disposal in this book. I am going to put you on the cutting edge of valuing stocks. You have a cost of capital, just as the firm does. I will show you how to find what your cost is. Then you will avoid the capital sin of investing — investing money that costs, say, 12 percent, in a stock that earns only a 10 percent return. I will show you how to use your cost to find what any stock is worth. Not what it is worth to some "average" investor; what it is worth to you. Once you know what a stock is worth, you can profit from the Golden Rule. You will be able to tell when a stock is low and worth buying. You will be able to tell when a stock is high and it is time to sell. You will become a confident and an intelligent investor.

What's Ahead

Let's take a moment for a quick walk down the path I have laid out to make you a more savvy investor. In Chapter 2 I will show you the basic method for finding what a stock is worth. The method requires that you forecast the cash the firm will generate for its stockholders in the future. We will track the cash flows a typical firm generates during its life cycle as it passes from the growth stage to maturity, and finally to senility in Chapter 3. These are the cash flows you will be concerned with when you evaluate a stock.

You will learn the basic SmartValue formula in Chapter 4. The formula is straightforward and easy to understand. That formula will reveal the key relations that govern how fast a firm can grow, how fast the price of its stock can grow, and how much the firm can pay in dividends.

Different investors may legitimately assign different values to the same stock, even when they share the same outlook for the firm's future. That is because each investor has a unique financial situation. Each investor may insist on a different minimum return, be in a different tax bracket, have a different time horizon, and have a different tolerance for risk. In Chapter 5 I will show you how to tune the analysis to your individual situation. Then you can use SmartValue to find what any stock is worth to you.

Stocks of mature firms are the easiest to value. You will learn how to use Smart-Value to find what mature firms are worth in Chapter 6. We will use Coca-Cola as an example of a mature firm. In Chapter 7 I will show you how to analyze Coca-Cola's historical performance and forecast its future performance. We will feed that forecast to SmartValue to find what Coca-Cola is worth in Chapter 8. In Chapter 9 I will show you how to find the rate of return you can expect from investing in any stock.

Many investors follow a "Buy-and-Hold" strategy. Buy-and-hold is not always a winning strategy. Chapter 10 will show you how to use SmartValue to find when buy-and-hold works, and when it does not.

Most investors are keenly interested in growth stocks. That is where the greatest profit potential lies. The problem is that other investors recognize the potential of growth stocks, too. They may have bid the price so high that growth stocks are no longer attractive. Chapter 11 will show you how to analyze growth stocks. You will learn how to allow for gradually slowing growth as a growth firm matures. Chapters 12 and 13 develop the worksheets for finding what growth stocks are worth. We will use those worksheets to find what Cisco Systems, a popular growth stock, is worth in Chapter 14. In Chapter 15 I will remove all restrictions on the formula for forecasting future performance. You will have unlimited forecasting flexibility. You can even forecast the firm's future by drawing free-hand forecast curves on a sheet of graph paper. I will show you how to use the Unlimited Flexibility Model to find what Microsoft is worth in Chapter 16.

Knowing whether to buy a stock is only half the battle. The other half is knowing when it is time to sell. In Chapter 17 I will show you how to use SmartValue to decide whether it is time to sell, or whether you should continue to hold the stock.

Stocks are risky. Professional analysts allow for risk by adding a risk premium to the minimum rate of return they will accept. I will show you a better way to allow for risk in Chapter 18. The better way shows you not only what a stock is worth, but also your chance of losing money. I will bring all the worksheets together in Chapter 19. That is the place to go after you understand SmartValue and are ready to apply it to the stocks of your choice.

How to Use This Book

Professional investors, impatient investors and devil-may-care investors will be tempted to go straight to the worksheets at the end of the book and begin using Smart-Value to find what their favorite stocks are worth. They want immediate results. They will skip the explanation of how SmartValue works. They will skip the demonstrations of how to use SmartValue to find what Coca-Cola, Cisco Systems, and Microsoft are worth. Resist the temptation. This book is not a "whodunit". You gain nothing by reading the last chapter first. SmartValue includes many new concepts about how to analyze a firm's performance and how to find what a stock is worth. Understand those concepts before you go crashing about in my worksheets. Be sure to read Chapter 4 so you understand the basic formula. Read Chapter 5 to find the minimum return on investment you should insist on. Learn how to analyze a firm's historical performance in Chapter 7. Study how SmartValue was used to find what Coca-Cola, Cisco Systems, and Microsoft are worth. Then you can go on and use the worksheets to find what your favorite stocks are worth.

Resist the temptation to skip ahead if you are a serious investor. You are investing hard-earned money. You want to be sure of what you are doing when you make investment decisions. Read every chapter. You will learn a lot about why stocks have value. You will understand how you arrived at what any stock is worth to you, and not to that "average" investor. And you will be much more confident when it comes time to decide whether to dig into your pocket, put up your money, and buy that stock.

SUMMARY

"Buy low, sell high!" is useless advice because investors do not know what stocks are worth. If you do not know what a stock is worth, you cannot tell when stocks are low and it is time to buy, or when stocks are high and it is time to sell. SmartValue will tell you what a stock is worth. SmartValue is quantitative. It will tell you what a stock is worth in dollars and cents. It tunes the analysis to your individual financial situation. SmartValue uses discounted cash flow analysis to tell what stocks are worth. Although Smart-Value uses cutting-edge methods, simple worksheets mask any difficult arithmetic and make the calculations easy. Grammar-school arithmetic does the job. You do not need a computer; a hand calculator will do nicely. Once you know what a stock is worth, you will be able to recognize when stocks are low and it is time to buy, and when stocks are high and it is time to sell.

Chapter **2**

How to Find What Stocks Are Worth

What Really Matters

What Are Future Dollars Worth Today?

Discounting

What Are Stocks Worth?

Forecasting

Investors, beware! It is a jungle out there. A bewildering jungle of statistics, indices, and ratios, all claiming to tell you what a stock is really worth. Proceed with caution, dear investor, or risk the fate of the Light Brigade:

> Statistics to the right of them,
> Statistics to the left of them,
> Volleyed and thundered.
> Yet into the Valley of Death
> Rode the innocent investors.

Statistics thunder from The Wall Street Journal and Barrons. They volley from Forbes and Money. Guests on Wall Street Week, Nightly Business Report, and CNBC's Money Wheel fire contradictory salvoes of them. One analyst says, "Keep your eye on sales," while another insists, "No, watch the cash flow a firm generates." Yet another advises. "No, no, keep your eye on earnings." And another screams, "No, no, no! It's dividends that count!" Who do you believe?

Even innocent investors know they should invest in profitable firms. But how do you measure how much money a firm is making? Rate of return, certainly, but which rate of return? The rate of return the firm earns on its sales? On total assets? On long-term capital? Or on stockholder equity?

Investors also know they should invest in rapidly-growing firms. But how do you track growth? Growth in sales? Growth in cash flow? Growth in earnings? Growth in dividends? Growth in stockholder equity? Growth in the stock's price?

Even the Golden Rule of investing can confuse you. "Buy low, sell high!" But how do you know if a stock has gone low enough to buy, or high enough to sell? Do you look at the price/earnings ratio? The price/book ratio? The earnings yield? The dividend yield?

What Really Matters?

A quandary, surely. What can a smart investor do in this minefield of numbers? What are you to make of all these statistics? That is easy. Ignore them. Ignore them all. At least for now. Go back to basics. Start with a clean slate, and write on it this simple rule: "Worry only about the money that enters and leaves your pocket as a result of buying a stock." Period. Case closed. Focus on the money traffic into and out of your pocket. That is what determines what a stock is worth. Then you will not have to worry about any statistic except those that measure that traffic. Only a few critical ones really matter, as you will soon see.

Which cash flows do you track as you keep a watchful eye on your pocket? Dividends, surely. They pour one stream of cash into your pocket. Another bundle tumbles into your pocket when you finally sell the stock. Not all cash flows in. Some flows out. The federal government has one hand out ready to tax your dividends. The other hand taxes capital gains when you sell. Your state needs money, too. They will be right behind, taking their cut of dividends and capital gains. Your broker does not work for nothing. He takes his commission when you buy and again when you sell. That is the money traffic that enters and leaves your pocket. That is the raw material that tells you what a stock is really worth.

> **Don't worry about the statistics. Concentrate instead on the money that enters and leaves your pocket as a result of buying a stock.**

What about all those statistics you see in the financial press? They are all interesting, but only a few are really critical. You will see which are the critical ones when we develop the SmartValue formula in Chapter 4.

What Are Future Dollars Worth Today?

You cannot simply add up all the dollars a stock will put into your pocket and say "That is what this stock is worth!" Why? Because stocks do not put dollars into your pocket immediately. Those dollars flow in over time. They flow in gradually. Dividends roll in once each quarter. The last bundle of dollars does not tumble in until you finally sell the stock. That could be years from now. How much are those dollars worth today? They are not worth face value. A dollar in your hand today is worth a full dollar. Not so with dollars you have to wait for. Future dollars are worth less. How much less? It depends. How long do you have to wait to get your hands on those dollars? What interest rate you can earn in the meantime?

Discounting

There is an easy way to tell what a dollar you will not receive until some future time is worth today. It is called discounting. Discounting is a simple process. Here is how it works. You can invest 50 cents today at 7 percent interest and watch it grow to $1 ten years from now. If you can earn 7 percent interest, you should not care whether you get 50 cents now or $1 ten years from now. As far as you are concerned, they are both the same. One dollar ten years from now is worth 50 cents today. Why? Because 50 cents is all you have to invest today at 7 percent interest to grow to that future dollar ten years from now.

That is all discounting does. It tells you what a dollar in the future is worth today. In the jargon of the trade, a dollar ten years from now has a present value of 50 cents when discounted at a 7 percent discount rate. Discount at a higher rate, and that future dollar is worth less. Discount at a lower rate and it is worth more. At a 10 percent discount rate, for example, that dollar ten years from now is worth only 37 cents today, not 50 cents. At a 5 percent discount rate, it is worth 61 cents. The sooner you get your hands on that dollar, the more it is worth today. The longer you have to wait for that dollar, the less it is worth today. Suppose you could get your hands on that dollar in only five years instead of ten. At a 7 percent discount rate, that dollar would be worth 70 cents today, not 50 cents. But if you had to wait 15 years, it would only be worth 35 cents. Don't worry about how to do the discounting. The worksheet for finding what stocks are worth will make discounting easy.

What Are Stocks Worth?

How do you put all of this together to find what a stock is really worth? Here is all you do:

How To Find What Stocks Are Worth

1. Forecast all the cash that enters and leaves your pocket. How many dollars? How soon do you get them?

2. Discount each dollar to find what it is worth today.

3. Add up all the discounted dollars.

Presto! The last step tells you what the stock is worth. A stock is worth the discounted value of the net cash that stock will put in your pocket. SmartValue's worksheets will make carrying out these steps easy.

Investing is much easier once you know what a stock is worth. No more buying on hunches. No more buying on tips. You can now buy low and sell high intelligently. Buy the stock if it is worth more than it costs. Sell the stock if you can get more for it than it is worth. It is as simple as that!

Forecasting

If investing is that simple, why aren't all investors rich? The problem is forecasting. How do you forecast how much cash enters and leaves your pocket? How do you forecast dividends? How do you forecast what the price of the stock will be when you sell? That is the rub. That is what makes investing risky. In the next chapter we will take our first look at forecasting the cash that a stock will put into your pocket. We will explore the cash a firm generates for its shareholders at various stages during its life cycle, and the problems investors face forecasting that cash in each stage. In Chapter 7 we will examine a real-life stock. I will show you how to forecast the cash Coca-Cola's stock might put into your pocket.

Summary

Ignore the bewildering array of statistics you read in the financial press. Concentrate instead on the cash that enters and leaves your pocket as a result of buying a stock. Concentrate on dividends, what the price of the stock will be when you sell, federal and state taxes on dividends and capital gains, and your broker's commission. Then you need only worry about the statistics that affect those cash flows.

Finding what a stock is worth requires forecasting the cash that enters and leaves your pocket. Forecast both the amount of cash and the timing. Then discount each dollar to see what it is worth today. Add up the discounted dollars. That is what the stock is worth. SmartValue's worksheets will make the computations easy.

Chapter 3

How Firms Generate Cash

The Firm's Life Cycle

How Investors See the Firm

Forecasting Cash Flows

What Is the Stock Worth?

The cash that enters and leaves your pocket — the dividends you receive, the proceeds when you finally sell the stock, the taxes and commissions you pay — that is the key to finding what a stock is worth. All you have to do is forecast the dividends the stock will pay while you hold it, and the price of the stock when you sell. Crunch a few numbers, and you can tell what any stock is worth. But how do you forecast future dividends and stock prices? That is the crux of the problem. That is what makes investing difficult. Forecasting is not easy. No forecast, not even those by experts, is 100 percent accurate.

Your forecast will not be 100 percent accurate, either. That is OK. Don't worry about it. Your forecast does not have to be 100 percent accurate to be useful. But it does have to be reasonable. How do you make reasonable forecasts? There is a way to go about it. There is a way to put boundaries around the process, boundaries that rule out wild forecasts. There is a way to insure that your forecast is at least reasonable. Let's begin by getting a feel for the problem. Let's follow a typical firm as it passes stage by stage from a new firm with hot new technology to a mature firm, and finally to a senile firm. We will examine how the firm generates cash for its shareholders along the way. Then we will consider the problems shareholders face when they try to forecast the dividends they will receive and what the price of the stock will be when they sell. The forecasting problem is different at each stage of the firm's life cycle.

The Firm's Life Cycle

Let's assume a firm has developed breakthrough technology that promises to be a bonanza on the internet. Call the firm Internet Communications. It has the potential of becoming the next Intel or Microsoft.

The Rapid Growth Stage

Like Apple Computer, the founder starts Internet Communications in his garage. He recruits a group of bright young computer wizards who are willing to work long hours in the hopes of becoming rich if the product succeeds. The founder interests a venture capitalist, who offers financial support until the product is developed, put on the market, and begins to generate sales revenue. The small development staff works late into the night and on weekends. As the product takes shape, the development staff grows, and production and marketing people join the group. They rent larger quarters, which quickly become crowded as more workers join the firm.

The first version of the product is ready for the market after three years of intensive development. It is a huge success. Customers love the product because it expands their business and lowers their costs. Orders come in faster than Internet can fill them. Internet needs to expand its plant in a major way. It needs a large infusion of cash to pay for that expansion. Internet decides to go public with an IPO — an initial public offering of stock. The initial offering price is set at $15 per share. But investors are so enthusiastic about Internet's bright prospects that they bid the price up to $36 the first day. With fresh cash available, Internet expands production. It hires more workers and adds to its development group. The development staff concentrates on solving problems customers find as they use the product. Part of the staff begins working on an improved version of the product.

Internet grows at the extraordinary rate of 100 percent per year as customers clamor for the product. Profits are high because customers are willing to pay a high price. There is no competition, so Internet is free to charge whatever price it chooses. Internet sets the price high initially, high enough to earn a 100 percent rate of return. They need the high return to pay for new production facilities. Investors are impressed by the firm's rapid growth, high return, and bright future. They bid up the stock's price and the P/E ratio (the price investors pay for each dollar of Internet's earnings) reaches 90. A P/E ratio of 90 is extraordinarily high based on current earnings. But investors are not buying current earnings. They are buying the much higher earnings they expect Internet to earn in the future.

Internet is under strong pressure to expand production and to improve the product. It needs every penny it generates to pay for these activities, and so reinvests all its earnings back into the business. There is nothing left for dividends. It will be years before the demands for more investment ease to the point where Internet has money left over and can afford to pay dividends.

The Maturing Stage

Such rapid growth, high profitability, and high P/E ratio cannot go on forever. Growth begins to slow as Internet satisfies the initial heavy demand. The product's price has to be lowered gradually to broaden the base of customers who can afford the product. Internet also lowers the price to discourage competitors from developing their own version of the product. Lower prices make Internet's rate of return gradually fall. Investors react to the slowing growth and the falling rates of return. They gradually lower the P/E ratio they are willing to pay for Internet's stock.

Internet goes on for ten years without paying any dividends. After ten years, Internet's earnings have grown enough, and growth has slowed enough, that Internet now has more earnings than it needs for reinvesting in its business. There is a small surplus. The surplus earnings are available for shareholders, and Internet begins to pay dividends.

The Mature Stage

Despite Internet's efforts to discourage competition, Internet's success attracts other firms. They develop their own versions of the product. They cut prices to gain a foothold in the market. The market settles into a long contest between Internet and its competitors. A delicate balance develops as competitors lower prices to gain a market edge, yet try to keep prices high enough so they can stay in the black. Product development continues, but major improvements become harder and harder to find. The market gradually matures. The days of heady growth are over. Growth slows to about the growth of the national economy, and stabilizes at that level. As growth slows, the demand for new investment falls, and Internet gradually raises dividends. At maturity, Internet pays half of its earnings out as dividends. High returns are also a thing of the past. Profits fall to a level just high enough that the most efficient firms keep their heads above water. The least efficient firms cannot survive at the lower prices. They lose money year after year, and are gradually either acquired or fall by the wayside.

After 50 years you will no longer recognize the original Internet Communications. The start-up company with the hot, new technology will have disappeared. A large, modern campus will replace the crowded rented quarters. The daily face-to-face contact between the owners and the development team who designed the product, the production team who made the product, and the marketing team who sold the product will be gone. Several layers of management will have intruded. A heavy traffic in memoranda and other paper will have displaced much of the face-to-face contact. The entrepreneurs who built the firm will have retired; many will be dead. They have been replaced by managers who are more concerned with preserving the firm than in taking risks in uncharted waters. Their goal is no longer rapid growth. They are pleased if they can maintain modest year-to-year growth. The law of diminishing returns plagues efforts to develop major new technology. The research staff is reduced to a series of minor improvements. Technological obsolescence creeps in, and sales slow to a crawl.

The Approach to Senility

As internally-developed products peter out, Internet turns to acquisitions. It has to pay a stiff premium over market price to acquire other firms. Usually it will not be able improve the acquired firm's performance enough to justify the acquisition premium, and Internet's rate of return will suffer. Internet will have to reduce costs to stay in business. Internet will go through a series of downsizing programs, and gradually shut down its least-profitable plants. Investors recognize that Internet is going downhill, and the stock price falls steadily.

Eventually some new technology displaces Internet's obsolete technology. Internet becomes senile. It can no longer afford product development. Downsizing shrinks Internet to a shadow of its former self, and Internet gradually disappears from the scene.

How Investors See the Firm

So much for Internet's history. How is this history reflected in terms that affect the firm's shareholders? How do shareholders assess the firm at each stage of its growth? How do they forecast the cash Internet's stock will put into their pocket? How do they forecast stock prices? How do they forecast dividends?

Growth Rate

Growth is a key concern. Internet's growth rate slows as it matures. Figure 3-1 shows how Internet's growth slows during the first 25 years. Growth is rapid at first. But rapid growth is something only small firms find easy. Large firms find it much more difficult to grow rapidly. So growth naturally tends to slow as Internet becomes larger. Internet's growth also slows as the initial strong product demands are satisfied, and as competitors eat into its market. Internet's growth slows from the initial 100 percent per year to 23 percent per year after ten years, then to only 12 percent per year after 25 years.

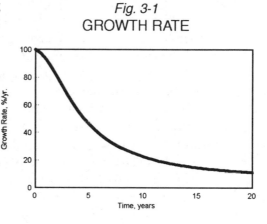

Fig. 3-1
GROWTH RATE

Stockholder Equity

Stockholders are not the only group that has a claim against Internet's assets. A number of other groups — suppliers, employees, banks, bondholders, the government — also have claims against Internet's assets. Someone has a claim against each dollar of assets. Stockholders own whatever is left after all other claims have been satisfied. The part of Internet that stockholders own is called stockholder equity. Stockholders focus on equity per share because they want to know what their share of Internet's business is worth. Internet starts with $0.40 of equity per share after its initial public offering. Figure 3-2 shows how equity per share grows. The equity curve

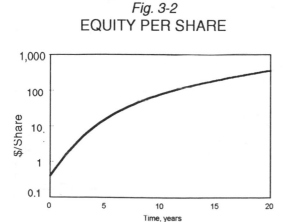

Fig. 3-2
EQUITY PER SHARE

is steep at first, reflecting Internet's rapid initial growth. The equity curve then gradually flattens as Internet approaches maturity and growth slows. It takes only five years for equity per share to grow to ten times its starting value. Because of slowing growth, however, it takes 11 years for the next tenfold increase. And it takes 19 years for the third tenfold increase.

Rate of Return and Earnings

Stockholders are concerned about how effectively Internet uses stockholder equity to generate earnings. That is what the rate of return on equity measures. Return on equity tells what earnings are as a percentage of stockholder equity. Internet's rate of return falls as it matures, as Figure 3-3 shows. The decay pattern in Figure 3-3 is similar to the decay in Internet's growth rate. Returns are high at first, then gradually fall as Internet lowers prices to broaden its market and as competitive pressures increase. What happens to earnings? Equity, the engine that is generating earnings, is growing steadily. That makes earnings grow. But the return Internet earns on that equity base is falling steadily. That makes earnings fall. What is the net result? Earnings grow as long as equity grows faster than return on equity falls. Figure 3-4 shows how the growing equity base and the falling return on equity balance out for Internet. Internet's equity base always grows faster than return on equity falls. That makes Internet's earnings grow steadily throughout the period. Earnings begin at 40 cents per share, and rise to $16 per share in 25 years. The return on equity stops falling and gradually stabilizes as Internet approaches maturity. When return on equity stabilizes, earnings per share and equity per share grow at the same percentage growth rate.

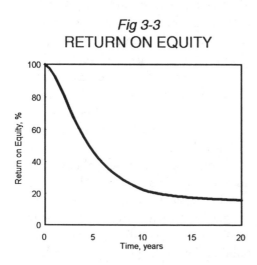

Fig 3-3
RETURN ON EQUITY

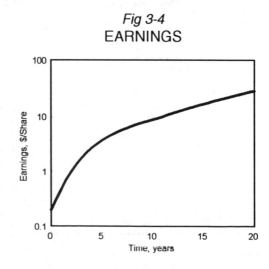

Fig 3-4
EARNINGS

Dividends

Earnings do not flow into investor's pockets. Dividends do. That is why share-holders are particularly interested in the dividends Internet pays. Internet reinvests all its earnings and pays no dividends for the first ten years of its existence. By that time, earnings have grown more than enough to pay for Internet's growth opportunities, and some earnings become available for dividends. Figure 3-5 shows how Internet's dividends grow. Dividends begin at year 10, and gradually grow as more of earnings become available for dividends. Ten years later, Internet pays out nearly one-third of earnings, or $9 per share, as dividends. Internet's growth rate and return on equity both stabilize as Internet approaches maturity. That makes dividends per share eventually grow at the same percentage rate as equity per share grows.

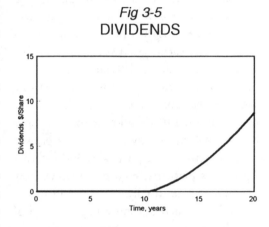

Fig 3-5
DIVIDENDS

Investors are willing to forego dividends at first. They recognize that they can earn more by letting Internet reinvest earnings in its profitable business than they can by taking dividends, paying taxes on those dividends, and then finding some other place to reinvest those dividends. They recognize that reinvesting all of Internet's earnings will make Internet grow faster. By the time Internet does begin paying dividends, that growth will lead to a much larger equity base which will be generating earnings and dividends. Investors wisely sacrifice small current dividends for much larger future dividends.

P/E Ratio

How much are investors willing to pay for Internet's stock? That is what the price/earnings (P/E) ratio measures. The P/E ratio is the price of the stock divided by earnings per share. It is the price investors pay for one dollar of earnings. Investors are willing to pay an extraordinary P/E ratio for Internet's stock at first because they anticipate strong growth in earnings. They are paying for future earnings. But they lower the P/E ratio they are willing to pay as Internet's growth slows, its return on equity falls, and Internet approaches maturity. Figure 3-6 shows how Internet's P/E ratio falls. The ratio begins at 90, and approaches a more normal level of 15 as Internet becomes a mature firm.

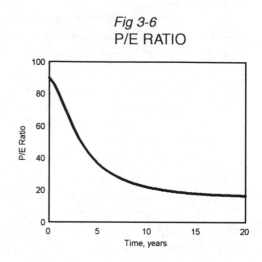

Fig 3-6
P/E RATIO

Stock Price

What does the drop in the P/E ratio mean for Internet's stock price? You can find

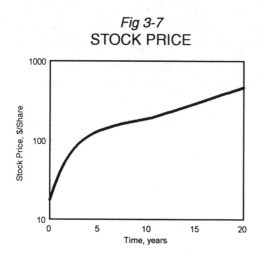

Fig 3-7
STOCK PRICE

Internet's stock price by multiplying earnings by the P/E ratio. Growing earnings make the stock price go up. A falling P/E ratio makes the stock price go down. Figure 3-7 shows the net result of growing earnings and the falling P/E ratio for Internet. Internet's price rises rapidly at first because earnings are growing faster than the P/E ratio is falling. Falling P/E ratios nearly offset growing earnings and cause the growth in the stock's price to slow from year 5 through year 10. The worst of the P/E ratio decay is over after year 5. P/E ratios stabilize as Internet matures, and the stock price rises again, paralleling Internet's growing earnings.

Figure 3-7 shows Internet's price heading towards very high levels. Most managements avoid high stock prices because investors find it difficult to buy the stock in round lots of 100 shares. Internet will therefore split its stock frequently to keep the price under about $100 per share.

Forecasting Cash Flows

Those are the cash flows Internet will generate for its shareholders during its lifetime. How do you go about forecasting those cash flows? It depends. Where in the life cycle are you making the forecast?

The Rapid Growth Stage

Forecasting the cash Internet is likely to put into your pocket is most difficult when Internet makes its initial public offering. You do not know whether Internet will succeed or fail. You have essentially no track record to go on. The historical record will not help much. Most of Internet's three-year development period will show a growing stream of losses as Internet pays for its growing staff, but has little or no sales revenue to offset those costs. There may be only a year or less of sales history to go on. Forecasts based on such a short track record are risky in the extreme. You have to forecast whether Internet will succeed or fail. If it succeeds, you have to forecast not only how fast Internet will grow and how profitable it will be, but also how rapidly growth, return on equity, and the P/E ratio will fall as Internet matures.

Investing when a firm makes its initial public offering is for risk takers. It is a gamble. It is for speculators. Unless you are an expert on Internet's business, or have a strong stomach for risk, it may be best to avoid stocks at this stage. Let them grow a while, at least long enough so they establish a track record. At least long enough so you can measure their growth rate, return on equity, and P/E ratio more reliably, and begin to judge how fast these critical factors might decay.

The Maturing Stage

The longer you wait before buying Internet's stock, the better your chances of making realistic forecasts of the cash Internet will generate. Internet will have built a track record. You will be able to measure Internet's growth rate, and observe how fast growth is slowing. You can measure the return on equity Internet is earning, and observe how fast it is falling. You can also track how the investment community changes its view of Internet by observing how the P/E ratio investors are willing to pay for Internet's stock is changing. That track record provides a basis for forecasting how growth will slow, and how the return on equity and the P/E ratio will fall while you hold the stock.

The Mature Stage

Forecasting will be much easier after Internet has become a mature company. Then its growth rate will have stabilized, perhaps to something approaching the growth of the national economy. That will make the equity Internet is using to generate cash for its shareholders easier to forecast. Its return on equity will also have stabilized to about the average return firms in Internet's industry are earning. That will make earnings easier to forecast. And Internet's P/E ratio will have stabilized to about the average P/E investors are paying for mature firms in Internet's industry. That makes Internet's stock price easier to forecast. The more reliably you can forecast, the more reliably you can find what a stock is really worth.

> **Forecasting is easiest for mature firms, more difficult for growth firms, and nearly impossible for start-up firms.**

Of course, the longer you delay investing, the lower is the potential return you can earn. If Internet is successful, it is the investors who buy in early when the price is low (and the risk is highest) who earn the highest return. They earn the high return because they take on the most risk. Those who wait until they can get a clearer view of how Internet is going to perform reduce their risk. But they pay for the lower risk by paying a higher price for the stock. That makes their return lower. Risk and return go together. If you insist on a high return, you will have to accept a higher risk. If you insist on low risk, you will have to accept a lower return.

You can see from the Internet Communications example how the problem investors have forecasting the cash a stock will put into their pocket changes depending on which stage of its life cycle a firm has reached. Forecasting is nearly impossible for firms just going public. Forecasting becomes easier as the firm builds up a track record. A track record gives you something to go on. Mature firms are the easiest to forecast. They have a long track record, and their operations have stabilized. In the next chapter I will develop quantitative formulas you can use to forecast how much cash a firm is likely to put into your pocket.

What Is the Stock Worth?

We saw in Chapter 2 that a stock is worth the discounted total of all the cash that stock will put into your pocket. When you buy a stock, you buy the right to all the dividends that firm will pay for as long as it stays in business. One way to measure what Internet is worth is to assume you will hold the stock forever. All your cash inflows will then be dividends. You do not have to worry about the price when you sell because you never sell. In that case, Internet's stock is worth the discounted value of all the dividends Internet will pay for as long as it stays in business.

You do not actually have to hold Internet forever. You can sell it whenever you like. But even if you sell, Internet will still be worth the discounted value of all the dividends it pays for as long as it stays in business. Why? Because when you sell, you sell the right to all those future dividends Internet will pay. What are all those future dividends worth when you sell? They are worth the discounted value of those future dividends. And that is what the selling price will be. That makes Internet's current value the discounted value of all future dividends — the dividends you receive while you hold the stock, plus the dividends Internet will pay after you sell. That is why it is legitimate to value a stock as the discounted value of all the dividends the stock will pay for as long as it stays in business, regardless of when, or even if, you sell.

Suppose you forecast the flow of dividends shown in Figure 3-5. You decide to discount each year's dividends at a 12 percent discount rate. (I will show you in Chapter 5 how to decide what discount rate you should use). Figure 3-8 shows how the value of discounted dividends builds up over time. There are no dividends until year 11. After year 11 dividends grow rapidly. That makes the curve grow. But successive dividends are farther and farther out in time, and so are discounted more and more heavily. Heavier discounting makes future dividends worth less; that makes the curve

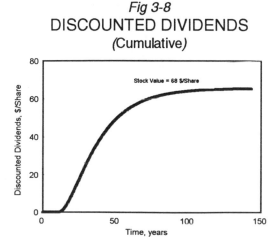

Fig 3-8
DISCOUNTED DIVIDENDS
(Cumulative)

Stock Value = 68 $/Share

flatten. Eventually dividends are discounted so heavily they make only a negligible contribution to the total. The curve then flattens out at some limiting value. That limiting value is what the stock is worth. In this example, the curve approaches a limiting value of $68 per share. That is what Internet is worth when the stock is first issued, given the forecast of dividends in this illustration and the choice of a 12 percent discount rate. Internet is earning only $0.40 per share when it first offers its stock to the public. That makes a fair initial P/E ratio 170. That P/E ratio is extraordinarily high, but the forecast of future dividends justifies it.

It may take a long time before discounting makes future dividends negligible. In this example, it takes about 100 years before the curve finally flattens and reaches a limiting value. Some analysts ignore dividends after 20 to 30 years. They reason that those late dividends are discounted so heavily they no longer amount to anything. That is a mistake. When the cash stream is growing, as dividends are in this example, the net discount rate is the difference between the dividend growth rate and the nominal discount rate. The net discount rate can be very small. That is why it can take such a long time before further discounted dividends become negligible. This example shows that dividends may have to be discounted for as long as 100 years to find what a stock is worth by discounting dividends.

You can buy Internet when it is first issued, hold it five years, and sell it at a gain without ever collecting a penny in dividends. Why does the stock price go up? Because all of Internet's future dividends are now five years closer. That means they are discounted less heavily. The lighter discounting is responsible for the increase in price.

SUMMARY

Firms typically pass through a number of stages during their life cycle. They grow rapidly and earn high profits at first. But growth slows and profits fall as firms approach maturity, and fall even further as they become senile.

Forecasting the cash a firm will put into your pocket is nearly impossible when the firm first goes public. There is no history to go on. You have to forecast whether the firm will succeed or fail, and, if it succeeds, what return it will earn, how fast it will grow, and the P/E ratio investors will pay for its stock. You also have to forecast how fast those critical factors will decay as the firm matures. Forecasting is easier after the firm has been in business several years. There is a historical record to go on. You have a better picture of those critical factors and how fast they are changing. Forecasting is easiest when the firm has matured. Mature firms tend to have stable operations. The rate of return they earn, how fast they grow, and the P/E ratio investors are willing to pay for mature firms all tend to stabilize and fluctuate in a relatively narrow band around some stable average level.

Chapter 4

The SmartValue Formula

The Steady-State Model

Forecasting

How Well Does SmartValue Fit Real Firms?

Key Operating Characteristics

Contact With Reality

How Firms Grow

Forecasting Tips

In the last chapter we saw how the problem of forecasting the cash a firm generates for its stockholders changes as the firm passes through the various stages of its life cycle. Knowing how cash flow changes from one stage of the cycle to the next is helpful. It puts the problem of forecasting future dividends and stock prices in perspective. But we saw those changes only in a qualitative way. Qualitative is not good enough. Now it is time to be quantitative. We want to make quantitative estimates of what a stock is worth. Dollars and cents estimates. We need a quantitative formula we can use to find the cash any stock is likely to put in our pocket.

Mature firms—that is the place to start. Mature firms are best because, as we found in the last chapter, forecasting the cash a stock will put into your pocket is easiest for mature firms. Mature firms are stable. Their key operating characteristics — their growth rate, the rate of return they earn, and the P/E ratio investors are willing to pay — all tend to fluctuate in a relatively narrow band around some stable trend line. Unless you expect some basic change in the firm, the most reasonable way to forecast the cash a mature firm will put into your pocket is to forecast that the firm will continue to operate along its historic trend lines. Of course, the key factors are not going to fall exactly on a trend line. They will deviate from the trend line. One year a key factor will fall above the line. The next year it may fall below. Don't worry about these year-to-year deviations as long as they are small. They are extremely difficult to forecast. Concentrate instead on the trend line. Forecasting that these key characteristics will continue to follow their historic trend is a reasonable way to forecast for mature firms.

Your time horizon is also important. If you intend to hold a stock for only a short time, you have a serious forecasting problem on your hands. If you hold the stock for only a short time you need to forecast those short-term deviations from the trend line. Good luck! But if you intend to hold the stock for a period of years, forecasting the trend line is more important than forecasting year-to-year deviations from the trend. That makes forecasting much easier.

In this chapter you will learn the SmartValue Formula for forecasting dividends and stock prices. The SmartValue Formula models how the firm operates. Here is the secret to building practical models. Keep them simple. As simple as possible. Every wrinkle you add means another factor you have to forecast. Every new wrinkle makes the stock's value more difficult to compute. You do not need to account for every wiggle in a firm's performance. A model that captures the basic trends will do nicely.

The Steady-State Model

There is a simple model for stocks that is extremely useful despite its simplicity. It is called the steady-state model. That is where we will begin. In the steady-state model the critical factors that determine what a stock is worth do not change. They stay constant. They hold at steady-state values, at least while you hold the stock. The steady-state model has important advantages — it is simple, easy to understand, and easy to use. Do real firms follow the steady-state model exactly? No, of course not. But mature firms are stable. They do operate reasonably close to steady-state conditions. Their key characteristics do fluctuate, but the fluctuations are contained in a narrow band around some steady-state trend line for extended periods. That is why steady-state models are appropriate for finding what stocks of mature firms are worth.

Growth stocks are a different story. Their key characteristics do not stay constant at steady-state conditions. Growth slows and profitability and P/E ratios fall as growth firms mature. We will have to adapt the model to account for these changes. We will do that in Chapter 11.

The SmartValue Formula consists of five simple models. Models? Did you say models? Do you mean mathematical models? Yes, I do, but stay cool. You will not have to solve any of them. They are all built into the worksheets in later chapters. When you get to those worksheets you will find just simple arithmetic. Add, subtract, multiply, and divide. The worksheets will lead you step by step through the computations. You do not have to be a rocket scientist. Grammar school arithmetic will do nicely. You will not even need a computer. You can do all the necessary computations easily on your hand calculator.

The models are not in this book just to test your tenacity. They are there to help you understand what is going on when you bet your money on a stock. You do not <u>have</u> to understand the SmartValue models. It is not absolutely essential. You could go ahead mechanically, fill in the worksheets, hope you are doing it correctly, and maybe find what a stock is worth. Don't. Know what you are doing when you invest your own hard-earned money. Take the time to understand at least the basic idea behind these models. If you understand what is going on, you will be much more confident about your investment. Try to follow the gist of the models. They will help you understand what is happening when you fill in the worksheet.

Forecasting

You have to make three basic forecasts to find what a stock is worth. You have to forecast how fast the firm is going to grow. You have to forecast how effectively the firm uses stockholder's equity to generate earnings and dividends. Finally, you have to forecast what the price of the stock will be when you sell. That is what the SmartValue formulas do.

Growth

There is a basic question we will ask repeatedly: "How fast will some key operating result — stockholder equity, earnings, dividends, the price of the stock — grow? What will its value be in the future?" Here is a simple formula to answer that question:

Future Value = (Growth Multiplier)(Current Value)

Finding the future value of any quantity is easy. Just multiply the current value by a growth multiplier. That is what the parentheses around the growth multiplier and the current value mean. It is a shorthand way of saying "Multiply the number in the first parenthesis by the number in the second." How do you find the growth multiplier? That is easy in steady-state models because the growth rate stays constant. Use the worksheet in Table 4-1:

Table 4-1
GROWTH MULTIPLIER WORKSHEET
Steady-State Growth Rate

1. Divide the Growth Rate (%/yr.) by 100 .... ————
2. Length of growth period, years .... ————
3. Multiply Line 1 by Line 2 .... ————
4. Growth Multiplier: Enter Line 3 in your calculator and
   tap the e^x key .... ————

The worksheet is easy to use. Here is an example:

Example 4-1 McDonald's Corporation has been growing 12.1 percent per year. If growth continues at that rate, what growth multiplier do we need to find how large McDonald's will be five years from now? Enter the 12.1 percent growth rate and the five-year time period in the worksheet and follow the instructions. The growth rate has to be in decimal form; that is why you divide by 100 in the first line.

Table 4-2
GROWTH MULTIPLIER - Example 4-1

1. Divide the Growth Rate (%/yr.) by 100	0.121
2. Length of growth period, years	5
3. Multiply Line 1 by Line 2	0.605
4. Growth Multiplier: Enter Line 3 in your calculator and tap the e^x key	1.831

The growth multiplier is 1.831. After growing 12.1 percent per year for five years, McDonald's will be 1.831 times larger than it is today.

Do not let the e^x (pronounced "e to the x") in line 4 throw you. If e^x is a strange beast to you don't worry. You do not have to know what it means[1]. Just think of e^x as another key on your calculator. When you find a line like line 4 in a worksheet, do what it says. In this example, enter the 0.605 from Line 3 in your calculator. Then tap the e^x key. The number in your calculator's display window changes to 1.831. That is the number that goes in Line 4. And that is all there is to it![2]

---

[1] "e" is 2.71828..., the base of natural logarithms. e^x just means to raise e to the x power. An addendum at the end of this chapter shows how e^x works.

[2] The keys on most calculators perform two arithmetic functions. One is written on top of the key. The other is written on the calculator just above the key. If you find e^x on top of a key, go ahead and tap it. If you find e^x written above the key, look for another key labeled "2nd", or something similar. Tapping that key tells your calculator to use the second arithmetic function on the next key you tap. Then tap the key with the e^x written above it. If in doubt, read your calculator's instruction manual.

Your calculator may not have an e^x key. Sorry! If it only adds, subtracts, multiplies, and divides you have a toy calculator! You need a real calculator to be a serious investor. Get a calculator that has an e^x key. Inexpensive calculators have this vital key; make one of them your first investment.

Forecasting Equity per Share

A number of parties — suppliers, banks, bondholders, employees, the government, and stockholders — all have claims against the firm's assets. They all "own" parts of the firm. Stockholder equity measures how much of the firm stockholders own. Stockholder equity is also known as "net worth" and "book value". As a stockholder, your primary interest is in your share of that equity. That is what you should focus on. Equity per share. That is your share of stockholder equity. Equity per share is an important measure. It is the engine that generates earnings and dividends per share. It determines, in large part, the price of the stock. Because it is so important, the SmartValue formula is based on stockholder equity per share.

Equity per share changes for two reasons. Most important, the firm continually reinvests part of its earnings in the business. Reinvested earnings add directly to the equity base and makes stockholder equity grow. Every time the firm reinvests a dollar of earnings stockholder equity grows by one dollar. The number of shares outstanding changes continually, too. The firm may issue new shares to acquire other firms, or to fund stock option and savings plans for its executives and employees. Issuing more shares dilutes your share of total equity. The firm may also buy back some of its own shares. Reducing the number of shares outstanding raises your share of total equity. When you focus on equity per share, you recognize how both reinvested earnings and changes in the number of outstanding shares affect your wealth.

Equity per share is a key factor. That is because the critical factors we are interested in — dividends and stock prices — depend on equity. Once we know equity, it will be easier to forecast the other key factors. The growth multiplier makes forecasting equity per share easy in the steady-state model. Forecast equity per share at any future time simply by multiplying the current equity per share by the growth multiplier:

Equity/Share = (Growth Multiplier)(Current Equity/Share)

Example 4-2 McDonald's Corporation had $11.24 of stockholder equity per share of stock at the end of 1995. Equity per share has been growing at 12.1 percent per year. If equity continues to grow at that rate, what will equity per share grow to in five years? Use the growth multiplier of 1.831 from Example 4-1. Equity per share in five years will be:

$$\text{Equity/Share} = (1.831)(\$11.24) = \$20.58/\text{Share}$$

Forecasting Earnings

The next question is "How effectively does a firm use stockholder equity to generate earnings?" That is what the rate of return on equity measures. Earnings are easy to model. Just multiply equity per share at any time by the return on equity the firm is earning. Return on equity has to be in decimal form, that is, you must enter a return like 15 percent as 0.15 in the formula. Here is the simple formula for earnings per share:

$$\text{Earnings/Share} = (\text{Return on Equity})(\text{Equity/Share})$$

Let's take a closer look at this simple model. We know what equity per share is at any future time from the equity model. Let's combine the two models. Replace the equity in the earnings model by its equivalent from the equity model:

Earnings/Share =
   (Return on Equity)(Growth Multiplier)(Current Equity/Share)

The last two parentheses in this formula are the equity per share from the equity model. Find earnings per share by multiplying the current equity per share by the growth multiplier and the return on equity. The combined model tells us something quite useful about how equity and earnings grow. Both equity and earnings depend on the same growth multiplier. That is an important result. When the return on equity stays constant, as it does in the steady-state formula, that makes both earnings and equity per share grow at the same percentage growth rate.

Example 4-3 McDonald's return on equity averaged 15.7 percent over the past five years. If McDonald's continues to earn a 15.7 percent return, what will earnings be in five years? Enter the 15.7 percent return (in decimal form), the 1.831 growth multiplier, and the current equity of $11.24 per share from Example 4-2 in the formula for earnings:

$$\text{Earnings/Share} = (0.157)(1.831)(\$11.24) = \$3.23 \text{ per share}$$

Forecasting Dividends

Forecasting dividends is a critical part of the SmartValue formula because dividends are one of the cash flows a stock puts in your pocket. Firms normally reinvest part of their earnings in the business and pay the balance to their shareholders as dividends. We can model dividends simply by multiplying earnings by the fraction of earnings the firm pays out in dividends:

Dividends/Share =
(Dividend Payout Fraction)(Return on Equity)(Growth Multiplier)(Current Equity/Share)

The last three parentheses in this model are earnings as defined by the earnings model. Here is another important result. Dividends, earnings, and equity per share all depend on the same growth multiplier. In the steady-state model the dividend payout fraction and the return on equity both stay constant. That makes dividends, earnings, and equity per share all grow at the same percentage growth rate. The simple formula for dividends makes forecasting dividends easy.

Example 4-4 McDonald's pays 13 percent of its earnings out as dividends and reinvests the balance. That makes the dividend payout fraction 0.13. What dividends can we expect in five years? Enter the 0.13 dividend payout fraction, the 15.7 percent return, the 1.831 growth multiplier, and the current equity of $11.24 per share from Example 4-3 in the formula for dividends:

$$\text{Dividends} = (0.13)(0.157)(1.831)(\$11.24) = \$0.42 \text{ per share}$$

Forecasting Stock Price

Forecasting the future price of the stock is normally the most critical forecast you will have to make to find what a stock is worth, particularly if you plan to hold the stock for only a short time. There are two ways to forecast stock prices. The first is to multiply your forecast of earnings by your forecast of the P/E ratio. The second is to multiply your forecast of equity per share by your forecast of the price/book (P/B) ratio. The P/B ratio is simply the stock price divided by book value per share. While both ways work, I have used the P/B formula in SmartValue because the P/B ratio tends to be a more stable series than the P/E ratio. That makes it easier to forecast. The P/E ratio is more erratic, particularly in years when earnings drop or when the firm reports a loss.

You can forecast stock price at any time by this simple formula:

Stock Price = (P/B)(Growth Multiplier)(Current Equity/Share)

The product of the growth factor and the current equity in the last two parentheses is equity per share as defined by the equity model. Here is another important result. The price of the stock, too, depends on the same growth multiplier as dividends, earnings, and equity. In the steady-state model the P/B ratio stays constant. That makes the price of the stock, dividends, earnings, and equity per share all grow at the same percentage growth rate. But it is the growth rate of equity per share that is the underlying growth rate.

Example 4-5 McDonald's stock sells at a P/B ratio of 4.3. What will the stock price be in five years if the P/B ratio stays constant? Enter the P/B ratio of 4.3, the growth multiplier of 1.831, and the current equity per share of $11.24 in the formula for the stock price:

Stock Price = (4.3)(1.831)($11.24) = $88.50/Share

You may be more comfortable thinking in terms of P/E ratios. No problem. The P/E ratio and the P/B ratio are related by the return on equity. Go ahead and forecast a P/E ratio. Then multiply the P/E ratio by the return on equity (in decimal form) to find the equivalent P/B ratio. If you are comfortable with the P/B ratio, you can always find the equivalent P/E ratio by dividing the P/B ratio by the return on equity (again, in decimal form).

Example 4-6 McDonald's stock sells at a P/E ratio of 27.4. What is the equivalent P/B ratio? McDonald's earns a 15.7 percent return on equity. Multiply the P/E ratio by the return on equity:

P/B Ratio = (0.157)(27.4) = 4.30

Forecasting Growth Rate

How fast a firm grows is a critical element in determining what a stock is worth. The firm's growth rate does not seem to appear the SmartValue formulas. Don't worry. It is there, all right. It is there in disguise —it is part of the growth multiplier. The Smart-Value formula is based on stockholder equity per share. That is the foundation. All the key factors we are interested in are tied to equity per share. That makes the growth rate of equity per share the basic measure of growth.

How fast equity per share can grow depends on how much of its earnings the firm reinvests in the business. Reinvested earnings add directly to stockholder equity, that is what makes equity grow. The firm's earnings are the total amount of money the firm has available to reinvest[1]. The firm usually reinvests only a fraction of those earnings in the business. It pays out the balance as dividends. The growth rate depends on the return on equity, which measures the total earnings the firm has available to reinvest, and the reinvestment fraction, which measures the fraction of those earnings the firm actually reinvests. The reinvestment fraction and the dividend payout fraction must add up to 1.0. That makes the reinvestment fraction one minus the dividend payout fraction. The firm's growth rate is simply the return on equity multiplied by the reinvestment fraction. Or, in terms of the dividend payout fraction:

Growth Rate = (1 - Dividend Payout Fraction)(Return on Equity)

Example 4-7 McDonald's earns a 15.7 percent return on equity and pays out 13 percent of its earnings as dividends. How fast can McDonald's grow? Substitute the payout fraction and the return on equity in the growth formula:

Growth Rate = (1 - 0.13)(15.7) = 13.7 percent per year

Oops! There is a problem. SmartValue's growth formula calls for growth of 13.7 percent per year. Yet McDonald's actually grew only 12.1 percent per year, as we saw in Example 4-1. What went wrong? Why did McDonald's grow only 12.1 percent per year instead of

---

[1] Cash flow is actually the amount of money the firm has available to reinvest in the business. But not all of cash flow contributes to growth. Cash flow is the sum of earnings and non-cash charges like depreciation. Reinvesting depreciation does not contribute to growth. It merely restores stockholder equity to the level it was before the depreciation was deducted. Only reinvested earnings contributes to growth. That is why SmartValue concentrates on earnings and ignores cash flow.

13.7 percent per year? The problem is that SmartValue applies exactly only to ideal firms. McDonald's is a real firm. Real firms do not behave exactly the way ideal firms behave. Not to worry. There is an easy way to make SmartValue's growth formula work exactly even for real firms. You will learn how to make SmartValue work exactly for real firms later in this chapter.

The growth formula fixes the relationship between three key factors — the growth rate, the return on equity, and the dividend payout fraction. You cannot forecast all three of these factors independently. You can only forecast two of these factors. Pick any two, it is your choice. But you cannot forecast the third. The growth formula determines the third factor. Most investors are more comfortable forecasting the growth rate and the return on equity. They need to know what dividend payout fraction is consistent with their forecasts of the equity growth rate and the return on equity. Let's rearrange the growth formula to find that dividend payout fraction. Simply divide the growth rate by the return on equity and subtract the result from 1.0:

Dividend Payout Fraction = 1 - (Growth Rate)/(Return on Equity)

Example 4-8 Verify from the payout fraction formula that a dividend payout fraction of 0.13 is consistent with the growth rate of 13.7 percent per year and a return on equity of 15.7 percent found in Example 4-7. Substitute the 13.7 percent per year growth rate and the 15.7 percent return in the payout fraction formula:

Dividend Payout Fraction = 1 - 13.7/15.7 = 0.13

Here is a major advantage of SmartValue. It forces your forecasts of the return on equity, the growth rate, and the dividend payout fraction to be consistent with each other. It keeps you from making mistakes like forecasting rapid growth and a high dividend payout at the same time. Both cannot be high at the same time. If growth is rapid, the firm will have to reinvest most of its earnings to finance that growth. There will be little left for dividends, and the dividend payout fraction will be low. If the payout fraction is high, there will not be much of earnings left to reinvest. That will make growth slow.

Don't worry about dividends. Forecast the return on equity you expect the firm to earn and how fast you expect the firm to grow. The worksheets for finding what a stock is worth in later chapters will automatically work out the dividend payout fraction that is consistent with your forecasts of return on equity and growth rate.

How Well Does SmartValue Fit Real Firms?

SmartValue is designed to be a simple formula, yet still be realistic enough for practical use. SmartValue is exact only for ideal firms. It fits them perfectly. The stock exchange, however, does not offer stocks of ideal firms. It only offers stocks of real firms.

How well does SmartValue fit real firms? There is one critical difference between ideal firms and real firms. That difference is the way stockholder equity grows. The only way stockholder equity grows in an ideal firm is by reinvesting part of the firm's earnings. The growth in equity is exactly equal to reinvested earnings. Every time the firm reinvests one dollar of earnings, stockholder equity increases by exactly one dollar. That leads to a simple formula for the growth of equity:

Growth of Equity = Reinvested Earnings

Real firms follow this simple formula too, but they do not follow it exactly. Reinvested earnings are still the major reason shareholder equity grows. But a number of other factors intrude. That makes the gain in equity in real firms a little more complicated:

Growth of Equity = Reinvested Earnings + Other Factors

Let's look at a real firm and see what those other factors can be. Table 4-3 shows the factors that were responsible for the growth in McDonald's equity in 1995. McDonald's began the year with $6,885.4 millions of stockholder equity. Reinvested earnings (earnings less dividends) account for most of the gain in equity. They are the numbers in bold type at the top of the table. Reinvested earnings increased equity by $1245.9 millions. A variety of other factors were also involved. Some made equity grow. Others made equity fall. The net effect of these other factors was to reduce equity by $270 million. That left a net gain in equity of $975.9 million for the year.

Table 4-3
GAIN IN STOCKHOLDER EQUITY

McDONALD'S CORPORATION, 1995
Millions of Dollars

Stockholder Equity, 12/31/94	6885.4
Plus: Earnings	1427.3
Less: Dividends on Common Stock	(181.4)
Equals: Reinvested Earnings	1,245.9
Other Factors:	
Preferred Dividends	(40.5)
Preferred Stock Conversion	(146.3)
ESOP Notes Payment	19.0
Treasury Stock Acquisition	(321.0)
Currency Translation	27.8
Common equity put options expiration	56.2
Stock Options plus Other	134.8
Total Other	(270.0)
Stockholder Equity, 12/31/95	7861.3
Gain in Stockholder Equity	975.9

Adjusted Reinvested Earnings

What to do? We cannot ignore these other factors. If we do, SmartValue will not track the firm's performance accurately. Somehow we need to account for them. We certainly do not want to forecast all the bits and pieces of those other factors. There is an easy solution. Lump all those other factors into the actual reinvested earnings. Lumping all these other factors into the actual reinvested earnings leads to a new kind of reinvested earnings. We need a way to distinguish this new reinvested earnings from the reinvested earnings the firm reports. Let's call this new form "adjusted reinvested earnings". That makes the SmartValue formula for the gain in equity for real firms:

Gain in Equity = Adjusted Reinvested Earnings

And that solves our problem! This formula fits real firms exactly. Adjusted reinvested earnings account for all of the gain in equity per share, not just most of the gain. And adjusted reinvested earnings are easy to measure. Just measure how much equity grows from one year to the next.

Adjusted Earnings

When we adjust reinvested earnings this way, we also have to adjust earnings to keep them both consistent with each other. In SmartValue, earnings are the sum of dividends and reinvested earnings. We get a new kind of earnings when we replace the reinvested earnings the firm reports by adjusted reinvested earnings. Let's call the new earnings "adjusted earnings". Just as earnings for ideal firms are the sum of dividends and reinvested earnings, adjusted earnings for real firms are the sum of dividends and adjusted reinvested earnings. And we can use the year-to-year change in equity to measure adjusted reinvested earnings. That leads to a simple formula for adjusted earnings:

Adjusted Earnings/Share = Dividends/Share + Gain in Equity/Share

Do not use the firm's reported earnings. They are entirely legitimate, but Smart-Value will not track the firm's growth exactly if you use them. Use adjusted earnings instead. Then you can be sure that SmartValue will track the firm's growth.

Do not use the earnings the firm reports. Use adjusted earnings instead. Adjusting earnings makes SmartValue track a real firm's growth exactly.

Here is a simple worksheet for adjusting earnings:

Table 4-4
ADJUSTING EARNINGS

1. Dividends, $/Share .... _____
2. Equity, $/Share, beginning of year .... _____
3. Equity, $/Share, end of year .... _____
4. Gain in Equity: Subtract Line 2 from Line 3 .... _____
5. Adjusted Earnings, $/Share: Add Lines 1 and 4 .... _____

Example 4-9 Find McDonald's adjusted earnings for 1995. McDonald's began the year with $6885.4 million of equity and 693.7 million shares, or $9.93 of equity per share, and ended the year with $7861.3 million of equity and 699.7 million shares, or $11.24 of equity per share. During the year McDonald's also paid $0.26 per share in dividends. Enter these values in the worksheet:

Table 4-5
ADJUSTING McDONALD'S 1995 EARNINGS

1. Dividends, $/Share 0.26
2. Equity, $/Share, beginning of year 9.93
3. Equity, $/Share, end of year 11.24
4. Gain in Equity: Subtract Line 2 from Line 3 .... 1.31
5. Adjusted Earnings, $/Share: Add Lines 1 and 4 .... 1.57

The adjusted earnings of $1.57 per share is significantly lower than McDonald's reported earnings of $1.97 per share. McDonald's reported earnings are completely legitimate. They conform to accepted accounting standards. But they do not account fully for the growth in equity. Adjusted earnings do. That is why it is important to adjust earnings.

Adjusted Return on Equity

You must also adjust the return on equity when you adjust earnings to keep the two consistent. Adjusting return on equity is easy. Simply divide adjusted earnings by the average equity per share during the year, then multiply by 100 to put the return on a percentage basis. Table 4-6 is a worksheet for adjusting return on equity.

Table 4-6
WORKSHEET FOR ADJUSTING RETURN ON EQUITY

1. Adjusted Earnings, $/Share .... _____
2. Equity, $/Share, beginning of year .... _____
3. Equity, $/Share, end of year .... _____
4. Average Equity: Add Lines 2 and 3; Divide the result
 by 2[1] .... _____
5. Adjusted Return, %: Divide Line 1 by Line 4,
 then Multiply by 100 .... _____

Example 4-10 Use Table 4-6 to find McDonald's adjusted return on equity for 1995. Enter the adjusted earnings and the beginning and ending equity per share from the previous example in the following table:

Table 4-7
ADJUSTING McDONALD'S 1995 RETURN ON EQUITY

1. Adjusted Earnings, $/Share 1.57
2. Equity, $/Share, beginning of year 9.93
3. Equity, $/Share, end of year 11.24
4. Average Equity: Add Lines 2 and 3; Divide the result
 by 2[1] 10.59
5. Adjusted Return, %: Divide Line 1 by Line 4,
 then Multiply by 100 .... 14.83

1. There is a better way to average equity/share in Chapter 7. The simple arithmetic average in this worksheet will do for now.

The adjusted return on equity of 14.83 percent is significantly lower than the 19.9 percent return McDonald's reported in its 1995 annual report.

Adjusting earnings and the return on equity is important; the adjustment makes SmartValue track how a firm grows much more closely. Table 4-8 shows how much closer SmartValue's growth formula reproduces McDonald's actual growth when using adjusted values in place of reported values:

Table 4-8
GROWTH OF McDONALD'S EQUITY PER SHARE - 1995

	Reported Values	Adjusted Values
Dividends, $/Share	0.26	0.26
Earnings, $/Share	1.97	1.57
Dividend Payout Fraction	0.132	0.166
Reinvestment Fraction	0.868	0.834
Return on Equity, %	19.9	14.83
Calculated Growth, %/yr.	17.3	12.37
Actual Growth, %/yr.	**12.39**	**12.39**

Using the adjusted values reproduces McDonald's growth rate almost exactly. The reported values seriously overstate McDonald's growth. That is why we did not calculate McDonald's growth rate correctly in Example 4-7 — we used reported values instead of adjusted values.

Adjusting earnings and the return on equity does not complicate finding what a stock is worth. You have to forecast a return on equity in any case. Forecasting an adjusted return is no more difficult than forecasting a reported return. And, as the growth rate example above shows, the improvement in how well SmartValue tracks the firm is well worth the small effort involved.

How to Use the SmartValue Formula

How do you use the SmartValue formula to find what a real stock is worth? You need to forecast future dividends and stock prices. Begin by forecasting the growth rate of equity per share. That allows you to find the growth multiplier and use the equity formula to find equity per share at any time in the future. Then forecast the firm's return on equity. Use the formula for the dividend payout fraction to find the payout fraction consistent with your growth and return on equity forecast. You now have all the information you need to forecast dividends from the dividend formula. Finally, forecast the P/B ratio. Then use the stock price formula to forecast the stock price at any future time. Do not worry about the details. This whole procedure is built in to the worksheets you will use in later chapters to find what any stock is worth.

Key Operating Characteristics

Why build models? There are two primary reasons. The first is to provide a quantitative tool for forecasting the dollars a firm will put into your pocket from dividends and the eventual sale of the stock. The second reason is to discover the key factors that drive the stock's performance. These are the factors you should pay attention to when you value a firm. This simple set of five models meets both needs. You will recognize the SmartValue formulas as you fill in the worksheets for finding what stocks are worth in later chapters.

The SmartValue formulas show that you need to concentrate on only three key factors to tell what any stock is worth:

> Rate of Return on Equity
> Growth Rate of Equity per Share
> P/B Ratio

Notice that the dividend payout fraction does not appear in this list. That is because the dividend payout fraction depends on the return on equity and the growth rate. Once you forecast the return and the growth rate, the payout fraction formula automatically fixes the dividend payout fraction. The P/E ratio does not appear, either. That is because the P/E ratio depends on the P/B ratio and the return on equity. Once you forecast the P/B ratio and the return on equity, you automatically forecast the P/E ratio.

Equity per share is important because all the cash flows that determine what a stock is worth depend on it. Some analysts object to models based on equity. They object because accountants base equity on arbitrary assumptions about how fast the firm depreciates its plant and equipment. So they do. But equity does not have to be accurate. It only has to be consistent, and calculated in a consistent way from one year to the next. Suppose equity per share is not really as large as the firm claims. What does that do to the Smart-

Value formulas for the stock price and dividends? Absolutely nothing! The P/B ratio multiplied by equity per share must equal the actual stock price. That means the P/B ratio must have an error that exactly compensates the error in equity per share. The dividend model is not affected, either. The payout fraction multiplied by the return on equity and equity per share must equal the actual dividends. That means the payout fraction and the return on equity must also have exactly compensating errors. Because of these offsetting errors models based on equity are perfectly acceptable.

The rate of return the firm earns on shareholder equity is a critical factor. It measures how well the firm fulfills its primary mission of earning a profit for its shareholders. It determines how much money is available to reinvest and to pay dividends. How the firm divides these earnings between dividends and reinvesting to make the firm grow is less important. You benefit either way. That is why the growth rate is less important that the return on equity. The P/B ratio is also a critical characteristic. It measures how the market judges what any stock is worth.

> **Three critical factors determine what a stock is worth:**
>
> **1. Return on Equity**
> **2. Growth Rate of Equity/Share**
> **3. P/B Ratio**

What about all those other statistics, indices, and ratios we worried about in Chapter 2? What happened to them? They are not important. If they were, they would have appeared in one of the SmartValue formulas. Don't worry about them. Concentrate on the three key characteristics that do show up in the SmartValue formulas. They determine what a stock is worth. The other statistics are all interesting. Read them, if you want. Enjoy them. But concentrate on the three key factors in the SmartValue formulas.

Contact With Reality

SmartValue is tied solidly to reality at two key points: stock prices and dividends. Earnings and stockholder equity are accounting devices. The firm's accountants have some leeway in deciding what numbers to report. Not so with stock prices and dividends. They are real. Money based on the stock price rolls out of your pocket when you buy and rolls in when you sell. Dividends roll into your pocket each quarter. Both are difficult to manipulate. The stock price is determined by the buying and selling pressures of many investors in public exchanges, and is reported in the financial pages of your newspaper each day. The Securities and Exchange Commission keeps the process honest. The SmartValue formula ties solidly to stock prices. If the accountants inflate stockholder equity by 20 percent, for example, the P/B ratio is automatically deflated by the same amount, because equity multiplied by the P/B ratio must equal the actual stock price.

Dividend checks arrive in your account each quarter. Once dividends are in your account they are beyond the reach of any games the firm might play. Remember that you are counting the cash that enters your pocket. Do not count stock dividends. Stock dividends are not cash, they are only pieces of paper. SmartValue's dividend formula ties you solidly to dividends. The firm's accountants have some leeway with only two of the three factors — equity per share, return on equity, and the dividend payout fraction — that determine dividends. Overstating any two of these factors forces exactly compensating understating of the third factor, because the three factors multiplied together must yield actual dividends.

How Firms Grow

The primary reason for developing the SmartValue Formula is to obtain a tool for forecasting dividends and stock prices. There is a valuable by-product. SmartValue also helps you understand how firms grow and generate the money that pours into your pocket.

Firms grow by reinvesting earnings. They grow the fastest when they reinvest all their earnings and pay no dividends. The dividend payout fraction then drops to zero and the reinvestment fraction rises to one. How does that affect growth? Remember that the growth rate is equal to the return on equity multiplied by the reinvestment fraction. Equity per share grows at a rate equal to the firm's return on equity when the reinvestment fraction is one. The reinvestment fraction cannot be any greater than one (i.e., the firm cannot reinvest more than all of its earnings). That limit on the reinvestment fraction has an important consequence. It sets a limit on how fast a firm can grow. Equity per share cannot grow any faster than the rate of return the firm earns on stockholder equity.

The fastest a firm can grow is at a rate equal to the firm's return on equity.

If the firm pays all of its earnings out as dividends, the dividend payout fraction rises to one and the reinvestment fraction drops to zero. The growth formula shows that the growth rate of equity per share also drops to zero. If the firm does not reinvest at least some of its earnings, it cannot grow.

A firm cannot grow rapidly and pay high dividends at the same time. If the firm grows rapidly, most of its earnings will have to be reinvested to pay for that growth, and dividends will be small. If the firm pays most of its earnings out as dividends, there will be few earnings left to reinvest, and growth will be slow.

Forecasting Tips

The SmartValue formula yields important guidelines to keep in mind when you forecast how any firm will perform. When you examine the firm's historical record, concentrate on the adjusted return on equity the firm has earned. What average return has it earned over the past few years? Is the return stable? Is it relatively constant? If not, the firm may not really be mature. You may need to use the worksheet for growth firms in later chapters because they allow for returns that do not stay constant.

Your forecast of the firm's growth rate is not quite as critical. Suppose the firm does not grow as fast as you forecast. Equity per share and the price of the stock will not be as high as you forecast when you eventually sell the stock. That will lower the value of the stock. But you will receive more dividends than you had forecast because the firm will have used less of its earnings to pay for growth. More will be available for dividends. That will make the stock more valuable. The two effects tend to balance. The higher dividends tend to offset the lower stock price. If the firm grows faster than you had forecast, the reverse is true. The price of the stock will be higher than you had forecast when you sell. But the firm will have reinvested more of its earnings to pay for the faster growth. You will receive less dividends than you had forecast. The smaller dividends tend to offset the higher stock price.

Once you forecast return on equity and the growth rate of equity per share, the growth formula determines a dividend payout fraction that is consistent with those forecasts. SmartValue thus forces your forecasts of growth, earnings, and dividends to be consistent with each other.

SmartValue demonstrates that a firm cannot grow at a rate faster than its return on equity. Be careful when you forecast growth rates. Make sure that you forecast a growth rate for equity per share no higher than your forecast of the return on equity. If you forecast a growth rate higher than the return on equity, the dividend payout fraction will be negative—you will pay dividends to the firm instead of the other way round!

Your forecast of the P/B ratio is also critical, particularly if you plan to hold the stock only a short time. If your time horizon is only a few months, your forecast of the P/B ratio is crucial. There is no time for dividends to amount to much. The reliability of a stock valuation depends primarily on how reliably you forecast the P/B ratio. As you lengthen your time horizon, dividends become more important and the future stock price less important. As we saw in Chapter 3, if you hold the stock forever, dividends become all important, and the future stock price becomes irrelevant because you never sell. As you lengthen your time horizon, the reliability of a stock valuation depends more on how reliably you forecast the return on equity and the growth rate of equity per share, and less on how reliably you forecast the P/B ratio.

Where to Next?

We now have a set of tools we can use to forecast both the dividends a mature firm will put in your pocket and the price you can expect when you eventually sell the stock. Before you use those tools to find what any stock is worth, you need to tune your analysis to your own situation. That involves choosing the right discount rate to find what those future dollars are worth today. You will learn how to do that tuning in the next chapter.

Summary

The SmartValue Formula consists of five simple models that allow you to make consistent forecasts of equity per share, earnings per share, dividends per share, the price of the stock, and the growth rate of equity per share. The SmartValue Formula shows that you need to focus on only three critical factors to find what a stock is worth:

> Return on Equity
> Growth Rate of Equity/Share
> Price/Book Ratio

All the other statistics you read in the financial media may be interesting, but they are not critical.

Using reported earnings makes SmartValue track a firm's performance only approximately. But a simple adjustment to reinvested earnings makes SmartValue track the firm exactly.

A firm cannot grow rapidly and pay high dividends at the same time. If the firm grows rapidly, it will need to reinvest most of its earnings to pay for that growth. There will be little or no earnings left for dividends. If the firm pays most of its earnings out as dividends, there will be little or no earnings left to pay for growth, and growth will be slow. The fastest stockholder equity can grow is at a rate equal to the firm's return on equity.

The SmartValue Formula forces your forecasts of growth rate, return on investment, and dividends to be consistent with each other.

The Exponential e^x

We will find the exponential e^x extremely useful when finding what any stock is worth. You might feel more confident when analyzing stocks if you understand how it behaves. Figure 4-1 tells all. As we will use the exponential in this book, the "x" in e^x is a rate multiplied by a time. The rate multiplied by time is plotted on the horizontal axis of Figure 4-1and e^x is plotted on the vertical axis. The rate is either a growth rate or a discount rate. When the rate is a growth rate the rate multiplied by time is positive, and e^x is a growth multiplier. That part of the curve on the right side of Figure 4-1 applies, and e^x has some value greater than 1.0. A discount rate is like a negative growth rate. When

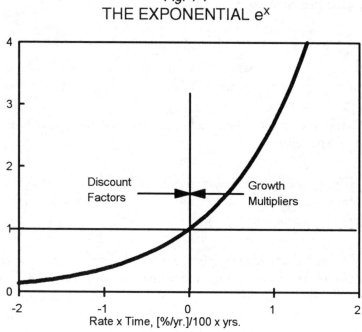

Fig. 4-1
THE EXPONENTIAL e^x

Rate x Time, [%/yr.]/100 x yrs.

the rate is a discount rate the rate multiplied by time is negative, and e^x becomes a discount factor. That part of the curve on the left side of Figure 4-1 then applies, and e^x has some value between zero and one.

When either the growth rate or the discount rate or time is zero, the rate multiplied by time is also zero, and e^x is 1.0. As you can see from Figure 4-1, the growth multiplier begins at 1.0 when the rate multiplied by time is zero, and increases towards infinity as either the growth rate, or time, or both, increase. The discount factor also begins at 1.0 when the rate multiplied by time is zero, and decreases towards zero as either the discount rate, or time, or both, increase.

Chapter **5**

Tuning The Analysis

Time Horizon

Taxes

What Your Money Costs

Risk Premium

Discount Rate

Broker's Commissions

A Typical Investor

We now have a model we can use to forecast future stock prices and dividends. How do we use that model to find what a stock is worth to you, and not to some "average" investor? How do we tune the analysis to your individual situation? To your time horizon? To your tax bracket? To your tolerance for risk? What discount rate should you use to find what all those dollars a stock will put into your pocket in the future are worth today? How do we compare the opportunity to invest in that stock with your alternative investment opportunities?

Different investors look at the same stock and place different values on it. That is why stocks trade. The buyer is convinced he is getting something worth more than the stock costs. The seller is convinced he is getting more than the stock is worth. Both may be right. Why? Certainly one major reason is that each investor has a different opinion about how the firm will perform, and how the price of its stock will respond. The buyer is more optimistic about the firm's prospects than the seller. But even if all investors shared an identical outlook for the firm, they would still place different values on the stock. Investors value stocks differently for a number of reasons. They may have different time horizons. They may be in different federal or state tax brackets. The money they are investing has a cost; the cost differs from one investor to the next. That is because different investors have different alternatives for investing their money. They may have different tolerances for risk. All of these factors affect how each investor decides what a stock is worth.

If all these factors are involved, you cannot simply take the SmartValue formulas from the last chapter and use them blindly to find what a stock is worth. That would tell you what a stock is worth to that average investor. You are not an average investor. You are special. You are an individual. You have your own outlook for the firm, your own time horizon, tax brackets, alternative investments, and tolerance for risk. You want to recognize your own characteristics and find out what a stock is worth to you, not to that average investor. In this chapter I will show you how to tune the analysis to your own individual situation. The tuning process will develop part of the input you will need for the worksheets in later chapters to find what any stock is worth.

Time Horizon

What kind of an investor are you? Are you the get-rich-quick type looking for a quick killing? Or do you have the patience to buy a solid company and hold on to the stock for a number of years? If getting rich quickly is your goal, you are not an investor. You are a speculator. There is too little time for dividends to make a significant contribution. You are looking for a quick, and largely unpredictable, rise in the stock's price. Everything rides on your forecast of tomorrow's stock price. Price forecasts, especially short-term forecasts, are extremely risky. Price movements are a combination of an underlying trend based on the firm's fundamentals, and an overlay of random price movements. You are not allowing enough time for the underlying trend to make itself felt. You are trying to forecast the random price movements. Good luck! But if you invest for a longer term, the underlying trend becomes more important, and the random price movements less important. You are in a much better position to make a reasonable forecast of future prices based on the firm's fundamentals. The first step in tuning the analysis is to decide on your time horizon. Are you a speculator or an investor? Do you plan to hold the stock for a few months or a few years? How many years?

Taxes

Taxes do not affect all stocks the same way. If you buy a growth stock that pays no dividends, all of your gains will come as a capital gain at the end of the investment period and will be taxed at that time. Deferring taxes is an advantage. Taxes have less of an impact the longer you can defer them. Remember that you have to discount those taxes. The longer you can defer taxes, the more heavily you discount them. That lowers their impact on the stock's value. Taxes have a greater impact if you buy a stock which pays most of its earnings out as dividends and grows slowly. Your gains will come more from dividends and less from capital gains. Taxes will be more important because you will have to pay them as you receive the dividends. Paying taxes sooner means those taxes will not be discounted as heavily. Allow for the different impact of taxes on low and high dividend-paying stocks by doing your analysis on an after-tax basis.

The federal government will tax any dividends you earn at your incremental tax rate, that is, at the tax rate you pay on your last dollar of taxable income. Suppose you have $40,000 of taxable income. That puts you in the 28 percent federal tax bracket; that is your incremental tax rate. If you add dividend income from a stock, that increment of income adds to your $40,000 of taxable income and will be taxed at your 28 percent incremental tax rate. State and local taxes add to your tax burden, but if you itemize deductions on your federal tax return you get a credit for the state and local taxes you paid.

Use the following worksheet to figure your net incremental tax rate on the combined federal, state, and local taxes. Use the same worksheet for both dividend income and capital gains:

Table 5-1
NET INCREMENTAL TAX RATE

1. Incremental Federal Tax Rate, % .... _____

2. Incremental State and Local Tax Rate, % .... _____

A. You Don't Itemize

3. Net incremental Tax Rate, %: Add Lines 1 and 2 .... _____

B. You Do Itemize

4. Multiply Line 1 by Line 2, then Divide by 100 .... _____

5. Net Incremental Tax Rate, %: Add Lines 1 and 2,
   then Subtract Line 4 .... _____

Example 5-1 An investor pays a 28 percent incremental federal tax rate and a 6 percent incremental state and local tax rate. He itemizes deductions on his federal tax return. What is his net incremental tax rate? Use Table 5-1.

Table 5-2
NET INCREMENTAL TAX RATE - Example 5-1

1. Incremental Federal Tax Rate, % 28

2. Incremental State and Local Tax Rate, % 6

A. You Don't Itemize

3. Net incremental Tax Rate, %: Add Lines 1 and 2 34

B. You Do Itemize

4. Multiply Line 1 by Line 2, then Divide by 100 .... 1.68

5. Net Incremental Tax Rate, %: Add Lines 1 and 2,
   then Subtract Line 4 .... 32.32

If this investor did not itemize, line 3 shows his total incremental tax rate would be 34 percent, the total of his federal, state, and local tax rates. Itemizing lowers his net tax rate to 32.32 percent, as line 5 shows. Check your tax federal and state returns, then use Table 5-1 to figure your incremental tax rate. After this investor pays his taxes, he will have 100 minus 32.32, or 67.68 cents left out of each dollar of taxable investment income.

Our investor is a long-term investor. He pays a 20 percent federal tax on capital gains. His state taxes capital gains at a 6 percent tax rate. He finds from Table 5-1 that his combined federal, state, and local capital gains tax rate will be 24.8 percent.

What Your Money Costs

What your money costs is one of the critical questions you must answer to decide what a stock is worth to you. If you do not know what your money costs, you risk the capital sin of investing. You risk the sin of investing money that costs, say, 12 percent, in a stock that earns a return of only 8 percent.

Alternative Investments

The money you use to buy a stock is not free. It has a cost. The cost is the return you could have earned if you had invested in the next best use of that money. Economists call that cost an "opportunity cost". It is the return you could have earned on the opportunity you have given up in order to buy a stock. Suppose you have some investment opportunity that promises a 10 percent return. If you use that money to buy a stock instead, you are giving up an opportunity to earn a 10 percent return on the alternative investment. Your opportunity cost is 10 percent. That cost sets a floor under the return you should accept from any other investment. If the stock you are considering does not promise at least a 10 percent return, do not buy it. Look for a better stock. Look for a stock that promises more than a 10 percent return. If you cannot find such a stock, put your money in that 10 percent opportunity instead. Know your opportunity cost, it is important.

How do you find your opportunity cost? Easy. Make a list of your alternative investment opportunities. Estimate the rate of return each one earns after taxes. Do not overlook paying off debt and avoiding interest payments. Paying off debt and avoiding interest payments is just as valuable as an investment that earns the same interest rate you are paying on the debt. Then rank your opportunities in order of their after-tax returns. The opportunity that promises the highest return determines your opportunity cost. Do not invest in any stock unless it promises a higher return than your opportunity cost.

What are your investment alternatives? You do not have to buy that stock you are considering. There are other alternatives. You can always invest that money somewhere else. If you are uneasy about risks in the stock market, you might invest in a certificate of deposit, a money market fund, or a Treasury Bill. They currently earn returns of about 5 percent. If you want a higher return and are determined to be in the stock market, you might invest with relative safety in an S&P 500 Index Fund. These funds invest in the 500 stocks that make up the S&P 500 stock index. They are a great way to lower your risk by diversifying. Vanguard's S&P 500 Index Fund has averaged a 13.7 percent return over the past ten years. Do you have any debt you might pay off? How about credit card debt? Paying off credit card debt could save you from paying 18 percent interest. What about your mortgage? Prepaying your mortgage also saves interest costs. Let's see how our investor from Example 5-1 would go about finding what his money costs.

Example 5-2 The investor from Example 5-1 sits down to find what his money costs. He would like to invest in the stock market, but recognizes that he has other reasonable alternative investments. He decides that reasonable alternatives for him include a certificate of deposit, a money market fund, one-year Treasury Bills, and Vanguard's S&P 500 Index Fund. He also considers paying off credit card debt and prepaying his mortgage, on which he pays 9 percent interest. His net incremental tax rate is 32.32 percent, so that his after-tax returns are 67.68 percent of his before-tax returns. That makes the net interest rate he is paying on his mortgage 9 times 0.6768, or 6.09 percent after allowing for deducting mortgage interest from his taxable income.

Table 5-3 shows how he values each opportunity and ranks them in order of the returns they promise after taxes. The most attractive alternative on this list is paying off credit card debt and avoiding 18 percent interest charges. Our investor knows better than to pay such high interest rates. He pays his credit charges promptly and avoids these high interest payments. His next best opportunity is the S&P 500 index fund. He estimates that fund will yield an after-tax return of about 9.3 percent. If he were willing to accept the risk that goes with this fund, that fund and its 9.3 percent after-tax return would establish his opportunity cost. He would not buy any stock unless it promised an after-tax return of at least 9.3 percent. If he could not find such a stock, he would put his money in the S&P 500 index fund instead. If he thought the index fund was too risky, his next best alternative would be to prepay his mortgage and save an after-tax interest rate of 6.09 percent. If he had no mortgage, a one-year Treasury Bill would be his next best investment. The one-year Treasury Bill would establish his opportunity cost at 4 percent.

Interest rates are not stable; they change with the supply and demand for credit and with the intervention of the Federal Reserve Board. Review your opportunity cost from time to time to make sure your assessment of what your money costs keeps abreast of changing interest rates.

Table 5-3
WHAT YOUR MONEY COSTS - Example 5-2

Alternative Investment	Cost or Return, %	
	Before Taxes	After Taxes
1. Pay off Credit Card debt	18	18
2. S&P 500 Index Fund	13.7	9.3
3. Prepay 9% Mortgage	9.0	6.09
4. 1-Year Treasury Bill	5.5	4.0*
5. 1-Year Certificate of Deposit	5.0	3.4
6. Money Market Fund	4.9	3.3

* Free of state taxes

Risk Premium

Stocks are risky. You buy a stock expecting that the price will go up. But no one can foretell the future. The price may, indeed, go up, particularly if you hold the stock long enough. But the unexpected may happen. A competitor may develop a better product and take markets away from your firm. Key personnel may leave. Fire may destroy the firm's plant. The firm may make a disastrous acquisition. The firm's product may harm customers and lead to serious legal problems. The Justice Department may file an antitrust suit. Such unexpected events may make the stock's price go down instead of up. Some stocks are riskier than others. Small firms making their initial public offering have little or no track record. Their stocks are extremely risky. Mature firms are much less risky; their long track record generates confidence in them. But they are still risky compared to the investments that determine your opportunity cost.

How can you allow for risk when deciding what a stock is worth? How can you allow for the difference between that risky start-up firm and a safer, mature firm? The easiest way is to add a risk premium to your opportunity cost. Do not settle for a stock that just earns your opportunity cost — that just earns the same return as one of the safer investments from the list you made to find what your money costs. Insist that the stock earn something extra to compensate for the additional risk you will shoulder. The total of your opportunity cost and the risk premium you add determines the minimum rate of return you should accept.

How do you decide on an appropriate risk premium? It is a very personal decision. It depends on your individual tolerance for risk. How much risk can you accept and still sleep nights? If even small amounts of risk make you nervous, choose a high risk premium. If you insist on low risk, you will have to accept a low return. If you want a higher return, you will have to accept the risk that goes along with high returns. If you are a risk taker, choose a low risk premium. You also have to consider the kind of firm whose stock you are thinking of buying. What kind of firm is it? A recent hi-tech start-up with little or no track record? If that description fits, choose a high risk premium. Or is the firm a stable, mature firm in a settled business? If that description fits, choose a lower risk premium.

Do not set your risk premium too high or too low. If you choose a high risk premium, you will have a high minimum acceptable return. You will find few stocks that meet such severe minimum return standards. You certainly reduce your risk, but you also reduce the number of stocks you have to choose from. Set the risk premium high enough, and you will not find any stocks that satisfy your requirements. Too low a risk premium causes the opposite problem. You will have too a low a minimum acceptable return. That means you run too high a risk of paying too much for stocks.

Remember that you are competing with a host of other investors for each stock. One of the dimensions of that competition is the minimum return each investor will accept. You need to set your risk premium at competitive levels. Otherwise, investors with a greater tolerance for risk will set lower risk premiums and have a lower minimum acceptable return. They will outbid you because they will put a higher value on stocks and be willing to pay a higher price.

Other Ways to Handle Risk

Adding a risk premium is not the only way to allow for risk. There is a better way in Chapter 18. It requires more work, but it provides a better feel for risk. If you are investing a large sum, use that method. It is well worth the extra work.

Discounting Future Cash Flows

Adding a risk premium to what your money costs establishes the minimum rate of return you should demand from any stock. Deciding what minimum rate of return you should accept from any stock is a critical step in finding what that stock is worth. Go ahead and work out your minimum acceptable return. What then? What do you do with your minimum acceptable return once you have it? Remember that you have to discount all the cash you expect a stock to put into your pocket in the future to find what that stock is worth. Discounting is a key step in finding what a stock is worth. That is where your minimum acceptable return comes into the analysis. Your minimum acceptable return is the discount rate you will use in the worksheet for finding what a stock is worth. The value you find when you discount the money you expect a stock to put into your pocket is a critical value. It is the most you can afford to pay for that stock and still earn at least your minimum acceptable return. If you pay anything more, you will earn some return below the minimum return you specified as being acceptable.

Do not worry about the details now. The worksheet for finding what stocks are worth takes care of all the details for you.

Here is the iron rule you must follow when you invest in stocks:

Do not buy any stock unless you can earn at least your minimum acceptable return — unless you can earn what your money costs plus a risk premium appropriate for your tolerance for risk and the riskiness of that stock.

Broker's Commissions

Broker's commissions can be an important factor in your analysis, particularly if you plan to hold the stock for only a short time, or if you use a full-service broker. Broker's commissions become less important the longer you hold the stock. Check with your broker and see what commissions he charges. Figure the commission as a percentage of the stock's market price; that is the way you will enter commissions in the stock valuation worksheet. Consider using a discount broker. After you use SmartValue to decide what a stock is worth, you will be in a better position to judge the stock than a full-service broker. Pay yourself his commission; you did the work!

A Typical Investor

We are now ready to use SmartValue to find what real stocks are worth. We need to tune the analysis to a specific investor. Let's use the investor we have been studying in this chapter as that investor, and tune the analysis to his situation.

Our investor invests for the long term. Let's assume he plans to hold any stock he buys for five years. He pays an incremental federal tax rate of 28 percent on dividends and a 20 percent tax on capital gains. He pays an incremental state and local tax rate of 6 percent on both dividends and capital gains. He itemizes deductions on his federal tax return. His net incremental tax rate is 32.32 percent on dividends, as we found in Example 5-1. His net federal, state, and local tax rate on capital gains is 24.8 percent. He needs to earn a higher return than he can get in safe investments like certificates of deposit. He is determined to invest in the stock market. He therefore decides that an S&P 500 index fund is his best alternative investment. It fits within his tolerance for risk. He chooses Vanguard's S&P 500 Index Fund, and concludes that the money he is investing costs 9.3 percent after taxes, as we saw in Example 5-2. He hopes to find stocks that earn higher returns. But he will buy no stock unless it promises a return of at least 9.3 percent, plus a risk premium he thinks appropriate for each stock he considers. We will follow this investor as he considers buying Coca-Cola, Cisco Systems, and Microsoft in subsequent chapters.

Summary

You need to make five choices to tune the analysis to your individual financial situation. You need to choose a time horizon — how long do you intend to hold the stock? You need to work out your net incremental tax rate so you can take taxes into account. You have to estimate the returns you could earn from alternative investments. The return you could earn from the best alternative investment determines what your money costs. That return is the minimum return you should insist on when you decide what any stock is worth. You also need to add a risk premium appropriate for your tolerance for risk and the riskiness of the particular stock you are considering. You should not buy any stock unless it promises a return at least as high as your cost of money plus a suitable risk premium. Finally, you have to decide whether you will use a discount broker or a full-service broker.

Chapter **6**

What Are Mature Firms Worth?

Where Do You Start?

1. Adjust Earnings and the Return on Equity

2. Examine the Historical Record

3. Forecast the Return on Equity, the Growth Rate, and the P/B Ratio

4. Use the Worksheet to Find What the Stock Is Worth

The Stock Valuation Worksheet

How much is the stock of a mature firm worth? We now have the tools we need to find out. The Stock Valuation Worksheet in this chapter does the job. It incorporates the SmartValue formulas and uses them to forecast the dollars that enter and leave your pocket — the dividends you receive while you hold the stock, and the net proceeds when you finally sell, and the taxes and broker's commissions you pay. Then it discounts those dollars to find what the stock is worth. It uses your analysis of your financial situation to tailor the valuation to your individual situation.

Where Do You Start?

How do you go about finding what a real stock is worth? The first step is to adjust the earnings and the return on equity the firm reports. Then analyze the firm's historical performance. Zero in on the rate of return the firm earns on stockholder equity, how fast the firm is growing, and the P/B ratio investors have been willing to pay for the stock. Use that analysis to forecast how the firm will perform in the future. If the firm appears to be mature and follow the steady-state model reasonably well use the worksheet in this chapter to find what the stock is worth. We will look at the basic procedure in this chapter. Then we will use SmartValue to find what Coca-Cola, a typical mature firm, is worth. We will analyze Coca-Cola's historical performance in Chapter 7 and use that analysis to forecast Coca-Cola's future performance. Then we will use the worksheet to find what Coca-Cola's stock is worth to our investor from the last chapter.

Get your hands on a record of the firm's historical performance. That is the place to start. The easiest way to get this information is from a service like Value Line. Value Line provides historical data for the past ten years and forecasts for the next two years. Your local library may subscribe to Value Line. If the stock looks promising based on your analysis, write to the firm and ask for a copy of their latest annual report. The firm's annual report is the primary source of information.

Step 1 - Adjust Earnings and the Return on Equity

The first thing to do when you want to know what any stock is worth is to convert the earnings and the return on equity the firm reports to adjusted earnings and adjusted returns on equity. You found why this adjustment is important and learned how to adjust the data in Chapter 4. I will give you a worksheet that makes adjusting earnings and the return on equity easy when we examine Coca-Cola in the next chapter. Work with adjusted earnings and returns rather than with the earnings and returns the firm reports. SmartValue will track a firm much more closely if you do.

Step 2 - Examine the Firm's Return on Equity, Growth Rate, and P/B Ratio

You need to make three key forecasts to find what any stock is worth. You need to forecast the rate of return the firm will earn on stockholder equity. You need to forecast how fast equity per share will grow. Finally, you need to forecast the P/B ratio investors will be willing to pay for the stock. What basis do you have for making these forecasts? Your primary information is the firm's historical record — how has the firm performed in the past? Although there is no guarantee that the firm will perform in the future as it has in the past, let's face it — the firm's historical record is frequently all you have to go on. It is the report card for the firm's management. By all means, read the financial press. It will give you a feel for the outlook for the national economy and the outlook for the particular industry the firm operates in. It may even feature articles on the firm itself. Your reading may alert you to changes in the business environment that might affect the firm. Use any information you come across in your reading to supplement the historical record and adjust your forecasts accordingly.

How do you examine a firm's performance? The best way is to take out a sheet of graph paper and plot how the key factors vary with time. How do the plots look? Are the key factors stable or do they gradually change? How badly do they scatter around their trend line? Do not expect the data to lie exactly on a trend line. This is not an experiment in a physical chemistry laboratory. We are dealing with economic data. The data do not have to lie exactly on a trend line. The data just has to be reasonably steady and reasonably close to the trend line. If the data scatter badly, forecasting future performance will be difficult. You might consider looking for another stock.

Return on equity is a critical factor. What return has the firm earned? Is the return stable? Is it growing? Is it steady? Or is it falling? Plot the adjusted return against time and see. The plot will show you whether the return is stable enough that you can use the steady-state model and the Worksheet for Mature Firms in this chapter to find what the stock is worth. If the return is reasonably stable, you can forecast that the firm will continue to earn the same average return in the future as it has in the past.

Mature firms earn adjusted returns on equity on the order of 15 percent per year. If the firm you are studying earns a much higher return, you should be concerned about the firm's ability to maintain that high return. Is it reasonable to forecast that the firm will continue to earn such a high return? Or is it more reasonable to forecast that the firm's return will gradually fall? If you expect the return to fall, do not use the steady-state worksheet in this chapter to find what the stock is worth. Use the worksheet for growth stocks in Chapter 12, or the worksheet for the Unlimited Flexibility Model in Chapter 15.

How fast equity per share grows is also critical. Plot the growth rate of equity per share against time. The plot will show you whether growth is rising, is stable, or is falling. If the firm is mature, it may be growing at about the rate the national economy grows measured in current dollars. With real (i.e., adjusted for inflation) GDP growing about 3 percent per year and inflation growing about 4 percent per year, that would be a growth rate of about 3 plus 4, or 7 percent per year in current (i.e., not adjusted for inflation) dollars. If the firm is growing much faster than about 7 percent per year, you should be concerned about the firm's ability to maintain such rapid growth. Can you reasonably expect the firm to continue growing that fast? Or is it more reasonable to forecast that growth will gradually slow? If you expect growth to slow, do not use the steady-state worksheet in this chapter to find what the stock is worth. That is what the worksheet for growth stocks in Chapters 12 and 13 is for. That is what the worksheet for the Unlimited Flexibility Model in Chapter 15 is for.

Finally, examine the P/B ratio investors have been willing to pay for the firm's stock. Value Line reports historical data on the P/E ratio, but not on the P/B ratio. No problem. A worksheet will make it easy to convert P/E ratios into P/B ratios. Remember that you can find the P/B ratio simply by multiplying the P/E ratio be the return on equity (in decimal form). Over the long run, the average stock sells at a P/E ratio of about 15. Mature firms tend to earn about a 15 percent return on equity. That makes the typical P/B ratio for mature firms about 0.15 times 15, or 2.25. If the stock you are considering sells at a much higher P/B ratio, you should be concerned about whether investors will continue to pay such a high P/B ratio. What will the P/B ratio be when you are ready to sell the stock? That is the key. The P/B ratio does not have to stay at steady-state levels in order to use the Worksheet for Mature Firms. Only the return on equity and the growth rate have to stay steady. The P/B ratio can vary. Your only concern is what the P/B ratio will be when you finally sell the stock.

Step 3 - Forecast the Firm's Return on Equity, Growth Rate, and P/B Ratio

The plots of the adjusted return on equity, the equity per share growth rate, and the P/B ratio will help you forecast the future values you can expect for these key factors. If those plots lead you to forecast that both return on equity and the growth rate of equity per share will continue at their historical levels, then the firm is mature, and the worksheet in this chapter is the one to use to find what that stock is worth. Go ahead and make those forecasts. Also forecast what you expect the P/B ratio to be when you eventually sell the stock.

Step 4 - Find What the Stock is Worth

Now you are ready for the final step — filling out the worksheet and finding what the stock is worth. Enter your forecasts of the firm's return on equity, growth rate of equity per share, and the P/B ratio when you eventually sell the stock in the Worksheet for Mature Firms. Enter your financial situation as well. Then follow the instructions in the worksheet and find what the stock is worth.

The Stock Valuation Worksheet

Table 6-1 is the worksheet for finding what the stocks of mature firms are worth. A stock is only worth whatever price allows you to earn the rate of return you specify as being the minimum return you will accept. The Worksheet for Mature Firms gives you that price. It tells you the most you can afford to pay for any stock, given your forecasts of how the firm will perform in the future, and your individual financial situation. If you buy a stock at that price and the firm performs as you forecast, you will earn the minimum return you specified. If you can buy the stock at a lower price, you will earn a higher return than the minimum return you specified.

The worksheet is divided into three sections. The first section describes the kind of an investor you are. It uses information on your individual financial situation to tailor the evaluation to you. Then SmartValue can tell you what the stock is worth to you, and not to some average investor.

The second section covers the firm. Here is where you enter your forecasts of the firm's return on equity, the growth rate of equity per share, and P/B ratio. Here is where you find how many dollars will flow into your pocket if the firm performs as you forecast.

The final section discounts all the dollars you forecast that stock will put into your pocket, adds up all the discounted dollars, and tells what the stock is worth.

Section I—The Investor

Each investor has his own value for a stock. SmartValue is going to tell you what a stock is worth to you, not to some other investor. We developed the information you need to tailor a stock's value to your individual financial situation in Chapter 5. That is the information that goes in Section I of the worksheet.

Table 6-1
WORKSHEET FOR MATURE FIRMS

Section I - The Investor

1. Investment Period, years .... _____
2. Divide Incremental Tax Rate on Ordinary Income (%)
   by 100; Subtract the Result from 1.0 .... _____
3. Divide Capital Gains Tax Rate (%) by 100 .... _____
4. Divide Minimum Acceptable Return (%) by 100 .... _____
5. Divide Broker's Commission (%) by 100;
   Add the Result to 1.0 .... _____
6. Divide Broker's Commission (%) by 100;
   Subtract the Result from 1.0 .... _____

Section II - The Firm

7. Initial Equity, $/Share .... _____
8. Projected Return on Equity, % .... _____
9. Projected Growth Rate, %/yr. .... _____
10. Dividend Payout Fraction: Divide Line 9 by Line 8,
    then Subtract the Result from 1.0 .... _____
11. Initial Dividend, $/Share: Multiply Line 7
    by Lines 8 and 10, then Divide by 100 .... _____
12. Multiply Line 1 by Line 9, then Divide by 100 .... _____
13. Growth Multiplier: Enter Line 12 in your calculator
    and tap the e^x key .... _____
14. Final Equity, $/Share: Multiply Line 7 by Line 13 .... _____
15. Projected Price/Book Ratio .... _____
16. Final Stock Price: Multiply Line 14 by Line 15 .... _____

Table 6-1
WORKSHEET FOR MATURE FIRMS (Cont'd)

Section III - What is The Stock Worth?

17. Multiply Line 1 by Line 4 .... _____
18. Enter Line 17 in your calculator, tap the change
    sign (+/-) key, then tap the e^x key .... _____
19. Multiply Line 13 by Line 18 .... _____
20. If Line 19 is less than 1.0:
    20a. Subtract Line 19 from 1.0 .... _____
    20b. Divide Line 9 by 100 and Subtract the Result
        from Line 4
    20c. Divide Line 20a by Line 20b .... _____
    If Line 19 is greater than 1.0:
    20a. Subtract 1.0 from Line 19 .... _____
    20b. Divide Line 9 by 100, then
            Subtract Line 4 from the Result .... _____
    20c. Divide Line 20a by Line 20b .... _____
    If Line 19 is equal to 1.0:
    20c. Copy Line 1 .... _____
21. Present Value of Dividends: Multiply Line 2 by
        Lines 11 and 20c .... _____
22. Present Value of Final Stock Price: Multiply Line 6
        by Lines 16 and 18 .... _____
23. Multiply Line 3 by Line 22 .... _____
24. Subtract Line 23 from Line 22 .... _____
25. Multiply Line 3 by Line 18 and
        Subtract the Result from 1.0 .... _____
26. Value of Stock: Add Lines 21 and 24, then
        Divide the Result by Line 5 and by Line 25 .... _____

Your time horizon is important. How many years do you plan to hold the stock? Enter that time in line 1 of the worksheet. Taxes are also important. Account for their impact in lines 2 and 3. You worked out your incremental tax rate on ordinary income such as dividends in Table 5-1 of Chapter 5. Divide the incremental tax rate by 100. Dividing by 100 expresses your tax rate as the fraction of your dividend income that goes to taxes. Then subtract that fraction from 1.0. Subtracting from 1.0 gives the fraction of dividend income you will have left after taxes. Enter that fraction in Line 2. You also used Table 5-1 to work out your incremental tax rate on capital gains. Divide that tax rate by 100 and enter the result in line 3.

The minimum acceptable rate of return you specify is a key factor in determining what any stock is worth to you. Your minimum acceptable rate of return is the discount rate SmartValue will use to discount all the dollars that roll into your pocket in the future. The higher the minimum return you specify, the less you can afford to pay for the stock and still earn that minimum return. Put the minimum rate of return you will accept in decimal form by dividing by 100 and enter the result in line 4.

Broker's commissions can also be important, particularly if you plan to hold the stock for only a short time. Ask you broker what his commission is and then convert it to a percentage of the stock's market price. Divide the percentage by 100. Then add the result to 1.0 in line 5 and subtract it from 1.0 in line 6. We will use line 5 to account for your broker's commission when you buy the stock and line 6 to account for his commission when you sell.

Section II—The Firm

Your forecasts of how the firm will perform in the future go in Section II of the worksheet. You need to enter the starting value of equity per share, and your forecasts of the return you expect the firm to earn on stockholder equity, how fast you expect equity per share to grow, and the P/B ratio you expect investors to pay when you sell the stock.

The current stockholder equity in dollars per share is the starting point for the computation. Your value for equity may be several months out of date. Bring it up to date. Suppose you are analyzing the stock in early July, and your latest value for equity per share comes from last year's annual report. Equity will have grown in the six-month interval since the annual report. Adjust for that growth; it is easy to do. Use Table 4-1 from Chapter 4 to find the growth multiplier for the six-month time period and the growth rate you are forecasting. Multiply last year's ending equity per share by that growth multiplier. That will give you a reasonable estimate of the current equity per share. Enter the result in line 7.

Your forecasts of the firm's return on equity and growth rate are critical elements of the analysis. Enter your forecast of the return on equity in line 8 and your forecast of the growth rate in line 9. The worksheet develops the dividend payout fraction consistent with your return on equity and growth rate forecasts in line 10, and uses that fraction to work out the initial dividend in line 11.

The worksheet finds the equity per share when you sell by multiplying the initial equity by a growth multiplier. The growth multiplier is developed in lines 12 and 13; these lines reproduce the growth multiplier computations in Table 4-1 of Chapter 4. Calculate the equity per share when you sell in line 14. Enter your forecast of the P/B ratio in line 15. Forecast the stock price when you sell by multiplying the equity per share by the P/B ratio in line 16.

Section III—What Is the Stock Worth?

You have now entered all the information you need to find what the stock is worth. Section II of the worksheet developed the dollars that will flow into and out of your pocket if you buy the stock. Section III discounts those dollars and adds them up to find what the stock is worth. The future dollars are discounted using the minimum acceptable return you specified in line 4 as the discount rate.

Lines 17 and 18 work out the discount factor used to discount those future dollars. The discount factor in line 18 must be some number between zero and one. That is why you are instructed to tap the change sign key in line 18. The number in your calculator's display window must have a minus sign in front of it before you tap the e^x key. Tapping the change sign key puts that minus sign in the display window. Your calculator may use the +/- symbol or the abbreviation CHS to identify the change sign key. If you find a number greater than one in line 18 you forgot to tap the change sign key. Go back and try again!

Lines 19 and 20 work out the discount factor that applies to the dividends you expect to receive. That discount factor depends on whether the minimum rate of return you specified in line 4 is greater than, less than, or equal to the growth rate you forecast in line 9. Line 20 is divided into three sections, one for each possibility. If line 19 is less than 1.0, your minimum acceptable return is greater than the growth rate. Use the first group of lines 20a through 20c to find the discount factor for dividends. That discount factor must be between zero and the number of years you entered in line 1. If line 19 is greater than 1.0, your minimum acceptable return is less than the growth rate. Use the second group of lines 20a through 20c to find the discount factor for dividends. That discount factor will be greater than the number of years you entered in line 1. If line 19 is equal to one the discount factor will be equal to the number of years you entered in line 1.

Find the discounted value of the dividends you receive while you hold the stock in line 21. Simply multiply the initial dividends in line 11 by the after-tax factor from line 2 and by the discount factor in line 20c. Find the discounted value of the stock price when you sell in Line 22. Multiply the final stock price in line 16 by the factor for broker's commissions in line 6 and by the discount factor in line 18. Lines 23 through 25 work out the effects of capital gains taxes.

What is the stock of a mature firm worth to you? What can you afford to pay for it and still earn at least the minimum rate of return you specified? Line 26 gives the answer. Once you know what a stock is worth you can use the Golden Rule. You can compare what the stock costs to what it is worth. Suppose the stock is available at the price you find from this worksheet. If you buy the stock at that price and the firm performs as you forecast, you will earn the minimum rate of return you specified as being acceptable. The stock may cost more than the value you find from the worksheet. If it does, the stock costs too much. Do not buy it! If you do and the firm performs as you forecast, you will earn a lower return than the minimum you specified. But if you can buy the stock at a price below the value you find from this worksheet, consider buying it. If you buy the stock and the firm performs as you forecast, you will earn a higher return than the minimum return you specified.

What Next?

The Worksheet for Mature Firms reduces the problem of finding what a stock is worth to a straightforward sequence of simple arithmetic. We will put the worksheet to work in the next chapter and use it to find what Coca-Cola, a good example of a mature firm, is worth.

Summary

Begin the analysis of what a stock is worth by converting the earnings and the return on equity the firm reports to adjusted earnings and adjusted returns on equity. Then examine the firm's performance by plotting the adjusted return, the growth rate of equity per share, and the P/B ratio against time for the historical period. See if the return on equity and the growth rate are stable enough to use the steady-state model to find what the stock is worth. If these key factors are not stable enough, use the worksheet for growth stocks in Chapters 12 and 13 or the worksheet for the Unlimited Flexibility Model in Chapter 15 instead. Then forecast the return on equity, the growth rate of equity per share during the period you expect to hold the stock, and the P/B ratio you expect when you sell.

Table 6-1 is the worksheet for finding what the stock of a mature firm is worth to you. Enter your financial situation in Section I of the worksheet. Enter the current equity per share and your forecasts of return on equity, growth rate, and the P/B ratio in Section II. Section III discounts the net cash that flows into your pocket and tells you what the stock is worth.

Chapter **7**

How to Analyze Past Performance - Coca-Cola

Where Do You Start?
Adjusting Reported Earnings and Returns
How To Analyze Performance
> **Return on Equity**
> **Growth Rate of Equity/Share**
> **P/B Ratio**

Forecasting Coca Cola's Future --
> **Return on Equity**
> **Growth Rate of Equity/Share**
> **P/B Ratio**
> **Adjusting the Beginning Equity/Share**

We have developed the SmartValue formula for defining a firm's performance in Chapter 4, learned how to tune the analysis to your individual financial situation in Chapter 5, and developed a worksheet for finding what the stocks of mature firms are worth in Chapter 6. Now it is time to get down to practical applications. It is time to use Smart-Value to find what real-life stocks are worth. Let's take Coca-Cola as an example of a mature firm. We will learn how to analyze Coca-Cola's performance and forecast its future in this chapter. In the next chapter we will feed that analysis into the Worksheet for Mature Firms and find what Coca-Cola's stock is worth.

The worksheet for finding what mature stocks are worth is for an idealized firm — for a firm that operates under steady-state conditions. That would be just the worksheet to use if the stock market offered shares of idealized firms for sale. But it doesn't. It only offers stocks of real firms. And real firms do not normally operate at pure steady-state conditions. At least, not exactly. The key factors do not hold steady, they fluctuate. The rate of return real firms earn fluctuates from year to year. Their growth rate fluctuates. And the P/B ratio investors are willing to pay for their stock changes from one day to the next.

Keep the task of finding what stocks are worth in perspective. No formula is going to forecast a real firm's future exactly. That is all right. It does not have to. You do not need to know what a stock is worth to the last penny in order to decide whether to buy it or not. A reasonable estimate of what the stock is worth will do nicely. A model that describes in a reasonable way how the firm is likely to perform will provide reasonable estimates of what a stock is worth. You are not likely to find a better estimate in this uncertain world. Mature firms do tend to operate near steady-state conditions. Not exactly at steady-state, of course. Their returns on equity, their growth rates, and their P/B ratios do fluctuate with time. But the fluctuations tend to stay within reasonably narrow bands around some steady-state average. Mature firms come close enough to the steady-state ideal that Smart-Value is a reasonable way to estimate what their stock is worth.

Now it is time to see what happens when we move from an idealized firm to a real firm. Coca-Cola is a good example of a mature firm. Coca-Cola is the world's largest soft-drink company. It sells soft drinks and fruit juices throughout the world. Coca-Cola is a solid, mature company. Large firms like Coca-Cola have a high degree of stability. They do not take off and grow suddenly. They do not collapse suddenly, either. They change, but they change gradually. They tend to move along trend lines for extended periods. That means that SmartValue's Worksheet for Mature Firms is a good way to find what a stock like Coca-Cola stock is worth. Do you know any reason why Coca-Cola might suddenly become more profitable? Or suffer a serious downturn? If not, the most reasonable way to forecast Coca-Cola's future is to forecast that it will continue to follow its historical trend, at least while you hold its stock.

Where Do You Start?

How do you begin to find what any stock is really worth? You know that you will have to begin with the firm's current equity per share and forecast how fast that equity will grow in the future. You will have to forecast the rate of return the firm will earn on that equity and the dividends it will pay. And you will have to forecast the P/B ratio investors will pay for the stock.

How do you go about making these forecasts? The first step is to gather historical data on the firm. The historical record tells you how the firm has performed in the past. It tells you whether performance is stable or erratic. It tells you whether the key factors stay relatively constant, so you can treat the firm as a mature firm and use the Worksheet for Mature Firms to find what the stock is worth. Or whether the key factors gradually decay with time, so that you have to treat that firm as a growth firm and allow for that decay. It tells you where you are starting from when you sit down to forecast the firm's future.

Examine that record. What return on equity does the firm normally earn? On average, how fast does equity per share grow? And what P/B ratio have investors been willing to pay for the stock?

Once you have analyzed the firm's historical record you can use the analysis to fit the SmartValue formula to the firm so that the formula tracks the firm's performance as closely as possible. Then you can forecast how the firm is likely to perform in the future and the dollars that will roll into your pocket if you buy the stock.

Value Line is an excellent source of historical data; it covers over 1,700 firms. Table 7-1 shows the data Value Line reports for Coca-Cola. The table at the top of the Value Line report includes ten years worth of operating results from 1987 to 1996 and Value Line's forecast for 1997 and 1998. Table 7-1 has all the data you need to find what Coca-Cola is worth. If SmartValue shows that Coca-Cola's stock is attractive, send for Coca-Cola's annual report. It will give you more detail on Coca -Cola's business, and how it plans to grow in the future.

Table 7-1
COCA-COLA'S HISTORICAL PERFORMANCE

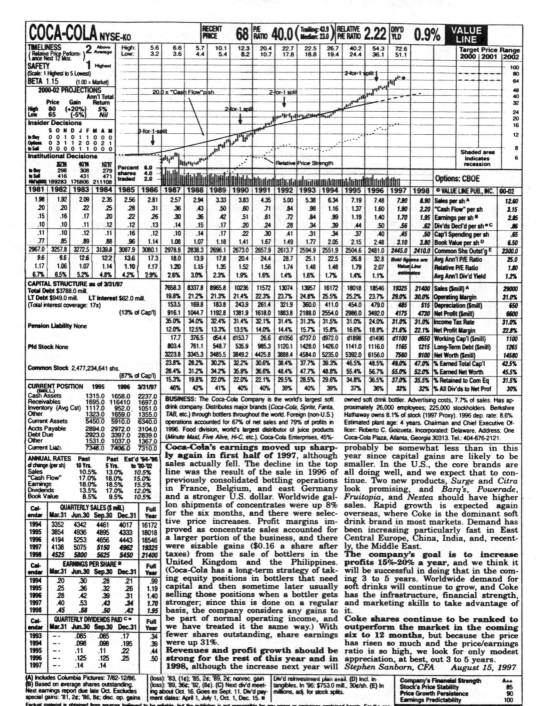

COCA-COLA NYSE-KO | RECENT PRICE **68** | P/E RATIO **40.0** (Trailing: 43.9 Median: 23.0) | RELATIVE P/E RATIO **2.22** | DIV'D YLD **0.9%** | VALUE LINE

TIMELINESS **2** Above Average (Relative Price Performance Next 12 Mos.)

SAFETY **1** Highest (Scale: 1 Highest to 5 Lowest)

BETA 1.15 (1.00 = Market)

2000-02 PROJECTIONS

	Price	Gain	Ann'l Total Return
High	80	(+20%)	5%
Low	65	(-5%)	Nil

High: 5.6 6.6 5.7 10.1 12.3 20.4 22.7 22.5 26.7 40.2 54.3 72.6
Low: 3.2 3.6 4.4 5.4 8.2 10.7 17.8 18.8 19.4 24.4 36.1 51.1

Target Price Range 2000 | 2001 | 2002

Options: CBOE

1981	1982	1983	1984	1985	1986	1987	1988	1989	1990	1991	1992	1993	1994	1995	1996	1997	1998	© VALUE LINE PUB., INC.	00-02
1.98	1.92	2.09	2.35	2.56	2.81	2.57	2.94	3.33	3.83	4.35	5.00	5.38	6.34	7.19	7.48	7.90	8.90	Sales per sh A	12.60
.20	.20	.22	.25	.28	.31	.36	.43	.50	.60	.71	.84	.98	1.16	1.37	1.60	1.90	2.20	"Cash Flow" per sh	3.15
.15	.16	.17	.20	.22	.26	.30	.36	.42	.51	.61	.72	.84	.99	1.19	1.40	1.70	1.95	Earnings per sh B	2.85
.10	.10	.11	.12	.12	.13	.14	.15	.17	.20	.24	.28	.34	.39	.44	.50	.56	.62	Div'ds Decl'd per sh ■ C	.86
.11	.10	.12	.11	.16	.12	.10	.14	.17	.22	.30	.41	.31	.34	.37	.40	.45	.50	Cap'l Spending per sh	.65
.77	.85	.89	.88	.96	1.14	1.08	1.07	1.18	1.41	1.67	1.49	1.77	2.05	2.15	2.48	3.10	3.80	Book Value per sh D	6.50
2967.0	3257.8	3272.5	3139.8	3087.9	3080.1	2978.8	2838.3	2696.1	2673.0	2657.9	2613.7	2594.9	2551.9	2504.6	2481.0	2445.0	2410.0	Common Shs Outst'g E	2300.0
9.6	9.6	12.6	12.2	13.6	17.3	18.0	13.9	17.8	20.4	24.4	28.7	25.1	22.5	26.8	32.8	Bold figures are		Avg Ann'l P/E Ratio	25.0
1.17	1.06	1.07	1.14	1.10	1.17	1.20	1.15	1.35	1.52	1.56	1.74	1.48	1.48	1.79	2.07	Value Line estimates		Relative P/E Ratio	1.80
6.7%	6.5%	5.2%	4.8%	4.2%	2.9%	2.6%	3.0%	2.3%	1.9%	1.6%	1.4%	1.6%	1.7%	1.4%	1.1%			Avg Ann'l Div'd Yield	1.2%

CAPITAL STRUCTURE as of 3/31/97
Total Debt $3788.0 mill.
LT Debt $949.0 mill. LT Interest $62.0 mill.
(Total interest coverage: 17x)
(13% of Cap'l)

Pension Liability None

Pfd Stock None

Common Stock 2,477,234,641 shs.
(87% of Cap'l)

	7658.3	8337.8	8965.8	10236	11572	13074	13957	16172	18018	18546	19325	21400	Sales ($mill) A	29000
	19.8%	21.2%	21.3%	21.4%	22.3%	23.7%	24.8%	25.5%	25.2%	23.7%	29.0%	30.0%	Operating Margin	31.0%
	153.5	169.8	183.8	243.9	261.4	321.9	360.0	411.0	454.0	479.0	485	515	Depreciation ($mill)	650
	916.1	1044.7	1192.8	1381.9	1618.0	1883.8	2188.0	2554.0	2986.0	3492.0	4175	4730	Net Profit ($mill)	6600
	35.0%	34.0%	32.4%	31.4%	32.1%	31.4%	31.3%	31.5%	31.0%	24.0%	31.0%	31.0%	Income Tax Rate	31.0%
	12.0%	12.5%	13.3%	13.5%	14.0%	14.4%	15.7%	15.8%	16.6%	18.8%	21.6%	22.1%	Net Profit Margin	22.8%
	17.7	376.5	d54.4	d153.7	26.6	d1056	d737.0	d972.0	d1898	d1496	d1100	d650	Working Cap'l ($mill)	1100
	803.4	761.1	548.7	535.9	985.3	1120.1	1428.0	1426.0	1141.0	1116.0	1165	1215	Long-Term Debt ($mill)	1265
	3223.8	3345.3	3485.5	3849.2	4425.8	3888.4	4584.0	5235.0	5392.0	6156.0	7560	9100	Net Worth ($mill)	14580
	23.8%	28.2%	30.2%	32.2%	30.6%	38.4%	37.7%	39.3%	46.5%	48.5%	47.0%	47.0%	% Earned Total Cap'l	42.5%
	28.4%	31.2%	34.2%	35.9%	36.6%	48.4%	47.7%	48.8%	55.4%	56.7%	55.0%	52.0%	% Earned Net Worth	45.5%
	15.3%	19.8%	22.0%	22.0%	22.1%	29.5%	28.5%	29.6%	34.8%	36.5%	37.0%	35.5%	% Retained to Com Eq	31.5%
	46%	42%	41%	40%	40%	39%	40%	39%	37%	36%	33%	32%	% All Div'ds to Net Prof	30%

CURRENT POSITION 1995 1996 3/31/97 ($MILL)

	1995	1996	3/31/97
Cash Assets	1315.0	1658.0	2237.0
Receivables	1695.0	116410	1697.0
Inventory (Avg Cost)	1117.0	952.0	1051.0
Other	1323.0	1659.0	1355.0
Current Assets	5450.0	5910.0	6340.0
Accts Payable	2894.0	2972.0	3104.0
Debt Due	2923.0	3397.0	2839.0
Other	1531.0	1037.0	1367.0
Current Liab.	7348.0	7406.0	7310.0

BUSINESS: The Coca-Cola Company is the world's largest soft drink company. Distributes major brands (Coca-Cola, Sprite, Fanta, TAB, etc.) through bottlers throughout the world. Foreign (non-U.S.) operations accounted for 67% of net sales and 79% of profits in 1996. Food division, world's largest distributor of juice products (Minute Maid, Five Alive, Hi-C, etc.). Coca-Cola Enterprises, 45%- owned soft drink bottler. Advertising costs, 7.7% of sales. Has approximately 26,000 employees; 225,000 stockholders. Berkshire Hathaway owns 8.1% of stock (1997 Proxy). 1996 dep. rate: 8.6%. Estimated plant age: 4 years. Chairman and Chief Executive Officer: Roberto C. Goizueta. Incorporated: Delaware. Address: One Coca-Cola Plaza, Atlanta, Georgia 30313. Tel.: 404-676-2121.

ANNUAL RATES

of change (per sh)	Past 10 Yrs.	Past 5 Yrs.	Est'd '94-'96 to '00-'02
Sales	10.5%	13.0%	10.5%
"Cash Flow"	17.0%	18.0%	15.0%
Earnings	18.0%	18.5%	15.5%
Dividends	13.5%	17.0%	12.0%
Book Value	8.5%	9.5%	10.5%

QUARTERLY SALES ($ mill.)

Cal-endar	Mar.31	Jun.30	Sep.30	Dec.31	Full Year
1994	3352	4342	4461	4017	16172
1995	3854	4936	4895	4333	18018
1996	4194	5253	4656	4443	18546
1997	4138	5075	5150	4962	19325
1998	4525	5800	5625	5450	21400

EARNINGS PER SHARE B

Cal-endar	Mar.31	Jun.30	Sep.30	Dec.31	Full Year
1994	.20	.30	.28	.21	.99
1995	.25	.36	.32	.26	1.19
1996	.28	.42	.39	.31	1.40
1997	.40	.53	.43	.34	1.70
1998	.45	.58	.50	.42	1.95

QUARTERLY DIVIDENDS PAID C ■

Cal-endar	Mar.31	Jun.30	Sep.30	Dec.31	Full Year
1993	--	.085	.085	.17	.34
1994	--	.098	.098	.195	.39
1995	--	.11	.11	.22	.44
1996	--	.125	.125	.25	.50
1997	--	.14	.14		

Coca-Cola's earnings moved up sharply again in first half of 1997, although sales actually fell. The decline in the top line was the result of the sale in 1996 of previously consolidated bottling operations in France, Belgium, and east Germany and a stronger U.S. dollar. Worldwide gallon shipments of concentrates were up 8% for the six months, and there were selective price increases. Profit margins improved as concentrate sales accounted for a larger portion of the business, and there were sizable gains ($0.16 a share after taxes) from the sale of bottlers in the United Kingdom and the Philippines. (Coca-Cola has a long-term strategy of taking equity positions in bottlers that need capital and then sometime later usually selling those positions when a bottler gets stronger; since this is done on a regular basis, the company considers any gains to be part of normal operating income, and we have treated it the same way.) With fewer shares outstanding, share earnings were up 31%.

Revenues and profit growth should be strong for the rest of this year and in 1998, although the increase next year will probably be somewhat less than in this year since capital gains are likely to be smaller. In the U.S., the core brands are all doing well, and we expect that to continue. Two new products, Surge and Citra look promising, and Barq's, Powerade, Fruitopia, and Nestea should have higher sales. Rapid growth is expected again overseas, where Coke is the dominant soft drink brand in most markets. Demand has been increasing particularly fast in East Central Europe, China, India, and, recently, the Middle East.

The company's goal is to increase profits 15%-20% a year, and we think it will be successful in doing that in the coming 3 to 5 years. Worldwide demand for soft drinks will continue to grow, and Coke has the infrastructure, financial strength, and marketing skills to take advantage of it.

Coke shares continue to be ranked to outperform the market in the coming six to 12 months, but because the price has risen so much and the price/earnings ratio is so high, we look for only modest appreciation, at best, out 3 to 5 years.
Stephen Sanborn, CFA   August 15, 1997

(A) Includes Columbia Pictures: 7/82-12/86.
(B) Based on average shares outstanding. Next earnings report due late Oct. Excludes special gains: '81, 2¢; '86, 8¢; disc. op. gains
(loss): '83, (1¢); '85, 2¢; '89, 2¢; nonrec. gain (loss): '89, 36¢; '92, (8¢). (C) Next div'd meeting about Oct. 16. Goes ex Sept. 11. Div'd payment dates: April 1, July 1, Oct. 1, Dec. 15. ■
Div'd reinvestment plan avail. (D) Incl. intangibles. In '96: $753.0 mill., 30¢/sh. (E) In millions, adj. for stock splits.

Company's Financial Strength A++
Stock's Price Stability 85
Price Growth Persistence 90
Earnings Predictability 100

Courtesy of Value Line Publishing, Inc.

Adjusting Earnings and the Return on Equity

Remember that you cannot use the data Coca-Cola reports on earnings and return on equity directly. The reported values are legitimate, but they do not account completely for how fast Coca-Cola grows. You have to adjust earnings and the return on equity to make SmartValue track Coca-Cola's growth. That is the place to begin with every stock. Adjust earnings and the return on equity first.

Coca-Cola does not report adjusted earnings or adjusted returns. No matter. Adjusting is easy. You can do it yourself. Remember from Chapter 4 that adjusted earnings for any year are the total of that year's dividends and the year-to-year gain in equity per share. The adjusted return on equity is simply adjusted earnings divided by the average equity per share during the year. Use the worksheet in Table 7-2 to adjust earnings and return on equity for any stock.

Adjusting Earnings

Adjusting earnings is straightforward. Look up the firm's equity per share and dividends in Value Line or in the firm's annual report. Let's use the Value Line data for Coca-Cola in Table 7-1. You will find equity per share in the sixth line of Table 7-1 (Value Line calls equity per share "Book Value per Share"). You will find dividends in the fourth line. Enter book value per share in Column 1 of the worksheet in Table 7-2 and dividends in Column 3. Then follow the simple directions at the bottom of the worksheet.

Find the change in book value per share by subtracting the previous year's book value from the current year's book value in Column 1. Enter the change in book value in Column 2. That is the gain in equity part of adjusted earnings. Dividends are in Column 3. That is the other part. Add the gain in equity per share in Column 2 and dividends in Column 3 to get adjusted earnings. List the adjusted earnings in Column 4. Now that you have adjusted earnings, you will be able to adjust the return on equity.

Adjusting the Return on Equity

Earnings are produced during the year. So it makes sense to base the return on equity on the average equity per share during the year, not on year-end equity. The computation of the average equity in Columns 5 through 7 may seem unnecessarily complicated. Why not simply take this year's equity and last year's equity and average them? That simple average is the right one to use when equity grows at a constant dollar rate during the year. But the SmartValue formula is not based on constant dollar growth. It is based on constant <u>percentage</u> growth. The average equity you calculate in Column 7 is the correct average to use when equity per share grows at a constant percentage rate. The difference between the two methods is small when growth is slow. But the difference

Table 7-2

ADJUSTING COCA-COLA'S EARNINGS AND RETURN ON EQUITY

Year	Col. 1 Equity, $/Sh.	Col. 2 Change in Equity, $/Sh.	Col. 3 Div., $/Sh.	Col. 4 Adjusted Earnings $/Sh.	Col. 5 ln(Col. 1)	Col. 6 Growth Rate, %/yr.	Col. 7 Average Equity, $/Sh.	Col. 8 Adjusted Return, %
1996	2.48	0.33	0.50	0.83	0.9083	14.28	2.31	35.92
1995	2.15	0.10	0.44	0.54	0.7655	4.77	2.10	25.76
1994	2.05	0.28	0.39	0.67	0.7178	14.68	1.91	35.13
1993	1.77	0.28	0.34	0.62	0.5710	17.22	1.63	38.13
1992	1.49	-0.18	0.28	0.10	0.3988	-11.40	1.58	6.33
1991	1.67	0.26	0.24	0.50	0.5128	16.92	1.54	32.54
1990	1.41	0.23	0.20	0.43	0.3436	17.81	1.29	33.30
1989	1.18	0.11	0.17	0.28	0.1655	9.78	1.12	24.89
1988	1.07	-0.01	0.15	0.14	0.0677	-0.93	1.08	13.02
1987	1.08	-0.06	0.14	0.08	0.0770	7.2	0.83	9.60
1986	1.14							

Cols. 1 and 3: Enter book value per share and dividends directly from Value Line or the Annual Report.

Col. 2: In Column 1 subtract last year's book value from this year's value and put the result in Column 2.

Col. 4: Add Columns 2 and 3.

Col. 5: Enter the number in Column 1 in your calculator and tap the ln(x) key.

Col. 6: Subtract last year's entry in Column 5 from this year's entry. Then multiply by 100.

Col. 7: Divide Column 2 by Column 6, then Multiply by 100.

Col. 8: Divide Column 4 by Column 7, then Multiply by 100.

becomes important for fast-growing growth stocks. Post the average in Column 7. Calculating the average equity this way is a little more work, but it is well worth it. Besides, there is a bonus. As a by-product, you get the year-to-year growth rate in Column 6. Finally, divide adjusted earnings in Column 4 by the average equity in Column 7. Then multiply by 100. That gives you the adjusted return on equity as a percentage. Post the adjusted return in Column 8.

Notice that a few negative numbers may appear in the worksheet. That means you may be asked to add, subtract, multiply, or divide a negative number. Oh-oh! You may have forgotten how. Don't worry. Your calculator knows how. Just make sure you enter a minus sign as a part of every negative number. The number in your calculator's display window must have a minus sign in front of it before you tap the add, subtract, multiply, or divide key. If you are asked to subtract a negative 5, for example, make sure there is a minus sign in front of the 5 in your calculator's display window before you tap the subtract key.

Column 5 asks you for the natural logarithm of the equity per share listed in Column 1. That is what the ln(x) key on your calculator is for. Like the e^x key, you do not have to know what a natural logarithm is. As far as you are concerned, it is just another key on your calculator. Rise to the challenge! Enter an equity per share from Column 1 in your calculator. Then tap the ln(x) key. Presto! The number in your calculator's display window changes. That is the number to enter in Column 5. And that is all there is to it!

Readers who have computers will find Table 7-2 easy to set up in a spreadsheet program. If you use a computer, add two more columns just before Column 1. Enter the firm's equity (in millions of dollars) in the first column and the number of shares of stock (also in millions) in the second. You will find the firm's equity in the fifth line up from the bottom of the Value Line table (Value Line calls equity "Net Worth"). The number of shares are in the seventh line of Value Line's table. Instead of using Value Line's equity per share in the sixth line, let your computer calculate it. Divide equity by the number of shares of stock to find equity per share, and post that result in Column 1 of Table 7-2. Value Line rounds off equity per share to the nearest penny. But your computer will retain a zillion decimal places. That will minimize round-off errors, which can become important in the early history of growth stocks.

Why go through all this trouble of adjusting earnings and returns on equity? Try calculating Coca-Cola's growth rate with reported and adjusted values, and you will see why. Table 7-3 shows what happens when you calculate Coca-Cola's growth rate for 1996. Remember that the growth rate is the return on equity multiplied by the reinvestment fraction. If you use the earnings Coca-Cola reports, you will calculate a growth rate of 38.9 percent per year — nearly three times Coca-Cola's actual growth of 14.28 percent per year. But when you use adjusted returns SmartValue's growth formula reproduces Coca-Cola's 1996 equity growth exactly.

Table 7-3
CALCULATED vs. ACTUAL GROWTH RATE
Coca-Cola, 1996

	Reported Results	Adjusted Results
Dividend, $/Sh.	0.50	0.50
Earnings, $/Sh.	1.40	0.83
Dividend Payout Fraction	0.357	0.602
Reinvestment Fraction	0.643	0.398
Return on Equity, %	60.5	35.92
Calculated Growth, %/yr.	38.9	14.30
Actual Growth, %/yr.	14.28	14.28

How To Analyze Performance

Now you are ready to examine Coca-Cola's performance. How do you examine a firm's performance? The best way is to take out a sheet of graph paper and plot how the key factors change with time. Whoever said that a picture is worth a thousand words is right on target. That is particularly true when analyzing financial data. Firms normally present their results in tables of data. But tables bury key changes in a mass of less important and often confusing detail. Don't waste your time looking for needles in haystacks. Plot the data. Plots bring those key changes to the forefront. They jump right off the page at you. That is why plots are so helpful.

Plot the key factors. How do the plots look? Are the key factors steady or do they gradually change with time? How badly do they scatter around their trend line? Do not expect the data to lie exactly on a trend line. This is not an experiment in a physics laboratory; we're dealing with economic data. The data do not have to lie exactly on a trend line. The data just has to be reasonably steady and reasonably close to the trend line. If the data scatter badly, forecasting future performance will be difficult. You might consider looking for another stock.

Make plots showing how the adjusted return has varied in the past. Do the same for the growth rate of equity per share. And do the same for the P/B ratio investors have been willing to pay. These plots will give you a clear picture of Coca-Cola's performance and help you forecast what these key factors are likely to do in the future.

Return on Equity

Figure 7-1 shows how Coca-Cola's adjusted return on equity has varied and how the adjusted return differs from the return Coca-Cola reports. Adjusted returns are normally close to reported returns. Not so with Coca-Cola. Adjusted returns are much lower than reported returns, particularly since 1986. The returns Coca-Cola reported grew steadily from 26 percent in 1987 to a whopping 60.5 percent in 1996! Adjusted returns are much lower. They were only 9.6 percent in 1987, peaked at 38 percent in 1993, then eased to 35.9 percent in 1996. The 1996 adjusted return of 35.9 percent was much lower than the 60.5 percent return Coca-Cola reported. And there were two serious dips, to 9.6 percent in 1987 and 6.3 percent in 1992. The dips are due to drops in shareholder equity in those two years. Drops in shareholder equity cause corresponding drops in adjusted earnings, but they are not reflected in reported earnings. "Extraordinary items" frequently cause such drops. Earnings are frequently reported "less extraordinary items" to make the earnings appear more stable. But the extraordinary items are included in stockholder equity. That automatically makes extraordinary items a part of adjusted earnings.

Coca-Cola's reported returns are legitimate. They are based on generally accepted accounting practice. But they do not fit the SmartValue formula. Adjust them, or you will not track Coca-Cola's growth closely.

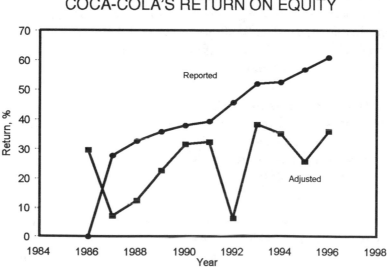

Fig. 7-1
COCA-COLA'S RETURN ON EQUITY

Value Line reports a return on equity as "% Earned Net Worth" near the bottom of its table of data. Value Line's return is based on reported, not adjusted, earnings. It is not an adjusted return. Value Line also bases its return on year-end equity, not on the average equity during the year. Do not use Value Line's return. Use the adjusted return calculated in Table 7-2 instead.

Growth Rate of Equity per Share

The best way to measure how fast Coca-Cola's equity per share is growing and see whether that growth is stable is to plot equity per share against time. But do not use regular graph paper. It is deceptive. It tends to make equity look like it is growing slowly in the early years, and then exploding in the later years. Here is the secret to measuring growth rates. Make your plot on semi-logarithmic graph paper. This graph paper is called semi-logarithmic because the vertical axis is graduated on a logarithmic scale. "Whoa!", you say. "Semi-logarithmic graph paper? You are getting over my head!" Do not panic! Logarithmic is just a word. So is semi-logarithmic. Semi-log paper is easy to use. If you do not have any you can make some. I will show you how in a moment.

Why semi-logarithmic graph paper? Because a semi-logarithmic graph is a powerful tool for analyzing growth rates. It works because anything that grows at a constant percentage growth rate, such as 15 percent per year, plots as a straight line on this special kind of graph paper. That is how to tell if the growth rate is reasonably constant. Plot equity per share against time on this special graph paper. Then draw a smooth trend line through the data. If equity per share plots as a reasonably straight line, you know that equity is growing at a reasonably constant percentage rate. That is an indication that the firm is mature, and that you can use the Worksheet for Mature Firms to find what the stock is worth. If equity per share plots as a curved line, the growth rate is not constant. The growth rate is changing with time. In that case, use the Worksheet for Growth Stocks in Chapters 12 and 13 to find what the stock is worth. The slope of the line tells you how fast equity per share is growing. A steep slope means rapid growth; a flatter slope means slower growth.

The data points lie exactly on a straight line for ideal firms. Not so for real firms. Real data normally scatter around the trend line, even if the firms are mature. The scatter reflects year-to-year variation in the growth rate. Some scatter is normal. Do not worry about it. But be wary if the data scatter badly. Bad scatter means erratic growth. That is a signal to look for a more stable firm.

You can also draw straight lines between any two adjacent annual data points. That is the way to measure year-to-year growth rates. The slopes of the year-to-year lines are more erratic. Some of these lines are steeper than the trend line. Other annual lines are flatter. That variation in slope simply reflects how year-to-year growth rates fluctuate around the growth rate of the trend line. In some years year-to-year growth is faster than trend growth. In other years year-to-year growth is slower. You have already calculated the variation in Coca-Cola's year-to-year growth rates in Column 6 of Table 7-2. Do not worry too much about how year-to-year growth rates vary, particularly if you are a long-term investor. Concentrate instead on the growth rate of the trend line. Trend line growth is more stable, and is usually a better indicator of future growth for mature firms.

Growth firms do not normally plot as a straight line. Growth gradually slows as growth firms mature. Slowing growth shows up as a curved line. The curve is steep when growth is rapid. But as growth slows the slope falls, and the curve gradually flattens. We will see how to account for slowing growth in Chapter 11.

You probably do not have semi-log paper in your desk drawer. No matter. You can make your own. All you have to do is plot the natural logarithm of equity per share against time on ordinary graph paper. Where do you find the natural logarithm? You already have it! You found the natural logarithm of equity per share when you filled out Column 5 of Table 7-2. All you need to do is plot the logarithms in Column 5 against time on ordinary graph paper.

How do you translate the slope on a semi-logarithmic plot into the corresponding growth rate? The worksheet in Table 7-3 does the job. Draw the best straight line you can through the data on the semi-logarithmic plot. Extend the line beyond the data at both ends for leverage. Read the values at each end of the straight line and enter those values into the worksheet. Use Part A of the worksheet if you made your plot on semi-logarithmic graph paper. Use Part B if you made your own semi-logarithmic paper.

Let's measure how fast Coca-Cola has been growing, and see how stable growth is. There is no semi-log paper in our desk drawer, so we will make our own. Simply plot the logarithms in Column 5 of Table 7-2 against time on ordinary graph paper. Figure 7-2 shows the result. Except for interruptions in 1986 and 1992, equity per share does plot on two reasonably straight lines. That means that Coca-Cola did grow at a reasonably steady rate during those two straight-line periods. The data cluster reasonably tightly around the trend lines during each straight-line period. That means Coca-Cola's growth was stable during those periods. And the two straight lines are nearly parallel. That means Coca-Cola's growth rate was nearly the same in both periods.

Here is how to find Coca-Cola's growth rate. The slope of the straight lines measures how fast Coca-Cola grew. Use the worksheet in Table 7-3 to translate the slope into a growth rate. Choose a period where the data plot reasonably well as a straight line. Let's use the 1992-1996 period as an example. Draw the best straight line you can through the data. Your calculations will be more accurate if you extend the line at both ends for leverage. Extend the line back to 1991 and forward to 1997 for leverage. Read the logarithm of

Table 7-4
WORKSHEET FOR FINDING GROWTH RATES

Part A - From Semi-Log Plot

1. Equity at right-hand end of the straight line, $/Sh. .... ⸺⸺⸺
2. Time corresponding to Line 1, years .... ⸺⸺⸺
3. Equity at left-hand end of the straight line, $/Sh. .... ⸺⸺⸺
4. Time corresponding to Line 3, years .... ⸺⸺⸺
5. Divide Line 1 by Line 3 .... ⸺⸺⸺
6. Enter Line 5 in your calculator and tap the ln(x) key ..... ⸺⸺⸺
7. Subtract Line 4 from Line 2 .... ⸺⸺⸺
8. Growth Rate, %/yr.: Divide Line 6 by Line 7,
     then Multiply by 100... ⸺⸺⸺

Part B - From ln(Equity/Share) Plot

1. ln(Equity/Sh.) at right-hand end of the straight line ...... ⸺⸺⸺
2. Time corresponding to Line 1, years .... ⸺⸺⸺
3. ln(Equity/Sh.) at left-hand end of the straight line .... ⸺⸺⸺
4. Time corresponding to Line 3, years .... ⸺⸺⸺
5. Subtract Line 3 from Line 1 .... ⸺⸺⸺
7. Subtract Line 4 from Line 2 .... ⸺⸺⸺
8. Growth Rate, %/yr.: Divide Line 5 by Line 6,
     then Multiply by 100... ⸺⸺⸺

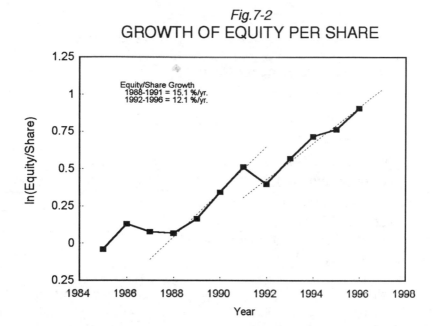

Fig.7-2
GROWTH OF EQUITY PER SHARE

equity per share and the time at each end of that line. The logarithm is 0.308 in 1991 and 1.036 in 1997. We are using regular graph paper, so enter the logarithms in lines 1 and 3 in Part B of Table 7-5. Calculate the growth rate in line 7. Table 7-6 shows that equity per share grew 12. 1 percent per year during the 1992-1996 period. In the same way, you will find that equity per share grew 15.1 percent per year during the 1987-1991 period.

The logarithm in line 1 or line 3 is negative whenever equity is less than $1 per share. That means you will be subtracting a negative number in line 5. Be sure that number has a minus sign in front of it in your calculator's display window before you tap the subtract key.

P/B Ratio

The last key factor to examine is the P/B ratio investors have been paying for Coca-Cola's stock. You will not find Coca-Cola's P/B ratio in Value Line. Value Line does not report it. It reports the P/E ratio instead. No problem. P/E and P/B ratios are related. You can calculate P/B ratios easily from P/E ratios and reported earnings.

Use the worksheet in Table 7-6. Enter the P/E ratio Value Line reports in Column 1. You will find the P/E ratio in line 8 of Value Line's table. Enter reported earnings in Column 2. You need to use reported earnings, not adjusted earnings, in this worksheet

Table 7-5
COCA-COLA'S GROWTH RATE, 1992 - 1996

Part B - From In(Equity/Share) Plot

1. In(Equity/Sh.) at right-hand end of the straight line	1.036
2. Time corresponding to Line 1, years	1997
3. In(Equity/Sh.) at left-hand end of the straight line	0.308
4. Time corresponding to Line 3, years	1991
5. Subtract Line 3 from Line 1	0.728
7. Subtract Line 4 from Line 2	6
8. Growth Rate, %/yr.: Divide Line 5 by Line 6, then Multiply by 100	12.1

because Value Line's P/E ratio is based on reported earnings. Reported earnings are in line 3 of Value Line's table. Copy the average equity per share from Column 7 of Table 7-2 into Column 3. Now multiply the P/E ratio in Column 1 by reported earnings in Column 2 (that gives you the stock's average price) and divide by the average equity per share in Column 3. The result is the P/B ratio; post it in Column 4.

Figure 7-3 shows how investors valued Coca-Cola's stock since 1985. There has been a remarkable increase in what investors were willing to pay for Coca-Cola. The price/book ratio increased steadily from about 5 in the mid 1980's to 20 in 1996. As this is written (November, 1997) the P/B ratio had climbed further to 24. Why such a large increase? The large drop in market interest rates that took place during the period is one factor. Remember that a stock's price reflects the discounted value of all future dividends investors expect from that stock. The discount rate investors use reflects the returns they could earn from alternative investments. When interest rates drop, the return investors can earn from alternative investments also drops. Investors then discount at lower rates, and the stock's price rises. That makes the P/B ratio rise, too.

Another factor may be the enormous return on equity that Coca-Cola reports. Investors may be willing to pay such a high P/B ratio when they see a solid, mature firm like Coca-Cola reporting a gigantic 60.5 percent return on equity. They do not realize that

Table 7-6
COCA-COLA'S P/B RATIO

Year	Col. 1 P/E Ratio	Col. 2 Reported Earnings, $/Share	Col. 3 Average Equity, $/Share	Col. 4 Average P/B Ratio
1996	32.8	1.40	2.31	19.9
1995	26.8	1.19	2.10	15.2
1994	22.5	0.99	1.91	11.7
1993	25.1	0.84	1.63	12.9
1992	28.7	0.72	1.58	13.1
1991	24.4	0.61	1.54	9.66
1990	20.4	0.51	1.29	8.07
1989	17.8	0.42	1.12	6.68
1988	13.9	0.36	1.08	4.63
1987	18.0	0.30	0.83	6.51

Cols. 1 and 2: Copy P/E ratios and reported earnings per share directly from Value Line.
Col. 3: Copy the average equity per share from Col. 7 of Table 7-3.
Col. 4: Multiply Column 1 by Column 2, then Divide by Column 3.

Coca-Cola's adjusted return on equity is only about 35.5 percent — about half the return Coca-Cola reports. The P/B ratio also reflects Coca-Cola's popularity among investors as well as investor's favorable outlook for Coca-Cola.

Forecasting Coca-Cola's Future

The key characteristic of a mature firm is that the return on equity it earns and how fast equity per share grows both fluctuate in a narrow band around a stable trend line. The most reasonable way to forecast how a mature firm will perform in the future is to forecast that both key factors will continue to move along those same trend lines. We have analyzed Coca-Cola's historical performance to establish what those trend lines are. Now we can get on with forecasting Coca-Cola's future.

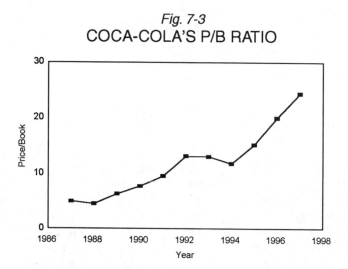

Fig. 7-3
COCA-COLA'S P/B RATIO

SmartValue requires three forecasts to tell what Coca-Cola's stock is worth. You need to forecast the adjusted return on equity you expect Coca-Cola to earn. You need to forecast how fast you expect equity per share to grow. And you need to forecast the P/B ratio you expect investors will pay when you are ready to sell the stock. Let's look at reasonable ways to make those forecasts.

Return on Equity

The plot of Coca-Cola's return on equity in Figure 7-1 shows that Coca-Cola's adjusted return is certainly not constant at some steady-state value, as an idealized firm's return would be. There is considerable scatter around the trend line. That is what happens when you look at a real firm instead of an idealized firm. But if we exclude the low returns in 1987 and 1992 as aberrations, adjusted returns do fall in a reasonably narrow band. Adjusted returns averaged 29.2 percent over the ten year period, and 33.4 percent over the last five years. Coca-Cola has been gradually increasing its return over the period. The more recent returns therefore probably indicate future returns better than the earlier returns do. Let's forecast that Coca-Cola will earn an average return of 33 percent over the next few years. Even though a 33 percent return is about half the return Coca-Cola reports, it is still an enviable return. Most firms would dearly love to earn such a high return.

Growth of Equity/Share

Except for the aberrations in 1986 and 1992, Figure 7-2 shows that Coca-Cola enjoyed stable growth over the past ten years. Coca Cola grew steadily at 15.1 percent per year from 1987 to 1991 and 12.1 percent per year from 1992 through 1996. Let's weigh the more recent growth rate more heavily, and forecast that equity per share will grow 12 percent per year.

Value Line reports growth rates in a box at the left side of the Value Line sheet. Value Line has an unusual way of calculating growth rates that is not consistent with the worksheet in Table 7-5. Do not use Value Line's growth rates. Use the process described here. Plot the natural logarithm of equity per share against time, draw the best straight line through the data, then use the worksheet in Table 7-4 to translate the slope of that line into a growth rate.

P/B Ratio

The key condition for finding what the stock of a mature firm is worth is that both the firm's return on equity and the growth rate of equity per share fluctuate in a narrow band around their trend lines. Both of these key factors must stay relatively constant while you hold the stock. The P/B ratio does not share this requirement. The P/B ratio may fluctuate up and down while you hold the stock. Your only concern is what the P/B ratio will be when you are ready to sell the stock. That is all you need to forecast.

The P/B ratio of 24 investors paid for Coca-Cola in late 1997 is an extremely high ratio, particularly for a mature firm like Coca-Cola. It is the highest that ratio has been in years. Do you think the market will maintain that high ratio while you hold the stock? Or will investors gradually lower the P/B ratio to levels more typical for mature firms? When the P/B ratio is extraordinarily high, it is unlikely that the ratio will continue to grow. It is more likely that the ratio will fall back to levels more typical of mature firms. Let's be a little conservative and forecast that investors will not continue to pay such a high ratio for a stock as mature as Coca-Cola. Let's forecast that Coca-Cola's P/B ratio will fall back to 18 in five years, the period we expect to hold the stock. Even a ratio of 18 is extraordinary for a mature firm.

Beginning Equity per Share

Coca-Cola reports $2.50 of equity per share in its 1996 annual report. But that was at the end of 1996. Suppose you are analyzing the stock in November, 1997. Eleven months have gone by. Equity per share has grown in the meantime. It is easy to adjust equity per share to account for that growth. Simply multiply the $2.50 of equity at the end of 1996 by a growth multiplier for a eleven-month period at the growth rate you are forecasting.

Table 7-8 shows how to allow for recent growth in equity per share. Enter the current equity in line 1, the eleven months since the last report in line 2, and the projected 12 percent per year growth rate (in decimal form) in line 3. Line 5 shows a growth multiplier of 1.116. Line 6 gives $2.79 as a good estimate of the equity per share eleven months after Coca-Cola's 1996 annual report.

Table 7-7
ADJUSTING FOR RECENT GROWTH IN EQUITY/SHARE

1. Initial Equity, $/Share	2.50
2. Divide the Growth Rate (%/yr.) by 100	0.12
3. Length of growth period, months	11
4. Multiply Line 2 by Line 3, then Divide by 12	0.110
5. Growth Multiplier: Enter Line 3 in your calculator and tap the e^x key	1.116
6. Current Equity, $/Share: Multiply Line 1 by Line 5	2.79

What Is Coca Cola Worth?

That completes the analysis of Coca-Cola's past performance. We have examined the adjusted return on equity Coca-Cola earned. We examined how fast equity per share grew. We also examined the P/B ratio investors were willing to pay for Coca-Cola's stock. On the basis of that examination, we forecast that Coca-Cola's starting equity will be $2.79 per share in late-1997, the time we make the analysis. We also forecast that Coca-Cola will earn a 33 percent adjusted return on equity and grow 12 percent per year. And we forecast that investors might pay a P/B ratio of 18 for Coca-Cola stock five years from now when our investor is ready to sell. In the next chapter we will enter those forecasts in the Worksheet for Mature Firms and find what Coca-Cola's stock is worth.

SUMMARY

The first thing to do when you analyze any stock is to adjust the earnings and the return on equity the firm reports. Then plot the adjusted return against time, and see whether the adjusted return is reasonably stable. If the returns fluctuate in a relatively narrow band around a stable average return you can forecast that the firm will continue to earn that average return.

Then plot the equity per share against time on semi-log graph paper. If you do not have semi-log paper, make your own. See how close the data come to a straight line. If equity per share plots as a reasonably straight line and the growth rate is not unusually high, assume the firm is mature and use the Worksheet for Mature Firms to find what the stock is worth. The slope of the straight line measures the growth rate of equity per share. Use the worksheet in Table 7-5 to translate the slope of that line into a growth rate. You can reasonably forecast that a mature firm will continue to grow at that same growth rate.

If equity per share plots on a curved line, the growth rate is not constant. It is gradually changing. If the growth rate is changing, you may want to use the worksheet for growth stocks in Chapters 12 and 13 and allow for that change.

Finally, plot the P/B ratio investors have been willing to pay for the stock. That plot will help you forecast the P/B ratio you can expct when you eventually sell the stock.

The equity per share the firm reported in its last annual report has grown since that report was issued. Use your growth rate forecast to estimate what equity per share is at the time you make your forecast.

Applying this procedure to Coca-Cola resulted in forecasts that Coca-Cola's equity had grown to $2.79 in late 1997, and that Coca-Cola will earn an adjusted return on equity of 33 percent, that equity per share will grow 12 percent per year, and that investors will pay a P/B ratio of 18 five years from now.

Chapter 8

What Is Coca-Cola Worth?

Stock Valuation Worksheet

   Section I - The Investor

   Section II - The Firm

   Section III - What is Coca Cola Worth?

Should You Buy?

Why Does Coca-Cola Cost Too Much?

Sensitivity Analysis

We have now established the procedure for finding what any stock is worth. Follow this sequence of steps:

1. Look up the firm's historical record for the past ten years.

2. Adjust the firm's reported earnings and return on equity.

3. Plot the adjusted return, equity per share, and the P/B ratio against time. Find the average growth rate from a semi-logarithmic plot of equity per share.

4. Decide whether the return on equity and the growth rate of equity per share are stable or are changing with time. If they are stable use the Worksheet for Mature Firms to find what the stock is worth. If you expect the return on equity and the growth rate of equity per share to change with time, use the Worksheet for Growth Stocks in Chapters 12 and 13.

5. Forecast the return on equity you expect the firm to earn, how fast you expect equity per share to grow, and the P/B ratio you expect when you eventually sell the stock.

6. Adjust the initial equity per share for the growth that has taken place since that equity was last reported.

7. Enter your forecasts in the appropriate worksheet and find what the stock is worth.

We analyzed Coca-Cola this way in the last chapter. Based on Coca-Cola's recent performance, we forecast that Coca-Cola would earn an adjusted return of 33 percent in the future. We also examined how fast equity per share grew, and concluded that equity per share would grow 12 percent per year over the next five years. We found that the P/B ratio investors were willing to pay for Coca-Cola skyrocketed from 5 in the 1980s to a high of 24 in late 1997. We did not believe that investors would continue to pay such a high P/B ratio for a firm as mature as Coca-Cola, and forecast that the P/B ratio would drop to perhaps 18 in five years. Based on the growth rate we forecast, we calculated that equity per share would grow from the $2.50 Coca-Cola reported in its 1996 annual report to $2.79 per share in late 1997, the time we make the analysis. We are now ready to enter those forecasts in the Stock Valuation Worksheet for Mature Firms and find what Coca-Cola's stock is worth.

Stock Valuation Worksheet for Mature Firms

We have done the hard part -- forecasting how Coca-Cola might perform in the future. The rest is easy. Just enter the forecasts from Chapter 7 in the worksheet for finding what stocks of mature firms are worth. Tap a few keys on your calculator. You will soon have the answer. You will know the most you can afford to pay for Coca-Cola's stock. If you can buy Coca-Cola at a lower price, go ahead. It is a bargain. But if Coca-Cola costs more than SmartValue says it is worth, it costs too much. Do not buy it. Look for a more attractive stock.

Tuning the Analysis

One of SmartValue's advantages is that it tunes the analysis to a particular investor's financial condition. Which investor shall we use? Let's go back to the investor we studied in Chapter 5, and see what Coca-Cola is worth to him. That investor is a long-term investor, and plans to hold Coca-Cola for five years. As we saw in Chapter 5, he pays a 32.32 percent combined federal and state incremental tax rate on ordinary income and a combined 24.8 percent tax rate on capital gains.

Our investor examined his alternative investments in Chapter 5, and concluded that his best alternative was to invest in Vanguard's S&P 500 Index Fund, which averaged a 9.3 percent return after taxes. That alternative established that his money costs 9.3 percent — he is giving up a 9.3 percent return if he invests that money in Coca-Cola instead of in the Index Fund. He needs to add a risk premium to his cost of money because Coca-Cola (and, indeed, any single stock) is riskier than his alternative investment in a diversified pool of 500 stocks. A risk premium is a highly personal choice. It depends on the investor's tolerance for risk, and how risky he views the stock he is considering relative to the alternative investment which established what his money cost. Our investor views Coca-Cola as a low-risk stock, just slightly more risky than the S&P 500 index fund he considers his alternative investment. He decides that a risk premium of about 1 percent is appropriate. That makes the minimum rate of return he will accept his 9.3 percent cost of money plus a 1 percent risk premium, or 10.3 percent. That is the discount rate SmartValue will use to discount the future cash Coca-Cola will put into that investor's pocket. That is the discount rate that determines the most he can pay for the stock and still meet his minimum return standard of 10.3 percent.

What Is Coca-Cola Worth?

Our investor is now ready for the key question: what is the most he can afford to pay for Coca-Cola and still earn a return of at least 10.3 percent? He turns to the Worksheet for Mature Firms and enters his financial situation and his forecasts for Coca-Cola. Table 8-1 shows the entries he makes in the worksheet.

Section I -- The Investor

Section I of the worksheet tells SmartValue what it needs to know to tune the valuation to this investor's financial situation. Our investor is a long-term investor and plans to hold the stock for five years. He enters the five-year investment period in line 1. His tax rates go in lines 2 and 3. Line 2 asks him to divide his incremental tax rate by 100 and subtract the result from 1.0. The result is an after-tax factor of 0.6768, which means he will have 67.68 cents left of each dollar of ordinary income after taxes. He enters the after-tax factor in Line 2. He will use that factor to find what dividends are worth after taxes. Line 3 asks him to convert his capital gains tax rate to a decimal. He divides his 24.8 percent tax rate by 100 and enters 0.248 in line 3. He also converts the 10.3 percent return he has decided is the minimum return he will accept to a decimal and enters 0.103 in line 4.

He uses a discount broker who charges a 1 percent commission. He enters 1.01 in Line 5; that will account for the broker's commission when he buys the stock. He enters 0.99 in Line 6; that will account for the commission when he sells. SmartValue now has all the information it needs to tune the valuation to this investor's financial situation.

Section II -- The Firm

Section II of the worksheet is where you enter Coca-Cola's beginning equity per share and your forecasts of the return on equity you expect Coca-Cola to earn, how fast you expect Coca-Cola to grow, and the P/B ratio you expect investors to pay for Coca-Cola's stock when you are ready to sell in five years. SmartValue will use your forecasts to find the cash that will flow into and out of your pocket if you buy Coca-Cola's stock.

Our investor enters his estimate that Coca-Cola's equity will have grown to $2.79 per share by late 1997, the time he is making the valuation, in line 7. He enters his forecast that Coca-Cola will earn a 33 percent return on equity in line 8, and his forecast that Coca-Cola's equity per share will grow 12 percent per year in line 9.

SmartValue finds that a dividend payout fraction of 0.636 is consistent with the forecasts of return on equity and growth rate in line 10. That dividend payout, combined with Coca-Cola's starting equity per share and the forecast return on equity, leads to initial dividends of $0.586 per share in line 11.

Lines 12 and 13 incorporate the growth multiplier from Table 4-1. His forecast of 12 percent per year growth over a five-year period leads to a growth multiplier of 1.8221 in line 13. He multiplies Coca-Cola's beginning equity per share by that growth multiplier in line 14 and finds that equity will grow to $5.08 per share in five years. He forecasts that investors will pay a P/B ratio of 18 for Coca-Cola when he is ready to sell the stock in five years. He enters that forecast in line 15. That forecast, combined with equity per share in line 14, leads to a stock price of $91.44 when he expects to sell five years from now.

Section III -- What Is Coca-Cola Worth?

The forecasts our investor entered in Section II establish the cash he expects will flow into his pocket if he buys Coca-Cola's stock. Section III of the worksheet discounts those cash flows using our investor's 10.3 percent minimum acceptable return as the discount rate. Adding up the discounted cash flows will tell him what Coca-Cola is worth.

He needs two discount factors, one for the money he will receive when he sells the stock, and one for the dividends he will collect while he holds the stock. The discount factors are different because the cash flows are different. Selling the stock results in a flow of cash at a single point in time. Collecting dividends results in cash that flows in over a period of time. Lines 17 and 18 develop the discount factor for discounting the net proceeds when he finally sells the stock. The discount factor in line 18 must be between zero and one. If you find a number greater than one, you forgot to tap the change sign key in line 18. Go back to line 18, and make sure there is a minus sign in front of the number in your calculator's display window before you tap the e^x key.

Line 19 tests whether dividends are growing faster than they are being discounted. That affects how you find the appropriate discount factor for dividends. In this example, line 19 is greater than 1.0. That means dividends are growing faster than our investor is discounting them. He uses the second section of line 20 and finds a discount factor of 5.22 for discounting dividends. Line 21 shows that the dividends he collects over the next five years are worth $2.07 per share today after taxes.

He expects to sell the stock for $91.44 in five years. After discounting and deducting broker's commissions, that $91.44 is worth only $54.09 today, as line 22 shows. Lines 23 through 25 account for capital gains taxes. What is Coca-Cola worth to this investor?

Table 8-1
What Is Coca Cola Worth?

I. The Investor

1. Investment Period, years   5
2. Divide Incremental Tax Rate on Ordinary Income (%)
   by 100; Subtract the Result from 1.0 .... 0.6768
3. Divide Capital Gains Tax Rate (%) by 100 .... 0.248
4. Divide Minimum Acceptable Return (%) by 100 .... 0.103
5. Divide Broker's Commission (%) by 100;
   Add the Result to 1.0 .... 1.01
6. Divide Broker's Commission (%) by 100;
   Subtract the Result from 1.0 .... 0.99

II. The Firm

7. Initial Equity, $/Share 2.79
8. Projected Return on Equity, % 33
9. Projected Growth Rate, %/yr. 12
10. Dividend Payout Fraction: Divide Line 9 by Line 8,
    then Subtract the Result from 1.0 .... 0.636
11. Initial Dividend, $/Share: Multiply Line 7
    by Lines 8 and 10, then Divide by 100 .... 0.586
12. Multiply Line 1 by Line 9, then Divide by 100 .... 0.6
13. Growth Multiplier: Enter Line 12 in your calculator
    and tap the e^x key 1.8221
14. Final Equity, $/Share: Multiply Line 7 by Line 13 .... 5.08
15. Projected Price/Book Ratio 18
16. Final Stock Price: Multiply Line 14 by Line 15 .... 91.44

Table 8-1 (Cont'd)
What Is Coca Cola Worth?

III. What Is the Stock Worth?

17. Multiply Line 1 by Line 4 ....   0.515
18. Enter Line 17 in your calculator, tap the change
    sign (+/-) key, then tap the e^x key 0.5975
19. Multiply Line 13 by Line 18 ....   1.0887
20. If Line 19 is less than 1.0:
    20a. Subtract Line 19 from 1.0 ....   _____
    20b. Divide Line 9 by 100 and Subtract the Result
        from Line 4
    20c. Divide Line 20a by Line 20b ....   _____
If Line 19 is greater than 1.0:
    20a. Subtract 1.0 from Line 19 ....   0.0887
    20b. Divide Line 9 by 100, then
        Subtract Line 4 from the Result 0.017
    20c. Divide Line 20a by Line 20b 5.22
If Line 19 is equal to 1.0:
    20c. Copy Line 1 ....   _____
21. Present Value of Dividends: Multiply Line 2 by
    Lines 11 and 20c 2.07
22. Present Value of Final Stock Price: Multiply Line 6
    by Lines 16 and 18 ....   54.09
23. Multiply Line 3 by Line 22 ....   13.41
24. Subtract Line 23 from Line 22 ....   40.68
25. Multiply Line 3 by Line 18 and
    Subtract the Result from 1.0 ....   0.8518
26. Value of Stock: Add Lines 21 and 24, then
    Divide the Result by Line 5 and by Line 25 ....   49.69

Line 26 has the answer. Coca-Cola is worth $49.69 per share. If our investor buys the stock at that price and Coca-Cola performs as he forecast, he will earn the 10.3 per cent return he specified as his minimum acceptable return.

To Buy or Not to Buy?

Our investor now knows what Coca-Cola is worth: $49.69 per share. He can now make an intelligent investment decision. Coca-Cola is a buy if he can buy it for less than $49.69 per share. If Coca-Cola performs as he forecast, he will earn a return higher than his minimum acceptable return of 10.3 percent after taxes. If Coca-Cola costs more than $49.69 per share, it costs too much. If he buys Coca-Cola anyway and it performs as he forecast, he will earn a return less than his minimum return standard.

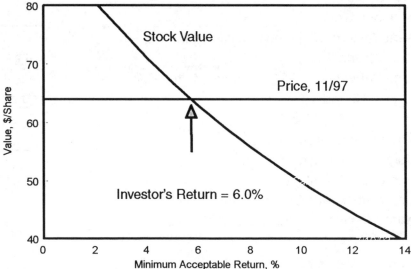

Fig. 8-1
THE BUY/DON'T BUY DECISION
COCA-COLA

At the time of this analysis Coca-Cola was selling for $64 per share. Should our investor buy? Of course not. Why spend $64 for a stock that is worth only $49.69? Our investor has two choices. He can either look for a more attractive stock, or he can put his money in the alternative investment, the Vanguard S&P 500 Index Fund, whose return established what this investor's money costs.

Figure 8-1 puts the buy/don't buy decision in broader perspective. The sloping line in Figure 8-1 shows what Coca-Cola is worth over a range of minimum acceptable returns. That line was developed simply by repeating the worksheet at a number of discount rates. The horizontal line locates Coca-Cola's current market price. The point where the two lines cross is a critical point. That is the point where Coca-Cola is priced exactly at what it is worth. Coca-Cola is a buy to the left of this crossing point. That is where Coca-Cola is worth more than it costs. Coca-Cola is not a buy to the right of the crossing point. That is where Coca-Cola costs more than it is worth.

The crossing point is important for another reason. The discount rate at the crossing point is the rate of return our investor can expect from Coca-Cola. The crossing point for Coca-Cola is at a discount rate of 6.0 percent. Given the forecasts our investor made in this chapter, he can expect an after-tax return of 6.0 percent if he buys Coca-Cola and Coca-Cola performs as he forecast. Our investor finds Coca-Cola unattractive because he insists on a minimum return of at least 10.3 percent. We will explore the investor's rate of return in the next chapter.

Why Does Coca-Cola Cost Too Much?

Why is the investing public willing to pay 64 dollars for a stock that is only worth $49.69? Other investors obviously do not value Coca-Cola the same way our investor does. They may be more optimistic about Coca-Cola's future, and forecast higher returns, faster growth, or higher P/B ratios. They may be in a lower tax bracket. They may be happy with a lower return. Or perhaps they did not use SmartValue. Perhaps they do not realize that Coca-Cola's reported return on equity of 60.5 percent is not consistent with Coca-Cola's growth rate and the dividends it pays. They do not know that a consistent return on equity is only about 35 percent, about half the return Coca-Cola reports. Or perhaps they have a low tolerance for risk, and flock to Coca-Cola because of its stability and maturity. They are paying a high price for stability. Perhaps they are investing on whims and hunches, and do not realize that Coca-Cola costs too much, and that they will earn such a low return on their investment.

SmartValue has done its job for our investor. It has warned him that Coca-Cola costs too much, and that he will be ahead of the game if he finds a more attractive stock, or invests in the S&P 500 Index Fund instead.

Sensitivity Analysis

The $49.69 value our investor found for Coca-Cola applies to one specific forecast of Coca-Cola's future performance. No stock is likely to perform exactly as forecast. Coca-Cola might earn a higher return. It might grow faster. Perhaps the P/B ratio will not drop as far as our investor forecast. How would different forecasts change the analysis? You can find out easily. You have the base analysis in the worksheet in front of you. It is easy to change a forecast, redo part of the worksheet, and see what happens.

The P/B ratio is a critical factor in this analysis. Suppose the P/B ratio did not drop to 18, as our investor forecast. Suppose it held at the current value of 24. How would that affect what Coca-Cola is worth? Go back to line 15 and change the P/B forecast to 24. That change raises the stock price in five years from $91.44 to $122.01 per share. There is no change in lines 17 through 21. Line 26 shows that Coca-Cola's value rises to $65.49 per share — slightly above the current market price of $64 per share. The P/B ratio was the most uncertain of our investor's forecasts. After seeing that Coca-Cola barely meets his minimum return standard even if the P/B ratio stays at its extraordinarily high current level of 24, our investor can be quite certain that Coca-Cola is not the stock for him.

SUMMARY

Once you have analyzed the historical record and forecast the return on equity you expect the firm to earn, how fast you expect equity per share to grow, and the P/B ratio you expect investors to pay for the stock, the rest is easy. Just enter your forecasts into the Worksheet for Mature Firms, do a few simple calculations on your hand calculator, and you will soon know what the stock is worth to you.

Based on the forecasts our investor made for Coca-Cola in the last chapter, he found that Coca-Cola was only worth $49.69 per share at a time when Coca-Cola was selling for $64 per share. Coca-Cola costs too much for this investor. He should look for another stock, or invest in his alternative investment, an S&P 500 Index Fund.

Chapter 9

The Investor's Rate of Return

Rate of Return

Dividend Discount Model

SmartValue Formula

How to Choose Stocks

Rate of Return for Real Stocks

The value SmartValue generates for any stock depends on the rate of return you specify as the minimum return you will accept. That is the return you will earn if you buy the stock at the SmartValue price and the firm performs as you forecast. The SmartValue price is important to know. That is the yardstick that tells you whether a stock is a bargain or whether it costs too much. If you can buy the stock for less than the SmartValue price, it is a bargain. If it costs more than the SmartValue price, it costs too much.

Rate of Return

There is another important yardstick for gauging the value of any investment. That is the rate of return you can expect from your investment. Rate of return measures how effectively you are using each of your investment dollars. Rate of return is the yardstick you should use to compare alternative investments. You can, for example, compare the rate of return you expect to earn from investing in a stock with the returns you could earn investing that money in other investments, like other stocks, mutual funds, bonds, certificates of deposit, and bank savings accounts, or the interest rate you can avoid by paying off debt.

Dividend Discount Model

The standard formula analysts use for the investor's return is the Dividend Discount Model. The model is deceptively simple:

Investor's Return = Dividend Yield + Dividend Growth Rate

Just add the dividend yield and the dividend growth rate (both in percent per year) and presto! You have the investor's return. But the model is deceptive. At first glance, the model says that the way to high returns is to find stocks that have a high dividend yield and a high dividend growth rate. Life is not that simple. You know from the SmartValue formula that dividends and the growth rate cannot both be high at the same time. If the dividend yield is high, the firm will have paid most of its earnings out as dividends. Reinvestment will be low. That will make growth slow. And if the growth rate is high, the firm will have reinvested most of its earnings to pay for that growth, and the dividend yield will be low.

The focus on dividends in the Dividend Discount Model led analysts to assume that the growth rate in this formula was the dividend growth rate. That caused a problem. How do you find your return for stocks which pay no dividends? They have no dividend growth rate and so could not be valued. SmartValue shows that the growth rate of equity per share is the underlying growth rate, not the growth rate of dividends. Stocks that pay no dividends still have an equity growth rate. When a stock pays no dividends, the dividend yield is zero and the investor's return is equal to the growth rate of equity per share.

The SmartValue Formula

The Dividend Discount Model is a steady-state model that ignores taxes and broker's commissions. Under those idealized conditions, SmartValue yields a more useful model for the investor's return. The model appears to be different from the Dividend Discount Model, but it is exactly equivalent. They both give identical results. The SmartValue formula is exquisitely simple:

Investor's Return = (Multiplier)(Firm's Return on Equity)

Your return is equal to the firm's return on equity multiplied by a return-on-equity multiplier. Want to earn a high return? Easy. Invest in a firm that earns a high return on equity. And choose a firm that has a high multiplier.

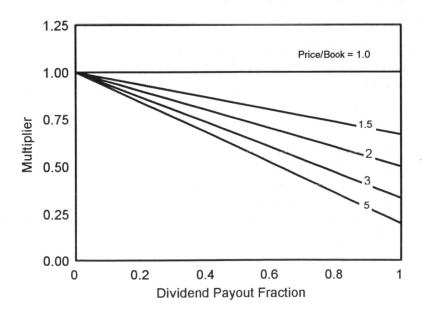

Fig. 9-1
RETURN ON EQUITY MULTIPLIER

The multiplier depends only on the dividend payout fraction and the P/B ratio, as shown in Figure 9-1. The multiplier is 1.0 at the extreme left side of Figure 9-1, where the dividend payout fraction is zero. A return on equity multiplier of 1.0 makes your return the same as the firm's return on equity. The multiplier falls as the dividend payout fraction increases. That drags your return below the firm's return. The multiplier falls slowly for stocks that sell at a low P/B ratio, and more rapidly for stocks that sell at high P/B ratios.

The multiplier is highest for firms which pay little or no dividends. These firms are growth firms; they are located at the left-hand side of Figure 9-1. Mature firms typically pay about half their earnings out as dividends. They have lower return-on-equity multipliers and are located near the middle of Figure 9-1. Firms like utilities pay most of their earnings out as dividends. They have still lower multipliers and occupy the right-hand side of Figure 9-1.

Figure 9-1 also shows that the P/B ratio is important only towards the right-hand side of the plot, where firms that pay most of their earnings out as dividends are located. The higher the P/B ratio, the lower is the multiplier. The drop in the multiplier is particularly severe for firms that have a high dividend payout fraction. If the dividend payout fraction is zero, it does not make any difference what P/B ratio you pay for the stock. The multiplier is 1.0, regardless of the P/B ratio. How can your return not depend on what you paid for the stock? That is a consequence of the steady-state assumption. If you pay a high P/B ratio when you buy a stock, in the steady-state model you will enjoy the same high P/B ratio when you later sell. That is why the P/B ratio does not affect your return for firms that do not pay dividends.

How do you find stocks that have high multipliers? Figure 9-1 shows that the multiplier is highest for firms that reinvest all of their earnings and pay no dividends. If the firm pays no dividends the payout fraction is zero. The multiplier is 1.0 when the payout fraction is zero. You return is then the same as the firm's return on equity.

What kinds of firms reinvest all their earnings and pay no dividends? Growth stocks. That is an important result. If you want to earn high returns, you should invest in growth stocks. There is a minor complication. The multiplier in Figure 9-1 is based on the steady-state model. That model is reasonable for mature firms near the middle and right-hand side of Figure 9-1. But the steady-state model does not work as well for growth stocks on the left-hand side of Figure 9-1. Their rate of return, growth rate, and P/B ratio does not hold at steady-state values. These key indicators all decay with time. That does not change the basic conclusion. Invest in growth stocks. The multiplier may be different than the multiplier in Figure 9-1. That is OK. We will get the multiplier right when we consider growth stocks in Chapter 11.

Worksheet for the Return-on-Equity Multiplier
Here is a simple worksheet to find the return-on-equity multiplier:

Table 9-1
WORKSHEET FOR RETURN ON EQUITY MULTIPLIER

1. Dividend Payout Fraction .... _____
2. P/B Ratio .... _____
3. Divide 1.0 by Line 2. Subtract the result from 1.0 .... _____
4. Multiply Line 1 by Line 3 .... _____
5. Multiplier: Subtract Line 4 from 1.0 .... _____

Example 9-1 A firm pays half its earnings out as dividends, sells at a P/B ratio of 5, and earns a 15 percent return on equity. What is its return-on-equity multiplier, and what rate of return can an investor expect? Table 9-2 shows how to fill out the worksheet:

Table 9-2
MULTIPLIER FOR EXAMPLE 9-1

1. Dividend Payout Fraction	0.5
2. P/B Ratio	5
3. Divide 1.0 by Line 2. Subtract the result from 1.0.	0.8
4. Multiply Line 1 by Line 3	0.4
5. Multiplier: Subtract Line 4 from 1.0	0.6

The firm has a multiplier of 0.6. An investor will earn a return of 0.6 times the firm's 15 percent return on equity, or a 9 percent return (before taxes).

Example 9-2 Demonstrate that the SmartValue formula gives exactly the same answer as the Dividend Discount Model for Example 9-1. Start by finding the dividend yield and growth rate for the firm in Example 9-1. Use a book value of $1 per share just to keep the numbers simple. You will get the same answer regardless of what book value you assume. Use the SmartValue formula to find dividends, the price of the stock, the dividend yield, and the growth rate:

$$\text{Dividends} = (\text{Payout Fraction})(\text{Return on Equity})(\text{Book Value})$$

$$\text{Dividends} = (0.5)(0.15)(1) = 0.075 \text{ \$/Share}$$

$$\text{Stock Price} = (\text{P/B})(\text{Book Value}) = (5)(1) = 5 \text{ \$/Share}$$

$$\text{Dividend Yield} = (100)(\text{Dividends})/(\text{Stock Price}) = (100)(0.075)/(5) = 1.5 \%$$

$$\text{Growth Rate} = (1 - \text{Payout Fraction})(\text{Return on Equity})$$

$$\text{Growth Rate} = (1 - 0.5)(15) = 7.5 \%/\text{yr.}$$

The Dividend Discount Model gives the investor's return as the sum of the 1.5 percent dividend yield and the 7.5 percent per year dividend growth rate, or 9 percent — exactly the same as the SmartValue formula.

How to Choose Stocks

Finding the investor's rate of return is only one use for this simple SmartValue formula. The formula is also useful because it leads to four key guidelines for choosing stocks:

1. Your return is proportional to return the firm earns. Choose profitable firms — firms that earn high rates of return.

2. Choose firms that carry a reasonable amount of debt. Debt leverages the firm's return on equity above its return on total capital. Your return is leveraged by the same proportion because it is a multiple of the firm's return on equity.

3. Choose firms that pay little or no dividends. The return-on-equity multiplier is highest for such firms. At the extreme, choose firms that pay no dividends. The multiplier is 1.0, and your return is equal to the firm's return on equity.

4. Ignore the price/book ratio if the firm pays no dividends. But choose stocks that sell at low price/book ratios if the firm has a high dividend payout fraction.

Not all financial advisors appear to appreciate these guidelines. Many analysts recommend investing in firms with "clean" balance sheets, that is, firms that carry no debt. One of the reasons firms carry debt is to leverage the firm's return on equity above its return on total capital. It is not just the firm's return that's leveraged. Your return is leveraged too, and by the same proportion. You might earn a 12 percent return on a firm that carried no debt. But if that firm took on enough debt to bring its capital pool up to 20 percent debt and 80 percent equity, your return would be leveraged from 12 percent up to 15 percent. Most firms could carry 20 percent debt with relative safety. Firms with "clean" balance sheets do their shareholders a disservice by denying them a leveraged return at little risk.

Many investors are too concerned about dividends. Dividends are important, and many investors depend on dividends to pay their living expenses. But as Figure 9-1 shows, you pay a heavy price for investing in stocks that pay dividends. A high dividend payout fraction makes the return-on-equity multiplier smaller, and your rate of return suffers. The rate of return you earn is more important than dividends. Why not choose stocks that earn high returns on equity and pay little or no dividends? Those stocks are growth stocks. They pay no dividends because they need to reinvest all their earnings to pay for their growth. Your rate of return will be higher because the return-on-equity multiplier is larger. Sell some of the stock every few months if you need money for living expenses. Use a discount broker to keep commissions under control. You should come out ahead of the game.

Some investors recognize that growth stocks yield higher returns, but shy away from them because growth stocks are riskier than stocks of mature firms. That is a legitimate concern. As you move from the middle towards the left-hand side of Figure 9-1 your return will go up. So will the risk. Move as far to the left-hand side — to stocks that pay small dividends and have higher multipliers — as your tolerance for risk will permit.

When you buy a stock that pays no dividends you do not have to worry about what the stock costs. At least in theory. The return-on-equity multiplier is 1.0 regardless of the P/B ratio. But that is only in the steady-state case, where the P/B ratio stays constant. Life is not that simple. In real life the P/B ratio does not stay constant at a steady-state value. It fluctuates. That means you cannot really ignore the price you have to pay for the stock. You are right to be concerned about the price. Use SmartValue to insure that you are not paying too high a price for any stock.

Rate of Return For Real Firms

Finding your rate of return is easy for idealized firms under steady-state conditions. Finding your rate of return is a little more complicated with real firms, where the key parameters may change with time, as they do for growth stocks, and where you need to take taxes and broker's commissions into account. The simple steady-state model is only an approximation in that case. It could be a very rough approximation. Your return is still the discount rate that makes the stock's value exactly equal to the stock's market price. Finding that discount rate is a trial-and-error process.

Use the Stock Valuation Worksheet to find what the stock is worth at several discount rates, i.e., at several minimum acceptable rates of return. Plot the resulting stock values against the discount rate on a sheet of graph paper. Add a horizontal line at the market price on the same plot. Your rate of return is the discount rate where the two curves cross. That is the point where the stock is priced exactly at what it is worth.

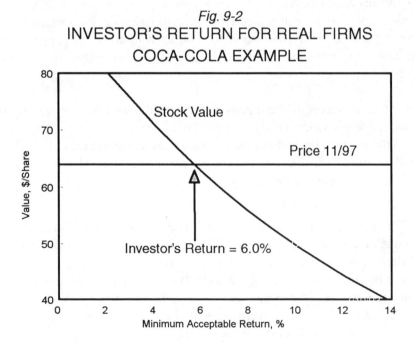

Fig. 9-2
INVESTOR'S RETURN FOR REAL FIRMS
COCA-COLA EXAMPLE

Our investor is curious about the rate of return he would earn if he did buy Coca-Cola. He repeats the worksheet over a range of minimum acceptable returns ranging from a low of 2 percent to a high of 14 percent. Figure 9-2 shows the values he finds for Coca-Cola over that range of discount rates. The curve for Coca-Cola's value crosses the market price line at a discount rate of 6.0 percent. If he buys Coca-Cola at $64 and Coca-Cola performs as he forecast, Figure 9-2 shows that he will earn a return of 6.0 percent after taxes.

Figure 9-2 shows the essence of the buy/don't buy decision. Buy the stock if your minimum acceptable return lies to the left of the crossing point. That is where the stock is worth more than it costs. Do not buy the stock if your minimum acceptable return lies to the right of the crossing point. That is where the stock costs more than it is worth.

Figure 9-2 is a convenient way to track a stock and look for a buying opportunity. The curve for Coca-Cola's value will change slowly as our investor reviews his analysis each time Coca-Cola issues a quarterly report. But the market price line moves up and down from one day to the next. A sudden dip in Coca-Cola's price could put the stock in a buying range. Whenever such a dip occurs, a glance at Figure 9-2 will show whether the dip is large enough to consider buying the stock.

Shortcut Method

There is a simpler way to estimate your rate of return with real stocks. The curve for the stock's value in Figure 9-2 is only slightly curved. You can approximate that curve by a straight line. That is a help because it is easy to find where two straight lines (the line for the stock's value and the line for the market price) cross. Table 9-3 does the job.

It takes two points to locate the straight line that approximates the value curve in Figure 9-2. You already have one of them. That is the value you calculated for the stock at your minimum acceptable return. Now go back to the stock valuation worksheet and calculate a second value for the stock at a discount rate five percentage points away from your minimum acceptable return. If the stock is worth more than the market price, pick a discount rate five percentage points higher than your minimum acceptable return. If the stock is worth less than the market price, pick a discount rate five percentage points lower than your minimum acceptable return. Now you have two different stock values at two different discount rates. Enter those values in Table 9-3 and work out your rate of return. If at least one of the stock values is higher than the market price, use Part A of the table. If both values are less than the market price, use part B.

Example 9-3 Coca-Cola is worth $49.69 per share to our investor at his 10.3 percent minimum acceptable return. Coca-Cola is a loser for this investor because Coca-Cola at $64 per share costs more than it is worth. To estimate his rate of return if he bought the

Table 9-3
ESTIMATING THE INVESTOR'S RETURN

1. Market Price, $/Share .... _____
2. Stock Value at low discount rate, $/Share .... _____
3. Low discount rate, % .... _____
4. Stock Value at high discount rate, $/Share .... _____
5. High discount rate, % .... _____
6. Subtract Line 4 from Line 2 .... _____
7. Subtract Line 3 from Line 5 .... _____

A. At Least One Value Above the Market Price

8a. Subtract Line 1 from Line 2 .... _____
8b. Multiply Line 8a by Line 7, then Divide by Line 6 .... _____
8c. Investor's Return, %: Add Lines 3 and 8b .... _____

B. Both Values Below the Market Price

9a. Subtract Line 2 from Line 1 .... _____
9b. Multiply Line 9a by Line 7, then Divide by Line 6 .... _____
9c. Investor's Return, %: Subtract Line 9b from Line 3 .... _____

stock he finds what Coca-Cola is worth at a second discount rate. Because Coca-Cola costs more than it is worth he chooses a discount rate about five percentage points lower than his minimum acceptable return. He chooses a discount rate of 5 percent. He finds that Coca-Cola is worth $68.02 per share at a 5 percent discount rate. One of the stock values is greater than Coca-Cola's market price, so he uses part A of the worksheet. He finds a return of 6.16 percent, as shown in Table 9-4.

A straight line is only an approximation to the stock value curve in Figure 9-2. That means the return you find from the worksheet is only an approximation of the actual return. Even so, the approximation is a good one. The estimated return of 6.16 percent is quite close to the 6.0 percent return found in Figure 9-2.

You can refine the estimated return by repeating the process. Our investor now knows that Coca-Cola is worth $66.80 per share at a 5 percent discount rate. He can use that value as the anchor point on a second straight line, and use the Stock Valuation Worksheet to find what the stock is worth at a discount near the return he found in his first pass through the rate-of-return worksheet. The second straight line will be a better

Table 9-4
ESTIMATING THE INVESTOR'S RETURN
Example 9-3

1. Market Price, $/Share 64
2. Stock Value at low discount rate, $/Share 68.02
3. Low discount rate, % 5
4. Stock Value at high discount rate, $/Share 49.69
5. High discount rate, % 10.3
6. Subtract Line 4 from Line 2 .... 18.33
7. Subtract Line 3 from Line 5 .... 5.3

A. At Least One Value Above the Market Price

8a. Subtract Line 1 from Line 2 .... 4.02
8b. Multiply Line 8a by Line 7, then Divide by Line 6 .... 1.16
8c. Investor's Return, %: Add Lines 3 and 8b 6.16

approximation of the actual curve because the line is shorter. Furthermore, the second line approximates the actual curve near the region where the two lines cross. Suppose he uses 6 percent as the new discount rate. That rate is close to the 6.16 percent return from the first pass through the worksheet in Table 9-1. At a 6 percent discount rate, he will find that Coca-Cola is worth $64.02 per share. He then enters the values he found at discount rates of 5 and 6 percent in the rate-of-return worksheet, and develops a refined estimate of 6.01 percent for his rate of return. The second pass through the worksheet agrees almost exactly with the 6.0 percent return read from the plot in Figure 9-2.

Summary

The investor's return is a multiple of the firm's return on equity when taxes and commissions are ignored in the steady-state model. The return-on-equity multiplier depends only on the dividend payout fraction and the P/B ratio. The multiplier is highest for firms that pay no dividends. The investor's return is then the same as the firm's return on equity.

SmartValue's simple formula for the investor's return gives the same result as the traditional Dividend Discount Model. The Smart-Value formula is more useful because it gives useful guidelines for choosing stocks. To earn a high return, choose firms that earn high returns, carry a reasonable amount of debt, and do not pay dividends. If the firm does pay dividends, choose stocks that sell at low P/B ratios.

Finding the rate of return is a trial-and-error process when you include taxes and commissions in the analysis. Find your rate of return by finding the discount rate that makes the value of the stock the same as the stock's market price.

Chapter 10

The "Buy and Hold" Strategy

Buy-and-Hold Coca-Cola?

Why Does Buy-and-Hold Work?

Does Buy-and-Hold Always Work?

When Does Buy-and-Hold Work?

"Buy-and-hold" is a time-honored investment strategy. Warren Buffet, the nation's most prominent investor, is a champion of the buy-and-hold strategy. The basic idea is simple. Buy stocks of sound firms. Then hold them for extended periods of time. How long is an "extended" period of time? Warren Buffet has the answer. His preferred holding period is "forever".

Is buy-and-hold really a good strategy? Does it always work? If not, how can you tell when buy-and-hold works and when it does not? Use SmartValue to find out. Measure what a stock is worth at a short investment period, say one year. Then use SmartValue to measure what the same stock is worth at a longer investment period, say five years. If the stock is worth more at the longer period, buy-and-hold works. If the stock is worth less, buy-and-hold fails.

Does Buy and Hold Work for Coca-Cola?

The investor we followed in Chapter 8 is a long-term investor. He believes in the buy-and-hold strategy. Unless something unusual happens, he prefers to hold any stock he buys for an extended period. How would buy-and-hold work if he bought Coca-Cola? Our investor believes Coca-Cola is a great company. It is an ideal candidate for buy-and-hold investing. He found in Chapter 8 that Coca-Cola costs too much. But that was for a five-year investment period. What if he plans to follow a buy-and-hold strategy, and hold Coca-Cola for a much longer time. Not forever, perhaps, but for a long time. It is, after all, one of Warren Buffet's favorites. What if he planned to hold it for ten years? Or twenty years? Would Coca-Cola then prove to be a worthwhile investment? To test the buy-and-hold strategy, he repeats his analysis of Coca-Cola over investment periods ranging from as short as six months to as long as 30 years. His individual situation and his forecasts are exactly the same as in Chapter 8. The only difference in the analysis is how long he plans to hold the stock.

He finds the results in Figure 10-1. Warren Buffet is right! Buy-and-hold works! The longer he holds the stock, the more it is worth. If he were a short-term investor and planned to hold the stock only a few years, Coca-Cola would be worth only $49 per share, well below Coca-Cola's current $64 market price. The longer he planned to hold the stock, the more Coca-Cola would be worth. But Coca-Cola still costs too much. He would have to extend his time horizon past 20 years before Coca-Cola was worth its current market price. At any investment period beyond about 20 years Coca-Cola would be worth more than it cost. The longer our investor held it, the more it would be worth. If he followed Warren Buffet's advice and held Coca-Cola forever, he would place an extremely high value on its stock. Coca-Cola's value would be infinite!

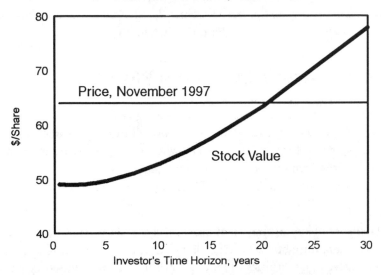

Fig. 10-1
BUY-AND-HOLD STRATEGY - COCA-COLA
10.3% Minimum Acceptable Return

While the Coca-Cola example shows that the buy-and-hold strategy works, Coca-Cola is still a poor investment for our investor. Sure, Coca-Cola is worth more the longer he plans to hold it. Sure, that means that buy-and-hold works. But he has to pay $64 for a stock that investors with a one to five-year time horizon would value at only $49 now. And he would need over twenty year's worth of patience waiting for the stock's value to grow to today's market price, all the while hoping that the forecasts he made today will hold up for the next twenty years. That is a mighty tall order. Our investor would be well-advised to look for some other stock not as overpriced as Coca-Cola.

Why Does "Buy-and-Hold" Work?

The basic reason buy-and-hold works for Coca-Cola is because Coca-Cola is growing faster than our investor is discounting the dollars Coca-Cola would put in his pocket. He forecast that Coca-Cola will grow 12 percent per year. But he is discounting future cash flows at only a 10.3 percent discount rate. Growth rates and discount rates pull in opposite directions. Faster growth makes the stock worth more. Higher discount rates makes the stock worth less. What is the net effect? The net effect depends on whether the growth rate is greater or smaller than the discount rate. In this example, Coca-Cola is growing faster than our investor discounts the dollars Coca-Cola generates. The net rate is the nominal growth rate of 12 percent per year minus a discount rate of 10.3 percent per year, or a net growth rate of 1.7 percent per year. Even after discounting, the discounted value of dividends and the proceeds from the eventual sale of the stock grow the longer he holds the stock. At that rate, the total discounted cash flow grows forever. The value of the stock (and the required investment period) is heading for infinity!

Does Buy-and-Hold Always Work?

Buy-and-hold works for firms that are growing faster than investors are discounting the dollars that firm puts in their pockets. But not all firms grow that fast. What happens with a slower growing firm? What happens when investors discount the dollars they receive faster than the firm grows? The net rate then is no longer a growth rate. The net rate is a discount rate. What happens then? Does buy-and-hold still work?

There are plenty of firms that grow slowly. Utilities are a good example. Utilities are normally in a mature business. They do not have great opportunities to grow. They do not have extensive opportunities to reinvest earnings. That is why they pay most of their earnings out as dividends. The SmartValue formula tells us that is a recipe for slow growth. Suppose our investor becomes interested in Con Edison, a major utility. Con Edison grows only about 3.5 percent per year. He considers Con Edison to be about as safe as Coca-Cola, and so decides to set the same minimum acceptable return of 10.3 percent. At that discount rate, he will be discounting the dollars Con Edison puts into his pocket much faster than Con Edison is growing. The net rate will be a discount rate of 6.8 percent -- the nominal discount rate of 10.3 percent less the 3.5 percent growth rate.

He finds whether buy-and-hold works the same way he did with Coca-Cola. He uses SmartValue to find what Con Edison is worth at several investment periods. Figure 10-2 shows how Con Edison's value changes with his investment period. Buy-and-hold is a disaster. The longer he holds Con Edison the less it is worth. Investing in Con Edison would be a serious mistake, at least for this investor.

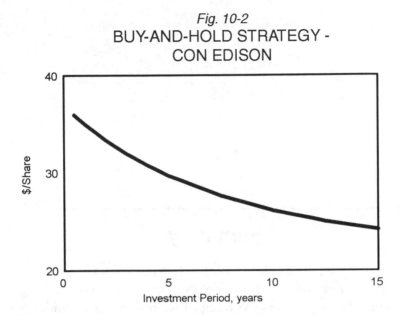

Fig. 10-2
BUY-AND-HOLD STRATEGY -
CON EDISON

When Does Buy-and-Hold Work?

How can you tell if buy-and-hold works? The relationship is more complicated than the simple difference between the growth rate and the discount rate. The only way to be sure is to use SmartValue. If you plan to follow a buy-and-hold strategy, work out the stock's value over a range of investment periods. You do not need to work out complete curves like Figures 10-1 and 10-2. Use the Stock Valuation Worksheet to find what the stock is worth for a short investment period, like one year. Then use the worksheet to find what the stock is worth for a longer period, like five years. If the stock is worth more at the longer investment period, buy-and-hold works. If the stock is worth less, buy-and-hold fails.

If you plan to follow a buy-and-hold strategy, follow this simple rule of thumb. Look for firms that are growing faster than you will be discounting the dollars you expect those stocks to put in your pocket. Look for firms whose growth rate is greater than the minimum return you specify as being an acceptable return.

Summary

"Buy-and-hold" is a time-honored investment strategy. It works when the firm is growing faster than the minimum return you specify as being an acceptable return. But if the firm is growing slower than your minimum acceptable rate of return, buy-and-hold fails. To be sure, use SmartValue to find what the stock is worth at a short and a long investment period. If the stock is worth more at the longer investment period, buy-and-hold works. If the stock is worth less, buy-and-hold fails.

Chapter **11**

Growth Stocks --
Allowing for Change

Decay Formula

Choosing Initial and Long-
     Run Limits

Forecasting Half Lives

Forecasting Dividends

The SmartValue formula is ideal for mature firms that follow the steady-state model. Finding what a stock is worth is easy when key factors like the firm's return on equity and growth rate all stay constant at steady-state values while you hold the stock. But many stocks do not follow the steady-state model. Their key factors do not stay constant. They change gradually with time. Growth stocks are the most important example. The return on equity growth firms earn, how fast they grow, and the P/B ratio investors are willing to pay gradually decay as the growth firm matures. The steady-state model is no longer appropriate when the key factors change as time goes on. Now it is time to extend SmartValue to growth stocks. It is time to find what a stock is worth when the key factors do not stay constant, but change with time.

The SmartValue formula for the investor's rate of return in Chapter 9 showed that you should invest in growth stocks. That is where you can earn the highest rate of return. That is the place to be if you can tolerate the risk. Growth firms normally do not pay dividends. They need every penny of their earnings to pay for their rapid growth. Growth stocks are extremely attractive. Growth firms are often at the leading edge of new technology. They are growing rapidly. They earn high rates of return. A growth firm may dominate a new market. Most likely it is adding capacity furiously to satisfy a strong demand for its product. Investors flock to growth stocks because they have such a bright future. Hype and glamour surround growth stocks. Buying growth stocks is the thing to do. Buy the hottest growth stock! Get rich quick! But all the hype and glamour may intoxicate innocent investors. They may bid the price so high these stocks are no longer winning investments. How can you tell if a growth stock is overpriced? How do you avoid paying too much? SmartValue will tell you what growth stocks are really worth, and which ones it pays to buy.

Rapid growth is great, but let's be realistic. Rapid growth cannot continue unchanged forever. Markets do not have an infinite capacity to absorb products. In time markets saturate, and growth slows. New competitors enter the market and put pressure on product prices. How does that affect growth firms? Their growth gradually slows. The rate of return they earn gradually falls. Investors react by lowering the P/B ratio they are willing to pay for the stock. As growth slows, growth firms no longer have the opportunities for new investment they had when they were younger. They no longer need to reinvest all of their earnings to finance growth. Part of the firm's earnings then become available for paying dividends. That makes dividends gradually increase as the maturing process progresses. By the time the growth firm is fully mature, it typically pays half of its earnings out as dividends.

Obviously the steady-state model is not going to work for growth firms. Those firm's current high growth rates, rates of return, and P/B ratios are not going to continue unchanged at steady-state values. We will have to adapt the SmartValue formula to make it recognize this gradual slowing of growth, the gradual fall in rate of return and P/B ratio, and the gradual increase in dividends as growth firms mature.

The great advantage of the steady-state model is that it is transparent and easy to understand. As we leave the assumption of steady-state conditions and allow the key factors to vary with time, our model is obviously going to become a little more complex. But it will still be easy to understand the fundamentals. Do not worry about understanding every last detail. That is not necessary. The worksheets will handle all the detail for you. Do try to get the gist of the expanded model. That will give you a degree of comfort when you apply the model to real stocks.

Decay Formula

Three key factors determine what a stock is worth. They are the rate of return the firm earns on stockholder equity, how fast equity per share grows, and the P/B ratio investors are willing to pay for the stock. If those key factors are not going to stay constant at steady-state values, we will need a formula that describes how they are likely to change as a growth firm matures. The basic requirements are obvious. Each factor begins at its current value. Each decays away gradually towards some long-run limit. What long-run limit? That is obvious, too. The most reasonable long-run limit is a value that is appropriate for a firm that has fully matured.

Each key factor is going to decay along a curve like the gradually falling curve in Figure 11-1. Let's model each key factor as the total of two parts. The first part is the long-run value we expect each key factor to settle down to when the growth firm has fully matured. The horizontal line in Figure 11-1 represents that long-run value. Each key factor will always be larger than that long-run value by some margin. That margin is the second part of the decay model. The margin is the gap between the actual value at any time and the long-run limit — the gap between the curved line and the horizontal line in Figure 11-1. The margin is the part that gradually decays away as the growth firm matures. Adding the two parts — the long-run value and the margin — yields the value of that factor. The curve in Figure 11-1 shows the value that factor has at any time. In the steady-state model that value would be represented by a straight horizontal line because that factor stayed constant. With growth stocks, however, each factor has to be represented by a curve because each factor gradually changes with time. As time goes on and the growth firm matures, the initial margin gradually decays away. That makes the sum of the two parts decay as well. When the growth firm has fully matured the margin will have decayed away completely. Only the long-run value will be left.

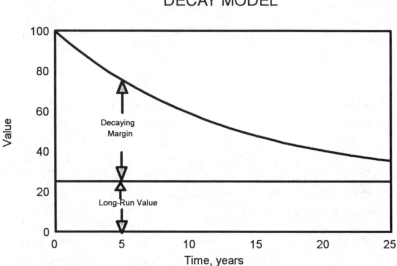

Fig. 11-1
DECAY MODEL

How fast will the margin decay? Let's take a page out of the physicist's book. Physicists use a half-life to describe how radioactive elements decay. SmartValue is a space-age formula; we can use a half life, too. In SmartValue, a half life is simply the time it takes to go halfway from any starting value towards the long-run limit.

The table below illustrates the idea of a half life. Some factor begins at an initial value of 100 and decays away towards a long-run limit of zero with a five-year half life. The first column shows the number of half lives that have passed. The second column

Table 11-1
DECAY MODEL WITH 5-YEAR HALF LIFE

Number of Half Lives	Years	Remaining Value
0	0	100
1	5	50
2	10	25
3	15	12.5
4	20	6.25
5	25	3.125

shows the corresponding number of years that have passed. The last column shows what is left of the initial value. Half is left after the first five-year half life. The initial value of 100 falls to 50. After a second half life, or at year ten, half of the 50 is left, and the value falls to 25. Each succeeding half life reduces the value at the beginning of that half life by one-half.

Here is a practical example of how to use a half life. Suppose a growth firm currently earns a return of 45 percent. That return is outstanding, but we know it cannot last. We forecast that the return on equity will fall and eventually level off at, say, 15 percent when the firm is mature. Figure 11-2 shows how we can use this two-part decay model and half lives to forecast how that firm's return on equity is likely to fall. Return on equity begins at 45 percent and gradually decays away towards the long-run limit of 15 percent. The plot shows how fast the return would decay for a series of half lives ranging from one year to 100 years. The half life offers great flexibility in forecasting how fast any factor will decay. A short half life makes return on equity fall quickly; a long half life makes return on equity fall slowly. How fast do you think a key factor will decay? Choose a half life that matches the decay you expect. If you think a key factor will decay slowly, use a long half life. If you think the factor will decay rapidly, use a short half life.

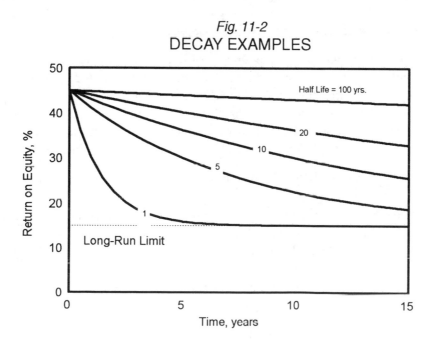

Fig. 11-2
DECAY EXAMPLES

Choosing Initial Values and Long-Run Limits

How do you go about using the decay model to make a forecast for some factor? The first step is to choose the initial and long-run values you expect for that factor. Choosing appropriate initial values and long-run limits is easier than you might think. Choosing the initial value is easy. The current value of any factor is the obvious choice for the initial value, unless you expect some significant near-term change.

Choosing the long-run limit is also easy. Let's begin with the growth rate. When the firm has fully matured, it is likely to grow at about the growth rate of the national economy. The growth rate of the Gross Domestic Product (GDP) measures how fast the national economy grows. GDP comes in two flavors. One is GDP measured in current dollars. The other is "real" GDP, which is measured in dollars adjusted for inflation. The firms whose history you will analyze report their results in current dollars, not inflation-adjusted dollars. Be consistent. Use the GDP in current dollars. That makes the growth rate of current-dollar GDP a reasonable estimate for a firm's long-run growth rate.

The financial press normally reports GDP growth as real (i.e., inflation-adjusted) growth. We want the growth in current dollars, not inflation-adjusted dollars. Converting growth rates from real dollars to current dollars is easy. Just add the inflation rate to the GDP growth in inflation-adjusted dollars. With real GDP growing about 3 percent per year and long-run inflation growing about 4 percent per year, for example, the long-run growth in current-dollar GDP would be 4 plus 3, or 7 percent per year. That is a good estimate of how fast today's hot growth firms will be growing, say, fifty years from now.

Now let's consider an appropriate long-run limit for the return on equity. The long-run return must be consistent with the long-run growth rate and the long-run dividend payout. The SmartValue formulas in Chapter 4 showed how the dividend payout fraction, the reinvestment fraction, the growth rate of equity per share, and the return on equity are related. Here is how to use that formula to find the return on equity that is consistent with any target dividend payout fraction and equity growth rate:

Return on Equity = (Equity Growth Rate)/(Reinvestment Fraction)

Remember that the reinvestment fraction is 1.0 minus the dividend payout fraction. Mature firms pay about half their earnings out as dividends. That means the reinvestment fraction is one minus one-half, or also about one-half. Suppose you forecast that equity growth in the long run will slow to the current-dollar GDP growth rate of 7 percent per year, and that the dividend payout and reinvestment fractions will both level out at 0.5. The return on equity that is consistent with these forecasts is:

Return on Equity = (7)/(0.5) = 14 %

If you forecast that equity per share will grow 7 percent per year in the long-run, and that the return on equity will stabilize at 14 percent, your forecasts will be consistent with the target long-run dividend payout fraction of 0.5.

How about the long-run P/B ratio? The financial press normally talks about the P/E ratio, not the P/B ratio. No problem. Remember that the P/B ratio is equal to the P/E ratio multiplied by the return on equity. P/E ratios for mature firms are typically about 15. If you forecast a long-run P/E ratio of 15 and a long-run return on equity of 14 percent, the corresponding long-run P/B ratio will be a long-run return of 0.14 (14 percent in decimal form) times a P/E ratio of 15, or 2.10.

Reasonable long-run limits are summarized in Table 11-2. Use the SmartValue formula to adjust these limits if you think a different long-run growth rate or dividend payout fraction is more appropriate for the particular stock you are considering.

Table 11-2
REASONABLE LONG-RUN LIMITS

Factor	Long-Run Limit
Return on Equity, %	14
Growth of Equity/Share, %/yr.	7
Dividend Payout, %	50
P/B Ratio	2.1

The long-run limit primarily affects the far-out part of your forecast. It will not be an important part of your analysis if you are a short-term investor, but will become more important as you extend your investment horizon.

Forecasting Half Lives

Forecasting half lives is more difficult. It is a matter of judgment. Describing decay in terms of a half life makes the process easier to visualize. Here is one way to estimate a half life. Suppose a firm is growing 30 percent per year, and you expect growth to slow and approach 10 percent per year as a long-run limit. The halfway point is 20 percent per year. How long do you think it will take before growth slows that much? The time you think it will take is the half life. History is often a useful guide. Examine the firm's historical record and plot each key factor for the past ten years or so. Draw a smooth curve through the data. Add a horizontal line on the plot to locate the long-run limit you expect that factor to approach. Now sketch in a forecast curve that appears to be a reasonable continuation of the historic trend. Let each key factor decay away about as rapidly as it has over the past few years, and gradually approach the long-run limit. Read how many years it takes for your forecast curve to go halfway from the starting value to the long-run limit. That time is the half life.

Another way to estimate half lives is to examine firms that once were hot growth stocks and have since matured. Look up their financial history, and see how many years it took for their growth to slow. Examining a number of firms this way will give you a better feel for what typical half lives are.

Which half life is the most critical? The half life for the P/B ratio is usually the most critical, particularly if you are a short-term investor. The half life for the return on equity is usually next. The half life for the growth rate is less critical. Suppose growth slows faster than you had forecast. That means that equity per share will not be as high as you had forecast when it is time to sell. That is bad. The stock price is tied to equity by the P/B ratio. That means the stock price will not be as high as you had forecast, either. But dividends will be higher because the firm will not have invested as much of its earnings to pay for growth if growth is slower. That is good. The higher dividends tend to offset the lower stock price.

How long should the half lives be relative to each other? Which half life is the longest? Which is the shortest? The half life for the return on equity is normally the longest. The half life for the growth rate of equity per share is normally shorter. A shorter half life for the growth rate makes the growth rate fall below the return on equity. That is the condition SmartValue formula requires for dividends to increase as the growth firm matures. A growth firm may not pay dividends now, but will start paying dividends as it matures. The firm will have a dividend payout fraction of zero if it does not pay dividends now. The SmartValue formula shows that the growth rate has to be equal to the return on equity to make the payout fraction zero. But if the payout fraction is to rise gradually above zero, the growth rate has to fall gradually below the return on equity. How do you make your forecast of the growth rate gradually fall below your forecast of the return on equity? There are two ways. One way is to make the long-run limit for the growth rate lower than the long-run limit for the return on equity. Another way is to make the half life of the growth forecast shorter than the half life of the return on equity forecast. Do both. Make the long-run limit for the growth rate smaller than the long-run limit for the return on equity. And make the half life for the growth rate shorter than the half life for the return on equity.

What about the half life for the P/B ratio? That half life is the shortest of all. Investors see what is coming. They know that growth will eventually slow and that profitability will fall. They want to hang on while the price goes up, but be the first one out before the price falls. It is a game of musical chairs. The last one out loses. Investors try to avoid being the last one out by anticipating slowing growth. They reduce the P/B ratio they are willing to pay before growth actually slows and the return on equity actually falls. That makes the P/B ratio fall faster than either the return on equity falls or growth slows. You can account for investor anticipation by forecasting a shorter half life for the P/B ratio than you forecast for either the equity growth rate or return on equity.

Forecasting Dividends

Don't worry about forecasting dividends. You will forecast them automatically, perhaps without realizing you have done so. How? The SmartValue formula fixes the relationship between the return on equity, the equity growth rate, and the dividend payout fraction. You can only forecast two of these factors. Once you forecast any two, the Smart-Value formula fixes the third. Once you forecast the return on equity and the growth rate of equity per share, you automatically forecast the dividend payout fraction. And once you forecast the growth rate of equity per share, you also automatically forecast future values of equity per share. Remember how the SmartValue formula finds dividends? Multiply equity per share by the return on equity to find earnings, and then by the dividend payout fraction to find dividends. Once you forecast the return on equity and the growth rate of equity per share, all these factors are fixed. The only thing left is crunching the numbers. You will do that in the worksheet for finding what stocks are worth.

Many growth stocks do not pay dividends. They reinvest all their earnings; there is nothing left for dividends. How do you build zero dividends into your forecast? The SmartValue formula shows that the dividend payout fraction is zero when the growth rate of equity per share and the return on equity are identical. If you do not expect the firm to pay any dividends for as long as you hold the stock, make your forecast of the return on equity and the growth rate of equity per share identical. That insures zero dividends forever. If you want to forecast that there will be no dividends initially, but that dividends will gradually grow while you hold the stock, make the initial return on equity and the nitial equity growth rate identical. That will force dividends to be zero initially. Then let the return on equity and the equity growth rate decay along different paths. Dividends will begin as soon as these paths diverge. You can make the paths diverge by forecasting different long-run limits for the return and the growth rate, or different half lives, or both.

Summary

The Half-Life Decay Model is a reasonable way to describe how the key factors gradually decay away as a growth firm matures. Each factor begins at its current value and gradually falls away towards some long-run limit appropriate for a mature firm. The long-run limit is one part of the model. The margin between the current value and the long-run limit is the other part. A half life describes how fast the margin decays towards zero, and the factor decays towards its long-run limit.

The growth rate of the GDP in current dollars is a reasonable long-run limit for the growth of equity per share. A mature firm typically pays half its earnings out as dividends. That makes the long-run limit for return on equity twice the growth rate of equity per share. Mature firms typically sell at P/E ratios of about 15. The long-run limit for the P/B ratio is the long-run limit for the P/E ratio multiplied by the long-run return on equity.

Estimating half lives is a matter of judgement. The half life for the return on equity is normally longer than the half life for the growth rate. The half life for the P/B ratio is normally the shortest half life.

Don't worry about forecasting dividends. Once you forecast the return on equity and the growth rate of equity per share, you automatically forecast dividends.

Chapter **12**

What Are Growth Stocks Worth?

Growth Multiplier

Forecasting the P/B Ratio

Worksheet for Non-Dividend Paying Stocks

Finding what a growth stock is worth is relatively easy if you forecast that the firm will reinvest all its earnings and pay no dividends. All you have to worry about is the price of the stock and the dollars that will roll into your pocket when you eventually sell the stock. There are no dividends to complicate the computation. Finding what a growth stock is worth is a little more complicated if you expect the firm to pay dividends. Then you have to forecast future dividends as well as the future stock price, and discount both. Let's begin with the simplest case, and find what a growth stock that does not pay any dividends is worth. We will study growth stocks that do pay dividends in the next chapter.

Many growth stocks do not pay any dividends. Those firms reinvest every penny of their earnings in the business instead. You may not expect that the growth firm you are studying will pay any dividends, at least while you hold its stock. If so, you already know the discounted value of dividends: zero. Good! You can simplify the analysis by skipping all the computations that have to do with dividends. There is another simplification. The SmartValue formula says that the growth rate of equity per share and the return on equity are identical when firms do not pay dividends. That means you only have to forecast the firm's growth rate. When you forecast the growth rate, you automatically forecast the firm's return on equity because it is the same as the growth rate. Of course, you also have to forecast the P/B ratio.

The Growth Multiplier

The growth multiplier we developed in Table 4-1 is for a mature firm that follows the steady-state model. Its growth rate stays constant. It does not vary with time. That is why it took only a simple four-line worksheet to find a growth multiplier in Table 4-1. Obviously, that growth multiplier is not going to work with growth stocks. Their growth rate does not stay constant. Growth decays gradually as time goes on. That makes calculating growth multipliers slightly more complicated. Provided you use the decay model described in the last chapter, finding the growth multiplier is still easy. Table 12-1 shows how.

Example 12-1 A growth firm is currently growing 45 percent per year. We expect that growth will slow to 7 percent per year when the firm is fully mature. We also expect growth to decay with a seven-year half life. We want to know how large the firm will be in five years. What growth multiplier do we need?

Enter the forecasts in Table 12-1 and follow the directions. Table 12-2 shows the results. If growth slows as forecast, the firm will be 6.35 times larger in five years. If we had forecast that growth would stay at 45 percent per year during those five years, the growth multiplier would have been 9.49, about 50 percent larger. This example shows how important it is to allow for growth to slow when analyzing growth stocks.

Table 12-1

GROWTH MULTIPLIER FOR THE DECAY MODEL

1. Investment period, years .... _____
2. Initial Growth Rate, (%/yr.)/100 (decimal form) .... _____
3. Long-Run Growth Rate, (%/yr.)/100 (decimal form) ...... _____
4. Initial Margin: Subtract Line 3 from Line 2 .... _____
5. Half Life, years .... _____
6. Divide 0.6931 by Line 5, then Multiply by Line 1 .... _____
7. Enter Line 6 in your calculator, tap the
   change sign (+/-) key, and then the e^x key .... _____
8. Subtract Line 7 from 1.0 .... _____
9. Multiply Line 4 by Line 8, then Divide by Line 6 .... _____
10. Add Lines 3 and 9. Multiply the result by Line 1. .... _____
11. Growth Multiplier: Enter Line 10 in your
    calculator and tap the e^x key .... _____

Table 12-2

GROWTH MULTIPLIER - Example 12-1

1. Investment period, years 5
2. Initial Growth Rate, (%/yr.)/100 (decimal form) 0.45
3. Long-Run Growth Rate, (%/yr.)/100 (decimal form) 0.07
4. Initial Margin: Subtract Line 3 from Line 2 .... 0.38
5. Half Life, years 7
6. Divide 0.6931 by Line 5, then Multiply by Line 1 .... 0.4951
7. Enter Line 6 in your calculator, tap the
   change sign (+/-) key, and then the e^x key 0.6095
8. Subtract Line 7 from 1.0 .... 0.3905
9. Multiply Line 4 by Line 8, then Divide by Line 6 .... 0.2997
10. Add Lines 3 and 9. Multiply the result by Line 1. .... 1.8485
11. Growth Multiplier: Enter Line 10 in your
    calculator and tap the e^x key 6.350

Table 12-3

WORKSHEET FOR FORECASTING THE P/B RATIO

1. Investment period, years .... _____
2. Initial P/B Ratio .... _____
3. Long-Run P/B Ratio .... _____
4. Initial Margin: Subtract Line 3 from Line 2 .... _____
5. Half Life, years .... _____
6. Divide 0.6931 by Line 5, then Multiply by Line 1 .... _____
7. Enter Line 6 in your calculator, tap the
   change sign (+/-) key, and then the e^x key .... _____
8. Final P/B Ratio: Multiply Line 4 by Line 7,
   then Add Line 3 .... _____

Table 12-4

P/B FORECAST - Example 12-2

1. Investment period, years 5
2. Initial P/B Ratio 10
3. Long-Run P/B Ratio 2.1
4. Initial Margin: Subtract Line 3 from Line 2 .... 7.9
5. Half Life, years 6
6. Divide 0.6931 by Line 5, then Multiply by Line 1 .... 0.5776
7. Enter Line 6 in your calculator, tap the
   change sign (+/-) key, and then the e^x key 0.5612
8. Final P/B Ratio: Multiply Line 4 by Line 7,
   then Add Line 3 .... 6.53

Forecasting the Final P/B Ratio

The P/B ratio will decay towards its long-run limit while you hold the stock. How do you find what the ratio will be when it is time to sell the stock? Forecast the initial and long-run P/B ratios and the half life, then use the worksheet in Table 12-3 to find how far this decay is likely to proceed, and what the ratio is likely to be when you sell the stock.

Example 12-2 A growth stock currently sells at a P/B ratio of 10. You forecast that it will decay towards a long-run limit of 2.1 with a six-year half life. If you buy the stock and hold it for five years, what is the P/B ratio likely to be when you decide to sell? Enter your forecast in Table 12-3 and use the worksheet to find that P/B ratio. Table 12-4 shows the calculations. Your forecast leads to a P/B ratio of 6.53 when you sell the stock in five years.

Worksheet for Growth Stocks That Do Not Pay Dividends

Table 12-5 is the worksheet for finding what growth stocks that do not pay dividends are worth. The worksheet follows the same pattern as the worksheet for mature stocks in Table 6-1. Describe your financial situation in Section I. Enter your forecasts for the firm in Section II. Discount the cash the stock puts into your pocket and find what the stock is worth in Section III of the worksheet.

Section I - The Investor

Section I is identical to Section I of the worksheet for mature stocks.

Section II - The Firm

Begin by forecasting the initial and long-run equity per share growth rates and the half life. Then use the worksheet in Table 12-1 to find the corresponding growth multiplier. Enter that growth multiplier in line 8 of the worksheet. Enter the starting equity per share in line 7. Then use Table 12-3 to forecast the P/B ratio you expect when you sell the stock at the end of the investment period, and enter that P/B ratio in line 9. Multiply the starting equity by the growth multiplier and the P/B ratio to forecast the final stock price in line 10.

Section III - What Is the Stock Worth?

The only dollars that rolls into your pocket when a growth firm pays no dividends is the net proceeds when you eventually sell the stock. That makes discounting in Section III much simpler. The computations are basically the same as those for mature firms, except that all the computations relating to dividends have been eliminated. The computations that remain allow for capital gains taxes and your broker's commission.

We will use this worksheet to find what Cisco Systems, currently a hot growth stock, is worth in Chapter 14.

Table 12-5
WORKSHEET FOR GROWTH STOCKS THAT DO NOT PAY DIVIDENDS

Section I - The Investor

1. Investment Period, years .... _____
2. Divide Incremental Tax Rate on Ordinary Income (%)
   by 100; Subtract the Result from 1.0 .... _____
3. Divide Capital Gains Tax Rate (%) by 100 .... _____
4. Divide Minimum Acceptable Return (%) by 100 .... _____
5. Divide Broker's Commission (%) by 100;
   Add the Result to 1.0 .... _____
6. Divide Broker's Commission (%) by 100;
   Subtract the Result from 1.0 .... _____

Section II - The Firm

7. Initial Equity, $/Share .... _____
8. Growth Multiplier (from Table 12-1) .... _____
9. Final P/B Ratio (from Table 12-3) .... _____
10. Final Stock Price: Multiply Line 7 by Lines 8 and 9 .... _____

Section III - What Is the Stock Worth?

11. Multiply Line 1 by Line 4 .... _____
12. Discount Factor: Enter Line 11 in your calculator,
    tap the change sign (+/-) key, then tap the e^x key .... _____
13. Present Value of Final Stock Price: Multiply Line 6
    by Lines 10 and 12 .... _____
14. Multiply Line 3 by Line 13 .... _____
15. Subtract Line 14 from Line 13 .... _____
16. Multiply Line 3 by Line 12 and
    Subtract the result from 1.0 .... _____
17. What the Stock is Worth: Divide Line 15 by Line 5
    and by Line 16 .... _____

Summary

If a stock does not pay dividends, you only have to worry about what the price of the stock will be when you decide to sell. The stock price will be the equity per share multiplied by the P/B ratio at that time. New worksheets give the required values of equity per share and the P/B ratio. A third worksheet finds what the stock is worth.

Chapter **13**

DIVIDEND-PAYING GROWTH STOCKS

Discounting Dividends

Forecasting:

    Growth Rates

    Equity/Share

    Return on Equity

    P/B Ratio

What Is the Stock Worth?

Finding what growth stocks are worth is a little more complicated if the growth firm pays dividends, or if you forecast that it will begin to pay dividends while you hold the stock. You need to make the same forecasts you made for the growth firm that does not pay dividends. But the growth rate forecast will no longer be the same as the forecast of the firm's return on equity. That means you will have to make independent forecasts of the firm's return on equity and how fast equity per share grows. Remember to forecast a return on equity greater than the equity growth rate to insure that the firm pays dividends to you, and not the other way around.

Your forecast that the return on equity and the growth rate of equity per share change continually with time has major implications. It means that equity per share, earnings, the dividend payout fraction, and dividends are also changing continually with time. We will need a way to discount this changing pattern of dividend payments.

Discounting Dividends

Discounting dividends was easy in the steady-state model. That is because dividends grew at a steady growth rate. The growth rate did not vary, it stayed constant. Constant percentage growth rates make discounting dividends easy. That is why it took only three lines in the Stock Evaluation Worksheet for Mature Firms to discount dividends. Discounting is not quite that simple with growth stocks. The SmartValue formulas still apply. You still multiply equity per share by the return on equity to get earnings, and then by the dividend payout fraction to get dividends. But these factors are no longer constant; they are all continually changing. Equity per share grows steadily, but at a slower and slower growth rate. The return on equity decays gradually towards its long-run limit. The dividend payout fraction is no longer constant. It gradually grows as the return on equity and growth rate decay along different paths. Because of all these changing conditions, the simple discounting process we used to discount dividends when all these factors stayed constant no longer works.

Figure 13-1 illustrates the problem. The top curve shows the dividends a growth firm might pay as it matures. How do you discount these dividends? It is easy in theory. You just multiply each point on the dividend curve by the discount factor for that point on the curve and draw a smooth curve through the resulting discounted dividends. Discounting generates the lower curve in Figure 13-1. The discount factor begins at 1.0 at zero time. That makes the discounted dividend curve begin at the same point the dividend curve begins. The discount factor then gradually drops below 1.0 and approaches zero as time goes on. Multiplying by a number that gradually approaches zero makes the curve for discounted dividends gradually fall below the curve for undiscounted dividend.

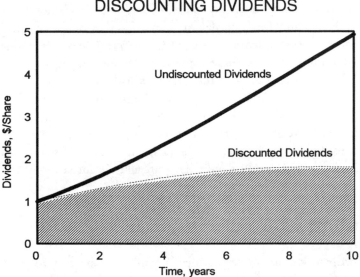

Fig. 13-1
DISCOUNTING DIVIDENDS

The lower curve in Figure 13-1 gives discounted dividends at each instant in time.[1] We want the total of all the discounted dividends that roll into our pocket while we hold the stock. To find the total we have to add up the discounted dividends at all these instants of time. How do you add up the discounted dividends at all these instants of time? The total of discounted dividends is equal to the area under the discounted dividend curve. That is the area that is shaded in Figure 13-1. All you have to do is measure the area under that curve during the investment period.

You are probably more at home measuring areas in square inches. Not this area. The height of the curve is not scaled in inches. It is scaled in discounted dividends per year. The width is not scaled in inches, either. It is scaled in years. When you multiply the width by the average height to find the area, you are not multiplying inches by inches. You are multiplying discounted dividends per year by years. The years cancel out in this process. That is why the area measures discounted dividends. And that is what we are looking for.

---

[1]SmartValue treats dividends as if they flowed into your pocket continuously, even though they actually roll in once each quarter. Continuous dividends make the arithmetic easier. The error caused by treating dividends as continuous rather than quarterly cash flows is trivial relative to the errors in forecasting those dividends. Don't waste time worrying about trivial errors.

Measuring the area under the curve was easy in the steady-state model. That is what made the steady-state model easy to use. Measuring areas is not as simple when the key factors are all changing from one day to the next, as they do for growth stocks. Do not worry, we are in luck. Carl Friedrich Gauss (1777-1855), one of the giants of mathematics, anticipated our problem. He found a simple way to measure areas under curves. All we have to do to find the area is to discount dividends at three points during the investment period, and average those discounted dividends. Not just any three points. Gauss specifies the three times where the dividends must be discounted. And not just a simple arithmetic average. Gauss uses a weighted average, and specifies the weights to be given each of the three discounted dividends. We will use the Gauss method to discount dividends in the worksheet. Don't worry about the details. They are all built into the worksheet for finding what the stock is worth

Forecasting

If a growth stock does not pay dividends, you only have to forecast the price of the stock when you are ready to sell. If the growth stock does pay dividends, however, you also have to forecast dividends at the three Gauss times. Use the SmartValue formula to find dividends. Develop three growth multipliers so you can find equity per share at each of the three Gauss times. Then forecast the return on equity and the growth rate at each of these three times and use the SmartValue formula to translate those forecasts into the corresponding dividend payout fractions. Multiply equity per share at those times by the return on equity to find earnings, and then by the dividend payout fraction to find dividends. Worksheets will make the process easy.

Forecasting the Growth Rate of Equity per Share

You need to forecast how fast equity per share grows and develop the appropriate growth multiplier whether the stock pays dividends or not. If the stock does not pay dividends, you only need a single growth multiplier to translate the growth rate forecast into the corresponding forecast of equity per share at the end of the investment period. If the growth stock does pay dividends, you also have to translate the growth forecast into the corresponding equity per share at the three Gauss times as well.

Use the worksheet in Table 13-1 to forecast growth rates and then to translate the growth rate forecast into the corresponding forecast of equity per share. Begin with Part A of the worksheet and enter your forecast of growth rates. The basic forecasts are the initial and long-run growth rates, the half life that tells how fast growth will decay, and the length of time you plan to hold the stock. Enter these forecasts in the first six lines of the worksheet. The worksheet expands into four columns starting in line 7. The four columns are for the three Gauss times and the time at the end of the investment period. Line 7

Table 13-1
WORKSHEET FOR FORECASTING RETURN ON EQUITY, GROWTH RATE, AND EQUITY PER SHARE

A. Forecast Return on Equity and Growth Rate of Equity/Share

		0.113	0.5	0.887	1.0
1.	Investment period, years				_____
2.	Initial Value				_____
3.	Long-Run Limit				_____
4.	Initial Margin: Subtract Line 3 from Line 2				_____
5.	Half Life, years				_____
6.	Divide 0.6931 by Line 5				_____
7.	Time, fraction of investment period	0.113	0.5	0.887	1.0
8.	Time, Years. Multiply Line 1 by Line 7	_____	_____	_____	_____
9.	Multiply Line 8 by Line 6	_____	_____	_____	_____
10.	Decay Factor: Enter Line 9 in your calculator, tap the change sign (+/-) key, then tap the e^x key	_____	_____	_____	_____
11.	Future Values: Multiply Line 4 by Line 10, then Add line 3	_____	_____	_____	_____

B. Translate Growth Forecast into Equity/Share Forecast

12.	Initial Equity, $/Share				_____
13.	Subtract Line 10 from 1.0, then Divide by Line 9	_____	_____	_____	_____
14.	Multiply Line 4 by Line 13, then Add Line 3	_____	_____	_____	_____
15.	Multiply Line 14 by Line 8, then Divide by 100	_____	_____	_____	_____
16.	Growth Multiplier: Enter Line 15 in your calculator and tap the e^x key	_____	_____	_____	_____
17.	Equity, $/Share: Multiply Line 12 by Line 16	_____	_____	_____	_____

shows the times where you need to make forecasts. These times are given as fractions of the investment period in line 7 and in actual years in line 8. The instructions starting in line 8 apply to each of the four columns on the right side of the worksheet. Line 11 shows the growth rates at the three intermediate times and at the end of the investment period. These growth rates are consistent with your estimates of the initial and the long-run growth rates and the half life.

Forecasting Equity per Share

When you forecast a growth rate for equity per share, you implicitly forecast equity per share as well. How do you translate these forecasts of growth rates into the corresponding forecast of equity per share? That is what Part B of the worksheet in Table 13-1 does. The SmartValue formula for equity per share is a simple one: multiply the initial equity by a growth multiplier. When the growth rate changes continuously, as it does in the decay model, the growth multiplier changes continuously too. You will need to find four growth multipliers — one at each of the three intermediate times, and one at the end of the investment period. Forecast the growth rate in Part A of the worksheet first. Then go on to Part B and translate the growth rate forecast into the corresponding forecast of equity per share. The four columns in Part B of the worksheet correspond to the same four columns in Part A.

Example 13-1 A growth firm has $5 of equity per share. Equity per share is currently growing 45 percent per year. We expect growth to slow to 7 percent per year when the firm is mature. We also expect growth to slow with a 7-year half life. We expect to hold the stock for five years. Use Part A of Table 13-1 to work out growth rates at the three intermediate times and at the end of the investment period. Then use Part B to translate this growth rate forecast into the resulting forecast of equity per share at those same times. The computations are shown in Table 13-2.

Part A of the worksheet shows that equity per share begins growing at 45 percent per year and gradually slows to 30 percent per year in five years. Part B of the worksheet shows that this pattern of decay in the growth rate makes equity grow from 5 $/Share initially to 31.75 $/Share at the end of the five-year investment period. If we had not allowed for slowing growth and forecast that growth would stay at 45 percent per year, equity would have grown to 47.44 $/Share in five years, 50 percent more than the forecast value.

Forecasting Return on Equity

If you do not expect a growth stock to pay dividends you can ignore the return on equity forecast. It will be identical to the equity growth rate. When you expect the growth stock to pay dividends, the return on equity forecast is no longer the same as the growth rate forecast. You will need to make an independent forecast of the return on equity. Forecast the initial return on equity and the long-run return, and the half life that tells how fast the return will decay. Remember that your forecast of the return on equity must

Table 13-2
GROWTH RATE AND EQUITY/SHARE FORECAST
Example 13-1

A. Forecast Return on Equity and Growth Rate of Equity/Share

1. Investment period, years				5
2. Initial Value				45
3. Long-Run Limit				7
4. Initial Margin: Subtract Line 3 from Line 2				38
5. Half Life, years				7
6. Divide 0.6931 by Line 5				0.0990
7. Time, fraction of investment period	0.113	0.5	0.887	1.0
8. Time, Years. Multiply Line 1 by Line 7	0.565	2.5	4.435	5
9. Multiply Line 8 by Line 6	0.0559	0.2475	0.4391	0.4950
10. Decay Factor: Enter Line 9 in your calculator, tap the change sign (+/-) key, then tap the e^x key	0.9456	0.7808	0.6446	0.6096
11. Future Values: Multiply Line 4 by Line 10, then Add line 3	42.93	36.67	31.49	30.16

B. Translate Growth Forecast into Equity/Share Forecast

12. Initial Equity, $/Share				5.00
13. Subtract Line 10 from 1.0, then Divide by Line 9	0.9732	0.8857	0.8094	0.7887
14. Multiply Line 4 by Line 13, then Add Line 3	43.98	40.66	37.76	36.97
15. Multiply Line 14 by Line 8, then Divide by 100	0.2485	1.0165	1.6747	1.8485
16. Growth Multiplier: Enter Line 15 in your calculator and tap the e^x key	1.2821	2.7635	5.3372	6.3503
17. Equity, $/Share: Multiply Line 12 by Line 16	6.411	13.817	26.69	31.75

be greater than your forecast of the equity growth rate to insure that the firm pays dividends to you, and not the other way round. You can insure that dividends flow in the right direction by making the initial growth rate equal to or less than the initial return on equity, and by forecasting a lower long-run value and/or a shorter half life for the growth rate than for the return on equity. Then use Part A of Table 13-1 to forecast the return on equity at the three intermediate times. Ignore Part B of the worksheet. Part B is used only to translate the growth rate forecast into the corresponding equity per share.

Forecasting the P/B Ratio

You only need the P/B ratio when you sell the stock at the end of the investment period. You can use the worksheet in Table 12-3 from the last chapter or Part A of the worksheet in Table 13-1. If you use Table 13-1 you need fill in only the right-most column. Either worksheet will estimate what the P/B ratio will be when you sell the stock.

What Are Dividend-Paying Growth Stocks Worth?

We are now ready to find what growth stocks that pay dividends are worth. The worksheet in Table 13-3 does the job. This worksheet has the same three sections as the worksheet for finding what stocks that do not pay dividends are worth. The primary difference is that the new worksheet has three additional columns to accept forecasts at the three intermediate times required for discounting dividends.

You will need to use the worksheet in Table 13-1 first. Use Part A of the worksheet to forecast the equity/share growth rate and the return on equity at the three intermediate times and at the end of the investment period. Also use Part A to find the P/B ratio when you sell the stock. Then use Part B of the worksheet to translate your growth rate forecast into a forecast of equity per share. Now you have all the data you need to use the worksheet in Table 13-3 to find what the stock is worth.

The worksheet for growth stocks is divided into the same three sections as the worksheet for mature firms.

Section I - The Investor

Section I contains data about the investor, and is identical in all stock valuation worksheets.

Section II - The Firm

Section II contains your forecasts for the firm. This section has four columns for data — three for the three intermediate times, and one for the end of the investment period when you sell the stock. Lines 7 and 8 are the same time fractions and times as lines 7 and 8 in Table 13-1. Copy the forecasts you developed in Table 13-8 for equity per share, the return on equity and the equity growth rate in lines 9 through 11 of Table 13-3. Line 12 develops a changing dividend payout fraction that is consistent with the changing return on equity and equity growth rates. The forecasts of return on equity and equity growth rate lead to the forecast of after-tax dividends in line 13.

Enter your forecast the P/B ratio when you eventually sell the stock in line 14. What will the price of the stock be when you sell? Multiply the final equity per share by this P/B ratio in line 15 to find out.

Section III - What is the Stock Worth?

Section III of the worksheet discounts the cash flows you forecast this stock will put into your pocket and adds up the discounted flows to find what the stock is worth. Line 17 develops the discount factors you need to discount dividends at each of the three intermediate times and to discount the cash you receive when you sell the stock at the end of the investment period. Line 18 contains the discounted dividends. Lines 19 through 21 carry out Gauss's averaging process, and find the discounted value of all the dividends you receive while you hold the stock. Work out the discounted value of the net cash you receive when you sell in line 22. Lines 23 through 25 account for capital gains taxes. Line 26 tells you what the growth stock is worth.

We will use this worksheet in the next chapter to find what Cisco Systems is worth to our investor.

Table 13-3

WORKSHEET FOR GROWTH STOCKS THAT PAY DIVIDENDS

Section I - The Investor

1. Investment Period, years .... _____
2. Divide Incremental Tax Rate on Ordinary Income (%)
    by 100; Subtract the Result from 1.0 .... _____
3. Divide Capital Gains Tax Rate (%) by 100 .... _____
4. Divide Minimum Acceptable Return (%) by 100 .... _____
5. Divide Broker's Commission (%) by 100;
    Add the Result to 1.0 .... _____
6. Divide Broker's Commission (%) by 100;
    Subtract the Result from 1.0 .... _____

Section II - The Firm

	0.113	0.5	0.887	1.0
7. Time, fraction of investment period	___	___	___	___
8. Time, Years. Multiply Line 1 by Line 7	___	___	___	___
9. Equity, $/Share*	___	___	___	___
10. Return on Equity, %*	___	___	___	
11. Growth Rate, %/yr.*	___	___	___	
12. Payout Fraction: Divide Line 11 by Line 10. Subtract the result from 1.0	___	___	___	
13. Dividends, $/Share: Multiply Line 2 by Lines 9, 10, and 12, then Divide by 100	___	___	___	
14. Final P/B Ratio*				___
15. Final Stock Price: Multiply Line 9 by Line 14				___

* From Table 13-1

Table 13-3 (Cont'd)
WORKSHEET FOR GROWTH STOCKS THAT PAY DIVIDENDS

Section III - What the Stock Is Worth

16. Multiply Line 8 by Line 4 ....   _____ _____ _____ _____
17. Discount Factor: Enter Line 16
    in your calculator, tap the change
    sign (+/-) key, then tap the e^x key   _____ _____ _____ _____
18. Discounted Dividends: Multiply
    Line 13 by Line 17 ....   _____ _____ _____ _____
19. Add the 1st and 3rd numbers
    in Line 18 and Multiply the
    result by 0.278 ....   _____
20. Multiply the 2nd number in
    Line 18 by 0.444 ....   _____
21. Discounted Dividends: Add Lines
    19 and 20 and Multiply the result
    by Line 1 ....   _____
22. Discounted Stock Price: Multiply
    Line 6 by Line 15 and by the last
    number in Line 17 ....   _____
23. Multiply Line 3 by Line 22 ....   _____
24. Subtract Line 23 from Line 22 ....   _____
25. Multiply Line 3 by the last number
    in Line 17 and Subtract the result
    from 1.0 ....   _____
26. What the Stock is Worth: Add Lines 21 and 24,
    then Divide by Line 5 and by Line 25 ....   _____

Summary

The worksheets for finding what a dividend-paying growth stock is worth take account of slowing growth, falling returns on equity, falling P/B ratios, and gradually increasing dividends as growth firms mature. A decay model describes how the return on equity, growth rate, and P/B ratio change over time. All these key factors start at their current levels and gradually approach long-run levels appropriate for mature firms. A half-life describes how rapidly this process occurs.

If the growth stock does not pay dividends, you only have to forecast the growth rate of equity per share and the price of the stock when you sell. The worksheet in the previous chapter tells you what stocks of growth firms that do not pay dividends are worth.

If the growth stock does pay dividends, you have to forecast dividends as well. The worksheet in this chapter tells you what stocks of growth firms that do pay dividends are worth. Discounting dividends is more complicated when all the factors that determine dividends are continually changing with time. A special weighted average of dividends discounted at three intermediate times during the investment period gives the total of discounted dividends.

Chapter **14**

Cisco Systems --
A Hot Growth Stock

Adjusting Earnings and Return on Equity

Analyzing Cisco's Performance

Forecasting Cisco's Future

What Is Cisco Worth?

  Scenario I - Cisco Pays No Dividends

  Scenario II - Cisco Pays Dividends

Chapters 12 and 13 provided worksheets to find what growth stocks are worth. How do we use these worksheets for a real stock? Let's take Cisco Systems as an example. Cisco is an excellent choice. It is a hot growth stock, and is heavily traded on the NASDAQ exchange. Cisco Systems is the leading supplier of hardware for linking computers together in local area (LAN) and wide area (WAN) networks. It is a major player in hardware for the internet. Computer scientists from Stanford University founded the company in 1984. Cisco shipped its first products two years later, and sales took off at an astounding rate. Sales nearly quadrupled the first year, and quintupled the next! Cisco's stock was first offered to the public in 1990 at $0.375 per share (adjusted for stock splits). At this writing (November, 1997) Cisco sells for $56 per share. Investors who bought Cisco when it was first issued, and accepted the risk that goes with a new firm with no track record and an uncertain future, did phenomenally well. They earned a 70 percent return on their investment!

But that day has passed. You cannot buy Cisco for $0.375 anymore. Sales are not growing at 150 percent per year, either. Growth has slowed. Even so, sales have still grown over 50 percent per year since 1990. Growth at that rate makes Cisco a hot growth stock. But if you want it now, you will have to pay $56, not $0.375. That is the problem. When Cisco first became public, few investors knew about it. It was an undiscovered gold mine. Now all investors know about it. They know that Cisco is a great firm. It is much less risky than it was when Cisco became public. Investors are so enthusiastic about Cisco they have bid the price of its stock sky high. The P/B ratio is 12, six times the ratio for a mature firm. Have investors bid the price too high? Is it now in the stratosphere? That is the question. Sure, Cisco is a great firm. Sales are growing over 50 percent per year. Cisco reported a sparkling 40 percent return on equity in 1997. But we know that fast growth and high returns cannot last forever. They are both going to decay with time. The P/B ratio is not going to stay at 12, either. It is sure to drop as well. With that kind of outlook for the future, can you afford to pay $56 for Cisco? We will use the worksheets from Chapters 12 and 13 to find out.

SmartValue will tell you what you can afford to pay for Cisco. We will use the Half Life Decay Model from Chapter 11 to allow for Cisco's inevitable slowing as it matures. And let's work out what Cisco is worth under two scenarios. Cisco has yet to pay a dividend. It is not likely to pay any dividends for a number of years. Let's assume that Cisco will not pay any dividends for at least the next five years. That will allow us to use the simpler worksheet to find what Cisco is worth. Then let's see what happens if we project that Cisco will begin to pay dividends. That is a less likely scenario, but it will show how to use the worksheet for growth stocks that do pay dividends.

Finding what a growth stock is worth involves three steps:

1. Adjust earnings and the return on equity. That is always the first step when finding what any stock is worth.

2. Use the decay model from Chapter 11 to forecast how the return on equity, the growth rate of equity per share, and the P/B ratio will decay while you hold the stock. If you do not expect the firm to pay dividends, you only have to forecast the growth rate and the P/B ratio. And you only have to forecast what the P/B ratio will be when you sell the stock. If you expect the firm to pay dividends, you also have to forecast the growth rate and the return on equity at the three intermediate times needed for discounting dividends.

3. Use the Worksheet for Growth Stocks to find what the sock is worth.

Adjusting Earnings and the Return on Equity

As always, begin the analysis by adjusting Cisco's earnings and return on equity. Use the same worksheet (Table 7-2) that we used in Chapter 7 to adjust Coca-Cola's earnings. Remember that adjusted earnings for any year are the total of that year's dividends and the gain in equity per share. Table 14-1 shows the historical record Value Line reports for Cisco. Look up Cisco's equity per share (Value Line calls it "Book Value per Share") in line 6 and dividends in line 4 of Table 14-1. Enter them in Table 7-2 and adjust Cisco's earnings and return on equity. Table 14-2 shows the results.

The equity per share in Column 1 is taken directly from Value Line for 1993 through 1997. Prior to 1993 equity per share was calculated by dividing book value (Value Line's "Net Worth") in the fifth line from the bottom of Value Line's table by the number of shares outstanding in line 6. Calculating equity per share this way avoids round-off errors when equity falls below about $1 per share.

Adjusting earnings is easy for growth stocks that pay no dividends. Simply subtract last year's equity per share from this year's equity per share in Column 1. The result is adjusted earnings; copy them into Columns 2 and 4. Cisco does not pay dividends. That makes Column 3 zero.

Table 14-1
CISCO SYSTEMS HISTORICAL PERFORMANCE

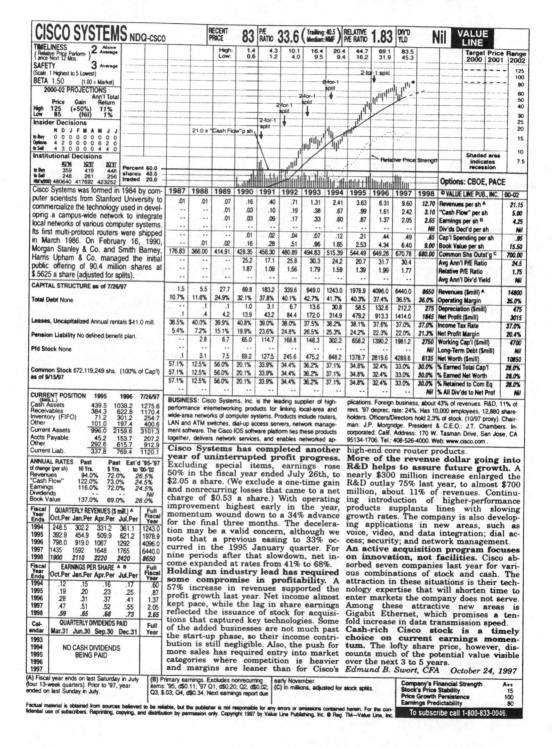

Courtesy of Value Line Publishing, Inc.

Table 14-2
ADJUSTING CISCO'S EARNINGS AND RETURN ON EQUITY

Year	Col. 1 Equity, $/Sh.	Col. 2 Change in Equity, $/Sh.	Col. 3 Div., $/Sh.	Col. 4 Adjusted Earnings $/Sh.	Col. 5 ln(Col. 1)	Col. 6 Growth Rate, %/yr.	Col. 7 Average Equity, $/Sh.	Col. 8 Adjusted Return, %
1997	6.40	2.06	0	2.06	1.8563	38.84	5.30	38.89
1996	4.34	1.76	0	1.76	1.4679	53.97	3.26	53.99
1995	2.53	0.88	0	0.88	0.9282	42.74	2.06	42.72
1994	1.65	0.69	0	0.69	0.5008	54.16	1.27	54.33
1993	0.96	0.45	0	0.45	-0.0408	63.25	0.711	63.29
1992	0.51	0.23	0	0.23	-0.6733	59.97	0.384	59.90
1991	0.28	0.12	0	0.12	-1.2730	55.96	0.214	56.07
1990	0.16	0.14	0	0.14	-1.8326	207.9	0.0673	209
1989	0.02				-3.912			

Cols. 1 and 3: Enter book value per share and dividends directly from Value Line or the Annual Report.

Col. 2: In Column 1 subtract last year's book value from this year's value and put the result in Column 2.

Col. 4: Add Columns 2 and 3.

Col. 5: Enter the number in Column 1 in your calculator and tap the ln(x) key.

Col. 6: Subtract last year's entry in Column 5 from this year's entry. Then multiply the result by 100.

Col. 7: Divide Column 2 by Column 6, then Multiply by 100.

Col. 8: Divide Column 4 by Column 7, then Multiply by 100.

Notice that the natural logarithm in Column 5 turns negative when equity drops below $1 per share. Be sure to have a minus sign in front of the number in your calculator's display window when you subtract negative numbers for Column 6. For the year 1991, for example, be sure the number in your calculator's display window is -1.2730 before you tell your calculator to subtract that number from -0.6733.

Adjusting the return on equity is easy once you have adjusted earnings. Simply divide adjusted earnings in Column 4 by the average equity per share in Column 7 and multiply by 100 to express the result as a percentage.

Notice that the growth rate in Column 6 is the same as the adjusted return in Column 8, except for round-off errors. The SmartValue formula says they must be the same for firms which do not pay dividends. They would not have been the same if we had used a simple arithmetic average to find the average equity in Column 7. That is why it is important to use the correct average as directed in Column 7.

Cisco split its stock 3 for 2 in December, 1997, shortly after the analysis in Table 14-2. Stock splits do not present a problem. The adjusted return on equity and the growth rate of equity per share, which are the key products of this analysis, are not affected. The only change the stock split requires is an adjustment in the starting value of equity per share.

Analyzing Cisco's Performance

Now that we have adjusted Cisco's return on equity, we can analyze Cisco's performance. That analysis will provide the basis for forecasting how Cisco is likely to perform in the future. We need to focus on three key factors: Cisco's adjusted return on equity, the growth rate of equity per share, and the P/B ratio investors have been willing to pay for Cisco's stock.

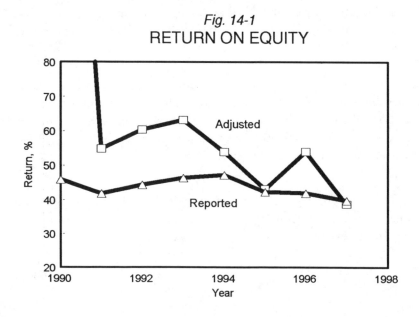

Fig. 14-1
RETURN ON EQUITY

Return on Equity

Cisco's adjusted returns are higher than the returns Cisco reported, as shown in Figure 14-1. The Cisco example is in sharp contrast to Coca-Cola in Chapter 7, where adjusted returns were much lower than reported returns. The adjusted return of 38.7 percent in 1997 was close to the return Cisco reported.

Adjusted returns are trending downward. Returns averaged 59.4 percent from 1991 to 1993. The average return dropped to 47.4 percent from 1994 to 1997; the return dropped further to 38.9 percent in 1997.

Growth Rate of Equity per Share

Find Cisco's growth rate the same way you found Coca-Cola's growth rate in Chapter 7. Plot the logarithm of equity per share against time, and use the worksheet in Table 7-4 to find the growth rate. Our investor does not have any semi-log graph paper in his desk drawer, so he makes his own. He already has the natural logarithm of Cisco's equity per share in Column 5 of Table 14-2. He simply plots that logarithm against time, and draws the plot shown in Figure 14-2. Here is an example of exceptional growth. Look how smooth the curve has been since Cisco became public in 1990. No jagged peaks. No deep valleys. Equity per share falls on a clean, smooth curve year after year. The curve is very nearly a straight line.

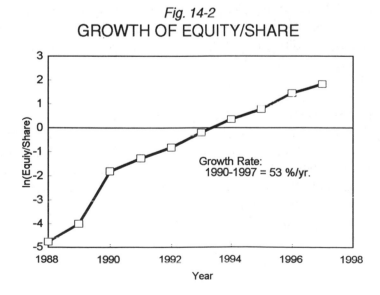

Fig. 14-2
GROWTH OF EQUITY/SHARE

Use the worksheet in Table 7-5 to find Cisco's growth rate. The logarithm of equity per share plots as a straight line from 1990 through 1996. Draw a straight line through the data and extend it from 1989 to 1997 for leverage. Read a natural logarithm of -2.283 in 1989 and 1.985 in 1997. Enter those readings in the worksheet and find the growth rate. The calculations are worked out in Table 14-3. Be careful to have a minus sign in front of the 2.283 in your calculator's display window before you tap the subtract key in line 5.

Table 14-3
MEASURING CISCO'S GROWTH RATE

1. ln(Equity/Sh.) at right-hand end of the straight line	1.985
2. Time corresponding to Line 1, years	1997
3. ln(Equity/Sh.) at left-hand end of the straight line	-2.283
4. Time corresponding to Line 3, years	1989
5. Subtract Line 3 from Line 1	4.268
6. Subtract Line 4 from Line 2	8
7. Growth Rate, %/yr.: Divide Line 5 by Line 6, then Multiply by 100	53.4

The slope of the line from 1990 to 1997 corresponds to a growth rate of 53.4 percent per year. That is what makes Cisco a hot growth stock. While past performance is no guarantee that equity will continue falling on this curve forever, it is certainly a reassuring sight to any investor. As Table 14-2 showed, however, growth did slow to 39 percent per year in 1997.

Measuring the growth rate from the slope of the curve in Figure 14-2 is the best way to average growth rates over a number of years. But growth rates scatter more in Figure 14-2 than meets the eye. You can see the scatter better by plotting the year-to-year growth rates in Column 6 of Table 14-2. Figure 14-3 shows how these growth rates fluctuated from one year to the next. If you are a short-term investor, you have the extremely difficult task of forecasting these year-to-year fluctuations. Good luck! If you are a long-term investor, you have an easier job. You can focus on the growth of the trend line in Figure 14-2 instead of year-to-year growth in Figure 14-3. Trend growth rates are more stable be-

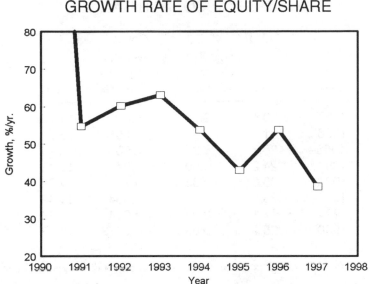

Fig. 14-3
GROWTH RATE OF EQUITY/SHARE

cause they are measured over a period of years, such as those measured along straight-line segments in Figure 14-2. Measuring the slopes of these curves damps out year-to-year fluctuations.

Notice the shape of the growth rate curve in Figure 14-3. Looks familiar, doesn't it? Where have you seen it before? Look at the curve for the adjusted return on equity in Figure 14-1. That is where you saw it! The two curves are identical. They have to be. Why? Because Cisco does not pay dividends. The SmartValue formula requires that the adjusted return on equity and the growth rate of equity per share must be identical when a firm pays no dividends.

P/B Ratio

Value Line reports P/E ratios, not P/B ratios. No problem. The worksheet in Table 7-6 translates P/E ratios to P/B ratios. Use that worksheet to find the P/B ratios for Cisco. The P/E ratio comes from line 8 of the Value Line table and reported earnings come from line 3. Table 14-4 shows how to make the translation. Cisco's P/B ratio is plotted in Figure 14-4.

Table 14-4
FINDING CISCO'S P/B RATIO

Year	Col. 1 P/E	Col. 2 Reported Earnings, $/Share	Col. 3 Average Equity, $/Share	Col. 4 P/B
1997	30.4	2.05	5.30	11.76
1996	31.7	1.37	3.26	13.32
1995	20.7	0.87	2.06	8.74
1994	24.2	0.60	1.27	11.43
1993	30.3	0.33	0.711	14.06
1992	25.8	0.17	0.384	11.42
1991	17.1	0.09	0.214	7.19
1990	25.2	0.03	0.0673	11.23

Cols. 1 and 2: Copy P/E ratios and earnings per share directly from Value Line.

Col. 3: Copy the average equity per share from Col. 7 of Table 14-2.

Col. 4.: Multiply column 1 by column 2, then divide by column 3.

Fig. 14-4
P/B Ratio

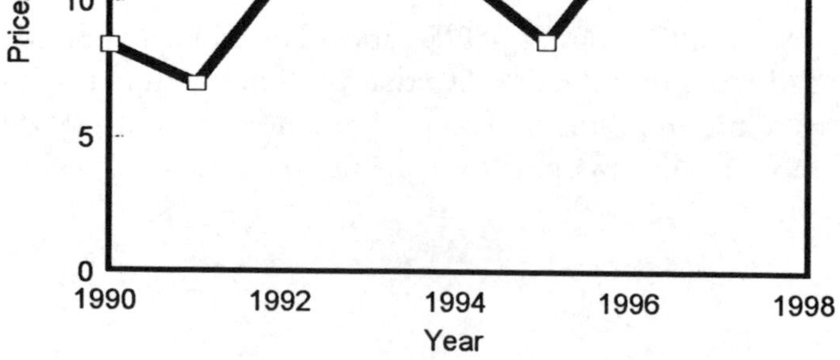

Investors are jittery when stocks sell at high P/B ratios. They should be. The slightest hint of bad news is likely to send investors scurrying towards the exits. They want to get out before some threatened catastrophe occurs and the price plummets. Investors are jittery about Cisco, as shown by the way they changed the P/B ratio they were willing to pay. Investors let the P/B ratio fall to 7.2 in 1991, bid the ratio up to 14.1 in 1993, let it drop again to 8.7 in 1995, and bid the ratio back up again to 11.8 in 1997. P/B ratios for mature firms are closer to 2, so there is still plenty of room for Cisco's P/B ratio to fall.

Forecasting Cisco's Future

The critical step in finding what any stock is worth is forecasting how that firm is likely to perform in the future. What return will it earn? How fast will it grow? What P/B ratio will investors be willing to pay? Analyzing the firm's historical performance is a great help. The analysis tells us how profitable the firm has been. The analysis tells us how fast the firm has grown. It tells us what P/B ratio investors have been willing to pay. And the analysis tells us how stable performance has been, and how fast the key factors are decaying with time.

That is a good start. We know how the firm is performing today. We also have a reasonably good idea of how the firm will perform when it is fully mature. Growth will likely have slowed to the current-dollar GDP growth rate of about 7 percent per year. The firm will pay about half its earnings out as dividends. The SmartValue formula shows that the long-run return on equiy must be 14 percent to be consistent with a 7 percent per year growth rate and a 50 percent dividend payout. The key forecasts we have to make is how fast the key factors will decay from their current levels towards their long-run values. What half life is appropriate for the return on equity, growth rate, and P/B ratio forecasts?

Growth Rate of Equity per Share

You are not flying blind when you sit down to forecast how fast Cisco might grow in the future. You know how fast Cisco has grown in the recent past. You know where the growth rate is heading as Cisco approaches maturity. An excellent way to maintain your perspective as you make a forecast is to plot your forecast. Include several years of recent history on the plot. That will tell you where you've been. Add a horizontal line at the long-run growth rate you expect. That will remind you of where you are heading. Then draw a curve representing your forecast. The forecast should start at Cisco's current growth rate and head towards your forecast of the long-run growth rate. How should you draw the forecast curve? The most reasonable way is to draw the curve as a smooth continuation of recent history. Our investor follows this approach, and draws the forecast curve in Figure 14-5.

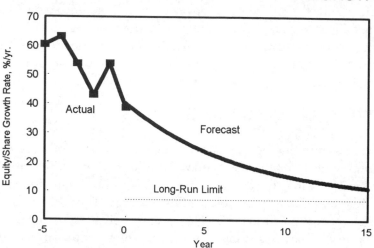

Fig. 14-5
FORECAST OF CISCO'S EQUITY/SHARE GROWTH

He forecasts that the growth rate of equity per share will begin at 40 percent per year, approximately the current growth rate, and approach a long-run growth of 7 percent per year. The halfway point is a 23.5 percent per year growth rate. His forecast curve takes five years to reach the halfway point. He therefore chooses a five-year half life to describe how fast the growth rate will decay. After studying Figure 14-5 for a while, he judges that his forecast is a reasonable continuation of the way Cisco's growth has been slowing in recent years

Return on Equity

Cisco does not yet pay dividends. The SmartValue formula shows that the equity/share growth rate and the return on equity must be identical when dividends are zero. Our investor does not expect Cisco to pay dividends while he holds the stock. He therefore forecasts that the return on equity will be identical to the growth rate. His forecast of the growth rate then serves a double purpose. It is also his forecast of the return on equity.

If he expects Cisco to begin paying dividends while he holds the stock, he should forecast that the growth rate and the return on equity are identical initially. That makes the initial dividends zero. But then he should forecast that the growth rate and the return on equity decay along different paths. The growth rate must gradually slip below the return on equity to insure that Cisco pays dividends to the investor, and not the other way round. He can make the growth rate drop below the return on equity by forecasting a longer half life for the return on equity, a higher long-run limit, or both. Figure 14-6 shows the return on equity forecast he might make if he expects Cisco pay dividends.

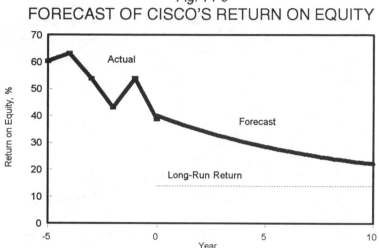

Fig. 14-6
FORECAST OF CISCO'S RETURN ON EQUITY

He starts his return on equity forecast at 40 percent, the same as his growth rate forecast. That makes the initial dividend payout zero. But then he forecasts the long-run return at 14 percent, double the long-run forecast of a 7 percent per year growth rate. That will lead to a 50 percent dividend payout when Cisco is fully mature. He also forecasts that the return on equity will decay more slowly than the growth rate. He forecast that the growth rate would decay with a five-year half life. He chooses a six-year half life for his return on equity forecast. The higher long-run limit and the longer half life will cause a gradual increase in dividends as Cisco matures. He steps back from Figure 14-6, looks at it for a while, and is satisfied that his forecast is a reasonable extension of how Cisco's return has decayed in the past.

P/B Ratio

Our investor uses the same approach to forecast the P/B ratio. Investors had bid the P/B ratio up to 11.9 in November, 1997. He forecasts that the P/B ratio will gradually decay towards 2.1, a typical ratio for a mature firm, in the long run. How fast will the P/B ratio decay? He recognizes that investors will anticipate that Cisco's growth is going to slow, and that its return on equity will fall. They will try to sell their stock ahead of that time. That means the P/B ratio is likely to fall faster than either the growth rate slows or the return on equity falls. He had forecast that the return on equity and the growth rate would decay with half lives of six and five years, respectively. He makes the P/B ratio decay faster by choosing a four-year half life. Figure 14-7 shows the resulting forecast.

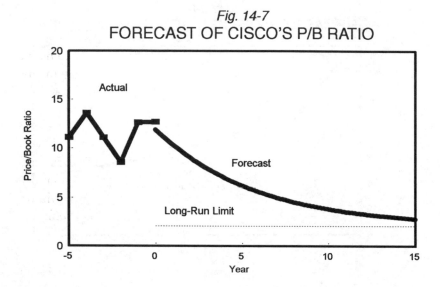

Fig. 14-7
FORECAST OF CISCO'S P/B RATIO

Initial Equity per Share

Cisco reported $6.40 of stockholder equity per share at the end of July, 1997. The 3-for-2 stock split in December of 1997 changes equity per share to two-thirds of $6.40, or $4.27 per share. Our investor is analyzing Cisco four months later. He decides to allow for the growth that has taken place in that time. Four months is a short time, but 40 percent per year is rapid growth. He uses the worksheet in Table 7-7 and finds a growth multiplier of 1.143, which brings Cisco's equity up to $4.88 per share at the time of his analysis. Table 14-5 shows his calculations.

Table 14-5
ADJUSTING INITIAL EQUITY/SHARE

1. Last Reported Equity, $/Share	4.27
2. Time since last report, months	4
3. Divide current growth rate (%/yr.) by 100	0.40
4. Multiply Line 2 by Line 3, then Divide by 12	0.1333
5. Growth Multiplier: Enter Line 4 in your calculator and tap the e^x key	1.143
6. Current Equity, $/Share: Multiply Line 1 by Line 5	4.88

What Is Cisco's Stock Worth?

Let's find what Cisco's stock is worth under two scenarios. Cisco has yet to pay a dividend. It reinvests all its earnings in the business. Cisco is not likely to pay any dividends in the near future. In Scenario I let's project that Cisco will not pay any dividends during the next five years, the period our investor plans to hold the stock. When a firm pays no dividends, the SmartValue formula requires that the growth rate of equity per share and the firm's return on equity be identical. That means you only have to forecast the growth rate. That forecast automatically generates a forecast of return on equity, because both forecasts must be the same. You also have to forecast the P/B ratio you expect investors to pay when you finally sell the stock. Forecasting that Cisco will not pay any dividends also allows using the simpler worksheet from the last chapter to find what Cisco is worth.

In Scenario II let's assume that Cisco will begin to pay dividends during the next five years. That forecast may not be as realistic as the forecast of no dividends. We will use it anyway, because it demonstrates how to use the worksheet for dividend-paying growth stocks.

Scenario I - Cisco Pays No Dividends

Finding what Cisco is worth is easier if you forecast that Cisco will not pay any dividends while you hold the stock. That simplifies the problem. You only have to forecast the growth rate of equity per share, then use Table 12-1 to develop the appropriate growth multiplier. You will not have to make an independent forecast of Cisco's return on equity. It will be identical to the growth rate forecast. You will also have to forecast the P/B ratio when you expect to sell the stock. Our investor expects to sell the stock in five years.

Forecasting the Growth Rate of Equity per Share

Our investor decides to use the forecast in Figure 14-5 as his forecast of the growth rate of equity per share. The return on equity forecast will be identical to the growth rate forecast because there are no dividends. He uses the worksheet in Table 12-1 to find the appropriate growth multiplier; Table 14-6 shows his calculations. He projects that Cisco's equity per share will be 4.667 times larger when he sells in five years.

Table 14-6

GROWTH MULTIPLIER FOR CISCO SYSTEMS

1. Investment period, years   5
2. Initial Growth Rate, (%/yr.)/100 (decimal form) 0.40
3. Long-Run Growth Rate, (%/yr.)/100 (decimal form) 0.07
4. Initial Margin: Subtract Line 3 from Line 2 ....   0.33
5. Half Life, years   5
6. Divide 0.6931 by Line 5, then Multiply by Line 1 ....   0.6931
7. Enter Line 6 in your calculator, tap the
    change sign (+/-) key, and then the e^x key 0.5000
8. Subtract Line 7 from 1.0 ....   0.5000
9. Multiply Line 4 by Line 8, then Divide by Line 6 ....   0.2381
10. Add Lines 3 and 9. Multiply the result by Line 1. ....   1.5405
11. Growth Multiplier: Enter Line 10 in your
    calculator and tap the e^x key 4.667

Table 14-7

CISCO'S FUTURE P/B RATIO

1. Investment period, years   5
2. Initial P/B Ratio 11.9
3. Long-Run P/B Ratio 2.1
4. Initial Margin: Subtract Line 3 from Line 2 ....   9.8
5. Half Life, years   4
6. Divide 0.6931 by Line 5, then Multiply by Line 1 ....   0.8664
7. Enter Line 6 in your calculator, tap the
    change sign (+/-) key, and then the e^x key 0.4205
8. Final P/B Ratio: Multiply Line 4 by Line 7,
    then Add Line 3 ....   6.22

P/B Ratio

Our investor only needs to forecast the P/B ratio at the time he sells the stock. He uses the worksheet in Table 12-3 to find that P/B ratio. He forecasts that Cisco's P/B ratio starts at the current value of 11.9 and decays towards a long-run limit of 2.1 with a four-year half life. Table 14-7 shows his calculations. His forecast leads to a P/B ratio of 6.22 in five years.

What Is Cisco Worth?

Table 12-5 is the worksheet for finding what growth stocks that do not pay dividends are worth. Our investor enters his own financial situation and his forecasts in that worksheet and finds what Cisco is worth. Table 14-8 shows his calculations.

Section I - The Investor

The investor we studied in Chapter 5 is investing money that costs 9.3 percent — the return he could have earned by investing that money in Vanguard's S&P 500 Index Fund instead of in Cisco's stock. He recognizes that Cisco is a riskier stock than the Coca-Cola stock he considered in Chapter 8. A 1 percent risk premium might be appropriate for a mature firm like Coca-Cola. But it is too small for Cisco. He ponders the variation in Cisco's historical record and his own tolerance for risk, and decides that a risk premium of about 5 percent is appropriate for Cisco. That brings the minimum return he will accept up to 14 percent. Except for the higher minimum acceptable return, the entries in Section I are identical to the entries he made in Section I of the worksheet for Coca-Cola.

Section II - The Firm

Enter Cisco's current equity of $4.88 per share in line 7. We found a growth multiplier of 4.667 in Table 14-6; enter that multiplier in line 8. We also found that the P/B ratio is likely to drop to 6.22 in five years. Enter that forecast in line 9. In line 10 multiply the starting equity by the growth multiplier and the P/B ratio to forecast a stock price of $141.66 per share when our investor sells in five years.

Section III - What Is Cisco Worth?

The only cash that rolls into your pocket if Cisco pays no dividends is the net proceeds when you eventually sell the stock. That makes discounting in Section III much simpler because you do not have to worry about dividends. There aren't any. The computations in Section III allow for capital gains taxes and broker's commissions, and discount the net cash this investor will receive when he sells the stock in five years. Line 17 shows that Cisco is worth $59.14 per share to our investor.

Should our investor buy? At the time of this analysis Cisco was selling for $56 per share, slightly below what Cisco is worth to this investor. Not a great bargain, perhaps, but Cisco is worth a little more than it costs. If our investor buys Cisco and Cisco performs as he forecast, he will earn a little more than the minimum he specified.

The Investor's Rate of Return

The analysis in Table 14-8 shows what Cisco is worth at only one discount rate. Our investor can find the rate of return he will earn if he buys Cisco by repeating the analysis over a range of discount rates, and finding the discount rate that makes the stock exactly worth the market price. Figure 14-8 shows the results. The point where the curve for Cisco's value crosses the market price line locates the investor's rate of return. The two

Table 14-8
WHAT IS CISCO WORTH?
Scenario I - No Dividends

Section I - The Investor

1. Investment Period, years	5
2. Divide Incremental Tax Rate on Ordinary Income (%) by 100; Subtract the Result from 1.0	0.6768
3. Divide Capital Gains Tax Rate (%) by 100	0.248
4. Divide Minimum Acceptable Return (%) by 100	0.14
5. Divide Broker's Commission (%) by 100; Add the Result to 1.0	1.01
6. Divide Broker's Commission (%) by 100; Subtract the Result from 1.0	0.99

Table 14-8 (Cont'd)
WHAT IS CISCO WORTH?
Scenario I - No Dividends

Section II - The Firm

7. Initial Equity, $/Share	4.88
8. Growth Multiplier (from Table 12-1)	4.667
9. Final P/B Ratio (from Table 12-3)	6.22
10. Final Stock Price: Multiply Line 7 by Lines 8 and 9	141.66

Section III - What Is the Stock Worth?

11. Multiply Line 1 by Line 4	0.7
12. Discount Factor: Enter Line 11 in your calculator, tap the change sign (+/-) key, then tap the e^x key	0.4966
13. Present Value of Final Stock Price: Multiply Line 6 by Lines 10 and 12	69.64
14. Multiply Line 3 by Line 13	17.27
15. Subtract Line 14 from Line 13	52.37
16. Multiply Line 3 by Line 12 and Subtract the result from 1.0	0.8768
17. What the Stock is Worth: Divide Line 15 by Line 5 and by Line 16	59.14

curves cross at a 15 percent return. Our investor can therefore expect a 15 percent return if Cisco performs as he forecast, somewhat higher than his 14 percent minimum return standard.

Figure 14-8 also shows where Cisco is a buy and where Cisco costs too much. The curve for Cisco's value lies above the market price line to the left of the crossing point. That is where Cisco is worth more than it costs. That is where Cisco is a buy. The curve for Cisco's value lies below the market price line to the right of the crossing point. That is where Cisco costs more than it is worth. The crossing point occurs at a minimum acceptable return of 15 percent. Investors who are willing to accept a return of 15 percent or less will conclude that Cisco is a buy. Investors who require a return greater than 15 percent will conclude that Cisco costs too much.

Fig. 14-8
INVESTOR'S RATE OF RETURN

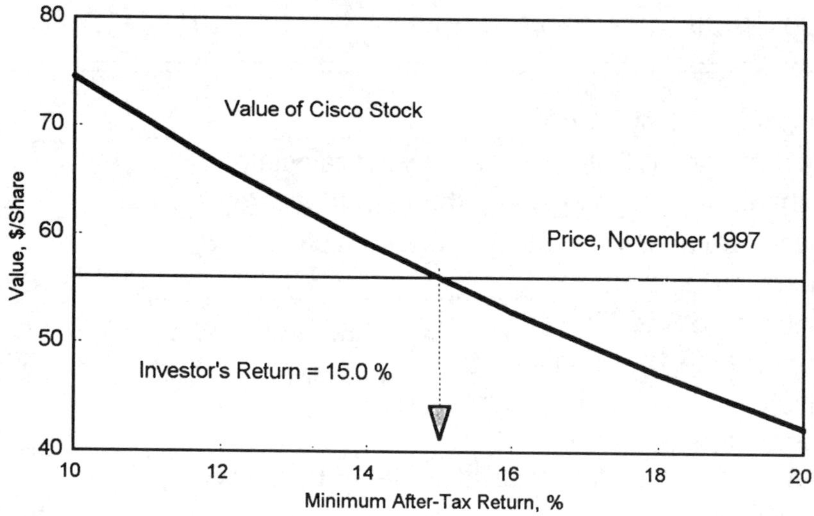

Risk

Our investor has calculated that Cisco is worth $59.14 per share. Does he really know what Cisco is worth to the last penny? No, of course not. His forecasts, after all, are only estimates. They are his best judgment. But there are bound to be errors. Cisco might perform better than some forecasts, and worse than others. That is why investing in stocks is risky. The primary source of risk is his choice of half lives — his forecast of how fast Cisco's performance is going to decay. He has forecast that the return on equity and the growth rate are both going to take five years to move halfway towards their long-run

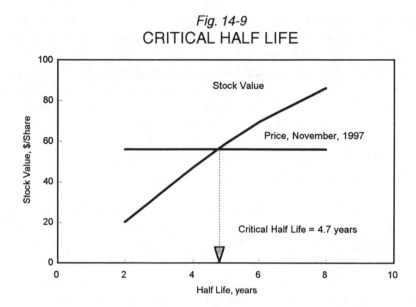

Fig. 14-9
CRITICAL HALF LIFE

values. He has forecast that the P/B ratio is going to take four years. He should be concerned about those forecasts. Perhaps he is too optimistic. There is an easy way to tell. Repeat the valuation at other half lives. Find the half life that makes Cisco's value just equal to the current market price. That half life is a critical half life. Figure 14-9 shows how Cisco's value depends on how fast Cisco's performance decays. The half life for the P/B ratio was kept at 80 percent of the half lives of the return on equity and growth rate in this calculation. The curve for Cisco's value crosses the market price line at a half life of 4.7 years. That is the critical half life. Our investor really does not have to forecast half lives all that accurately. All he has to decide is whether he thinks Cisco will decay faster or slower than this critical half life. If he believes Cisco will decay slower than the critical half life, Cisco is indeed a buy. But if he thinks Cisco will decay faster, Cisco costs too much.

The uncertainty in forecasting how fast Cisco will mature is a major reason Cisco's stock is risky. We will look at Cisco again when we study a better way to handle risk in Chapter 18.

Scenario II - Cisco Pays Dividends

Let's also find what Cisco would be worth if Cisco started to pay dividends while our investor held the stock. That requires forecasting that Cisco's growth rate and return on equity will not be identical, but will instead decay along different paths. That will make dividend payments begin and gradually grow.

Let's use the same forecasts we used in Scenario I. We will need a separate forecast of the return on equity because it will no longer be the same as the growth rate forecast. Cisco's return on equity and growth rate will both decay, but the return on equity must stay above the growth rate to build dividends into the analysis. Use the return on equity forecast from Figure 14-6 that has the return starting at 40 percent and decaying towards a long-run limit of 14 percent with a half life of six years. And use the growth rate forecast of Figure 14-5, which has growth starting at 40 percent per year and decaying towards a long-run rate of 7 percent per year with a half life of five years. The different long-run limits and half lives will make the return on equity and growth rate decay along different paths. That will generate dividends while our investor holds the stock.

We will use Gauss's three-point averaging process to discount these changing dividends. That means we will need to forecast dividends at the three intermediate times during the investment period. We will find dividends by multiplying equity per share by the return on equity to get earnings, and then by the dividend payout fraction to get dividends. The worksheet for finding what Cisco's stock is worth works out the dividends and does the discounting. Before we can use that worksheet there is an intermediate step we must complete. We need to find the return on equity, the growth rate, and equity per share at the three intermediate times. That is what the worksheet in Table 13-1 does. Use Part A of the worksheet to convert the forecast of the initial and the long-run return on equity and its half life into forecasts of the return on equity at the three intermediate times. Do the same for the forecast of how fast equity per share grows. Then use part B of the worksheet to translate the growth rate forecast into the corresponding forecast of equity per share at the three intermediate times. We can still use the forecast for the P/B ratio from Scenario I.

Tables 14-9 and 14-10 show how to forecast the returns on equity and the growth rates of equity per share at the three intermediate times. Table 14-10 also shows how to translate the forecast of growth rates into the corresponding forecast of equity per share.

The worksheets show that the return on equity will fall from 40 percent now to 28.6 percent at the end of the five-year investment period. The growth rate will slow from 40 to 23.5 percent per year in the same period. That pattern of slowing growth rates will cause equity per share to grow from $4.88 per share now to $22.77 per share at the end of the investment period.

Table 14-9
INTERMEDIATE RETURNS ON EQUITY

1. Investment period, years				5
2. Initial Value				40
3. Long-Run Limit				14
4. Initial Margin: Subtract Line 3 from Line 2				26
5. Half Life, years				6
6. Divide 0.6931 by Line 5				0.1155
7. Time, fraction of investment period	**0.113**	**0.5**	**0.887**	**1.0**
8. Time, Years. Multiply Line 1 by Line 7	0.565	2.5	4.435	5
9. Multiply Line 8 by Line 6	0.0653	0.2888	0.5122	0.5776
10. Decay Factor: Enter Line 9 in your calculator, tap the change sign (+/-) key, then tap the e^x key	0.9368	0.7492	0.5992	0.5612
11. Future Values: Multiply Line 4 by Line 10, then Add line 3	38.36	33.48	29.58	28.59

What Is Cisco Worth?

Use Table 13-3, the worksheet for growth stocks that pay dividends, to find what Cisco is worth if it begins paying dividends during the investment period. The computation is detailed in Table 14-11.

Section I — The Investor

There are no changes in our investor's situation. Section I of the worksheet is therefore identical to Section I in Table 14-8.

Table 14-10
INTERMEDIATE GROWTH RATES AND EQUITY/SHARE

A. Forecast Return on Equity and Growth Rate of Equity/Share

1. Investment period, years				5
2. Initial Value				40
3. Long-Run Limit				7
4. Initial Margin: Subtract Line 3 from Line 2				33
5. Half Life, years				5
6. Divide 0.6931 by Line 5				0.1386
7. Time, fraction of investment period	0.113	0.5	0.887	1.0
8. Time, Years. Multiply Line 1 by Line 7	0.565	2.5	4.435	5
9. Multiply Line 8 by Line 6	0.0783	0.3119	0.6147	0.6931
10. Decay Factor: Enter Line 9 in your calculator, tap the change sign (+/-) key, then tap the e^x key	0.9247	0.7321	0.5408	0.5000
11. Future Values: Multiply Line 4 by Line 10, then Add line 3	37.52	31.16	24.85	23.50

B. Translate Growth Forecast into Equity/Share Forecast

12. Initial Equity, $/Share				4.88
13. Subtract Line 10 from 1.0, then Divide by Line 9	0.9617	0.8589	0.7470	0.7214
14. Multiply Line 4 by Line 13, then Add Line 3	38.74	35.34	31.65	30.81
15. Multiply Line 14 by Line 8, then Divide by 100	0.2189	0.8835	1.4037	1.5405
16. Growth Multiplier: Enter Line 15 in your calculator and tap the e^x key	1.2447	2.4194	4.0702	4.6669
17. Equity, $/Share: Multiply Line 12 by Line 16	6.07	11.81	19.86	22.77

Section II — The Firm

The worksheet expands to four columns from lines 7 through line 18. The extra columns are needed for discounting dividends. Line 7 shows the fractions of the investment period where forecasts are required. Line 8 works out the corresponding times in years. We worked out forecasts of Cisco's equity per share, return on equity, and growth rate at the three intermediate times in Tables 14-9 and 14-10. Enter those forecasts in lines 9, 10, and 11. Use the SmartValue formula to find the dividend payout faction in line 12, and after-tax dividends at the three intermediate times in line 13.

There has been no change in the forecast of the P/B ratio. Use the same forecast as the no-dividend case, and enter it in line 14. Line 15 shows that Cisco's stock should sell for $141.63 at the end of the investment period. Except for rounding errors, this is the same price we found in the no-dividend case.

Section III — What Is Cisco Worth?

The forecasts you entered in Section II establish the dividends and the proceeds from selling the stock. In Section III we'll discount those cash flows and then add them up to see what Cisco is worth.

Line 17 develops the discount factor at each of the three intermediate times and at the end of the investment period. All these discount factors must be less than 1.0. If you find a discount factor greater than 1.0, you did not tap the change sign key before you tapped the e^x key. Repeat the calculation, and be sure you tap the change sign key. Make sure there is a minus sign in front of the number in your calculator's display window before you tap the e^x key. Lines 19 through 21 do the averaging procedure for discounting dividends. Line 21 shows that the dividends you should collect over the next five years are worth only $1.20 per share today.

The stock price of $141.63 when our investor sells in five years is worth only $69.63 today after discounting and deducting broker's commissions, as line 22 shows. Lines 23 through 25 account for capital gains taxes.

What is Cisco worth? Line 26 shows that Cisco is worth $60.48 to our investor. This value is slightly higher than the $59.14 found in Scenario I. The change in value is due to the more optimistic return on equity forecast in Scenario II. The half life was lengthened from five to six years, and the long-run limit was raised from 7 to 14 percent.

Table 14-11
WHAT IS CISCO WORTH?
Scenario II - Cisco Pays Dividends

Section I - The Investor

1. Investment Period, years	5
2. Divide Incremental Tax Rate on Ordinary Income (%) by 100; Subtract the Result from 1.0	0.6768
3. Divide Capital Gains Tax Rate (%) by 100	0.248
4. Divide Minimum Acceptable Return (%) by 100	0.14
5. Divide Broker's Commission (%) by 100; Add the Result to 1.0	1.01
6. Divide Broker's Commission (%) by 100; Subtract the Result from 1.0	0.99

Section II - The Firm

7. Time, fraction of investment period	0.113	0.5	0.887	1.0
8. Time, Years. Multiply Line 1 by Line 7	0.565	2.5	4.435	5
9. Equity, $/Share*	6.07	11.81	19.86	22.77
10. Return on Equity, %*	38.36	33.48	29.58	
11. Growth Rate, %/yr.*	37.52	31.16	24.85	
12. Payout Fraction: Divide Line 11 by Line 10. Subtract the result from 1.0	0.0219	0.0693	0.1599	
13. Dividends, $/Share: Multiply Line 2 by Lines 9, 10, and 12, then Divide by 100	0.051	0.274	0.939	
14. Final P/B Ratio*				6.22
15. Final Stock Price: Multiply Line 9 by Line 14				141.63

* From Tables 14-9 and 14-10

Table 14-11 (Cont'd)
WHAT IS CISCO WORTH?
Scenario II - Dividends

Section III - What is Cisco Worth?

16. Multiply Line 8 by Line 4	0.0791	0.35	0.6209	0.7
17. Discount Factor: Enter Line 16 in your calculator, tap the change sign (+/-) key, then tap the e^x key	0.9239	0.7047	0.5375	0.4966
18. Discounted Dividends: Multiply Line 13 by Line 17	0.047	0.193	0.505	
19. Add the 1st and 3rd numbers in Line 18 and Multiply the result by 0.278				0.154
20. Multiply the 2nd number in Line 18 by 0.444				0.086
21. Discounted Dividends: Add Lines 19 and 20 and Multiply the result by Line 1				1.20
22. Discounted Stock Price: Multiply Line 6 by Line 15 and by the last number in Line 17				69.63
23. Multiply Line 3 by Line 22				17.27
24. Subtract Line 23 from Line 22				52.36
25. Multiply Line 3 by the last number in Line 17 and Subtract the result from 1.0				0.8768
26. What the Stock is Worth: Add Lines 21 and 24, then Divide by Line 5 and by Line 25				60.48

SUMMARY

Cisco Systems was evaluated for an investor who planned to hold the stock for five years and who insisted on a minimum return of 14 percent. The investor based his valuation on the analysis of Cisco's performance and forecasts that the growth rate and the return on equity would fall from 40 percent towards a long-run value of 7 percent with a five-year half life, and that the P/B ratio would fall from 11.9 towards a long-run value of 2.1 with a four-year half life.

Cisco does not pay dividends; it reinvests all its earnings back into the business. Our investor assumed that Cisco would not pay dividends during the five years he planned to hold the stock. In Scenario I he made his forecast of the return on equity identical to his forecast of the growth rate of equity per share to build zero dividends into the analysis. He used the SmartValue Worksheet for growth Stocks and found that Cisco was worth $59.14 per share.

The value our investor found for Cisco's stock was higher than the $56 market price at the time of the analysis. If he buys the stock and Cisco performs as he forecast, he will earn a return of 15 percent, which is higher than the 14 percent minimum return he specified.

He also tested what would happen if Cisco began to pay dividends while he held the stock. To build dividends into the analysis he forecast that the return on equity would decay more slowly than the growth rate, and would decay towards a higher long-run value. The more optimistic return on equity forecast raised Cisco's value slightly to $60.48 per share.

Chapter **15**

The Unlimited Flexibility Model

Similarity to Half-Life Decay Model

Making Forecasts

Scenario I - Stock Pays No Dividends

Scenario II - Stock Pays Dividends

What Is the Stock Worth?

The Half-Life Decay Model of Chapter 11 is a good model for finding what growth stocks are worth. It captures the essence of the growth stock problem — how do you allow for gradually slowing growth as a growth firm matures? How do you allow for gradually falling returns? For gradually falling P/B ratios? The model gives realistic values for growth stocks. But the model is restricted to decay patterns that you can describe by a half life. The Half-Life Decay Model is useful. It is easy to use. It is a good approximation for the way the key factors actually decay in real firms.

The Half-Life Decay Model fits a wide variety of growth stocks. But it does not fit all of them. You may prefer some other decay pattern than the one a half life describes. When we studied Cisco Systems in Chapter 14, for example, we wanted to forecast that Cisco would not pay dividends for some time. The Half-Life Decay Model gave us only two choices. We could make the forecasts for the growth rate and the return on equity identical. When the growth rate and return on equity forecasts are identical, SmartValue forces dividends to be zero. If the two forecasts are identical forever, SmartValue forces dividends to be zero forever as well. The second choice was to make the growth rate and the return on equity identical only at the start of the investment period, and then let them decay away along different paths. That makes dividends zero only at the start of the investment period. But as soon as the growth rate and the return on equity begin decaying along different paths, dividends begin to grow. There was no in-between choice. Either zero dividends forever, or zero dividends just at the start. You may not want just those two choices of zero dividends forever or zero dividends only at the start. You may want some intermediate choice. You may want more flexibility.

In this chapter we will pull out all the stops. No restrictions at all. Let freedom ring! You will have complete flexibility in how you make your forecasts. I will retain the basic framework of the Half-Life Decay Model because it makes a lot of sense. Each key factor begins at its current value and decays gradually towards some appropriate long-run limit. But you will not be restricted to just those decay patterns that a half life describes. You will have unlimited flexibility in forecasting the path each key factor travels as it goes from here to there. You can even make your forecasts by drawing free-hand curves on a sheet of graph paper. Use graph paper because you will have to read values off of your forecast curves to find what the stock is worth.

How do you think a key factor like the return on equity will decay? You might want it to hold near current levels for a year or two, and then have it begin to decay. You might even want it to increase for a while, and then decay. Have it your way. Draw the forecast curve any way you like. You might want to keep zero dividends for just the first few years of the investment period. No problem. Just make your forecasts of the return on equity and the equity growth rate identical for those first few years. Then let them begin to decay along different paths. You will have all the flexibility you will ever need. But be reasonable. Stay with smooth curves. Let them bend this way and that if you like. That is OK. But stay away from stepped "curves" that look like a staircase. Smooth curves, yes. Staircases, no.

Similarity to Half-Life Decay Model

You might expect the computations for the Unlimited Flexibility Model to be much more complicated than the computations for the Half-Life Decay Model. Not so. The Unlimited Flexibility Model is identical to the Half-Life Decay Model in its essentials. You still need to make the same three forecasts the Half-Life Decay Model required. You need to forecast how the firm's return on equity will change with time. You need to forecast how fast equity per share will grow, and how the growth rate will change with tome. And you need to forecast what the P/B ratio will be when you sell. There are only two major differences:

1. In the Unlimited Flexibility Model you forecast the return on equity, the growth rate of equity per share, and the P/B ratio by drawing free-hand curves on a sheet of graph paper. The Half-Life Decay Model used a worksheet to develop each of these forecasts.

2. The Unlimited Flexibility Model has a new worksheet for translating your forecast of growth rates into the corresponding forecast of equity per share.

Except for these differences, the analysis is the same as the analysis for the Half-Life Decay Model. There are the same two scenarios. Scenario I covers growth stocks that do not pay dividends. Scenario II covers growth stocks that do pay dividends. Use the same worksheets to find what the stock is worth that you used for stocks that followed the Half-Life Decay Model in Chapters 12 and 13. Use Table 12-5 to find what stocks that do not pay dividends are worth. And use Table 13-3 for stocks that do pay dividends.

How to Proceed

In this chapter you will learn why and how the Unlimited Flexibility Model works. Understanding how the model works will give you confidence when you apply the model to a real stock. In the next chapter you will get hands-on experience by using the Unlimited Flexibility Model to find what Microsoft, a hot growth stock if there ever was one, is worth. You do not really have to read this chapter. It is not essential. If you are a daredevil investor, or you are in a great hurry, you can go on to the next chapter, and learn the mechanics of filling out the worksheets. But if you are a serious investor, you want to know what you are doing when you invest hard-earned dollars. You want to understand the process well enough that you can judge how reliable it is. By all means, work your way through this chapter, and try to grasp the essence of the analysis.

Making Forecasts

The basic difference between the decay model using half lives and the Unlimited Flexibility Model is that you are not restricted to half lives when you make your forecasts. You can forecast any way you like. The sky is the limit.

Let's forecast by drawing free-hand curves on a sheet of graph paper. That provides the ultimate in flexibility. Suppose we want to forecast the firm's return on equity. Take out a sheet of regular graph paper. First plot several years of historical returns. The historical returns are important because they give you perspective. They give you a basis to go on. They show where the firm has been. They show you how fast the return has been decaying. They tell you where you are starting from. Then draw a dashed horizontal line where you expect the return to line out when the firm is fully mature. That horizontal line will be a useful boundary for the long-run part of your forecast. Your forecast will gradually approach that horizontal line as time goes on. Good! Now you have drawn some reasonable boundaries around your forecast. Examine the historical returns and see how stable the firm's return has been. Is the return on equity fairly stable? Or does it wobble around? Has it been falling off?

Now make your forecast. Here is where judgment comes into play. Extend the historical returns into the future. Start your forecast at the firm's current return on equity. What do you see for the firm's future? Does it have hot new technology that is going to lead to faster growth and higher profits in the coming years? Or do you expect just a gradual slowing as the firm matures? Draw a smooth curve showing how you expect the return to decay as it approaches its long-run limit. There are no restrictions on the curve you draw. Shape it any way you like. You may want to redraw it several times before you are satisfied the curve reflects how you expect the firm's return on equity to change. When you are satisfied with your forecast, forecast the growth rate of equity per share and the P/B ratio the same way.

Remember not to let your growth rate forecast creep above your return on equity forecast. If you do, you will be paying dividends to the firm instead of the other way round. A good way to keep the growth rate forecast reasonable relative to your return on equity forecast is to plot them both on the same sheet of graph paper. Then you can see at a glance whether the growth rate forecast is at or below the return on equity forecast. Also remember to make your P/B forecast decay faster than both your return on equity and growth rate forecasts decay.

Finding What the Stock Is Worth

When you are satisfied with your forecasts, you are ready to find what the stock is worth. You have the same two options you had with the Half-Life Decay Model. You can forecast that the stock will not pay any dividends while you own it. That makes the analysis easier. You can forget about dividends — there will not be any. If there are no dividends, the firm's growth rate and the return on equity will be identical. That means you only have to forecast the growth rate of equity per share. You can forget about forecasting the return on equity; it will be the same as your growth forecast. You also have to forecast what the P/B ratio will be when you sell the stock. Then you can use the simpler worksheet in Table 12-5 to find what the stock is worth.

Or you might choose the second option, and forecast that the stock will pay dividends while you own it. You will need the same forecasts that are required for the first option. If the stock pays dividends, the return on equity forecast will be different from the growth rate forecast. That means you will need to forecast the return on equity in addition to forecasting the growth rate. Use the same method for discounting dividends as you used in the Half-Life Decay Model of Chapter 11. Make your forecasts, then use the worksheet in Table 13-3 and find what the stock is worth

Scenario I - Stocks That Do Not Pay Dividends

You can find what a growth stock that does not pay dividends is worth in four easy steps:

1. Forecast how you expect the growth rate of equity per share to change while you hold the stock.
2. Find the growth multiplier that corresponds to your growth rate forecast in step 1.
3. Forecast what you expect the P/B ratio to be when you sell.
4. Use the worksheet in Table 12-5 and find what the stock is worth.

That is it. The first three steps give you all the input you need to find what the stock is worth. There is no need to forecast the return on equity. That forecast will be identical to the growth rate forecast if the stock does not pay dividends.

Growth Multiplier

In the Half-Life Decay Model you used the worksheet in Table 12-1 to find the growth multiplier that corresponded to your growth rate forecast. That worksheet only works when you use the Half-Life Decay Model to forecast growth rates. It will not work if you are now going to forecast growth rates by drawing a free-hand curve on a sheet of graph paper. You will need a new way to find the growth multiplier that corresponds to your free-hand growth forecast.

Remember how easy it was to find a growth multiplier for the Steady-State Model back in Chapter 4? All you had to do was multiply the growth rate by the investment period and then tap the e^x key. What could be easier? Let's examine that process more closely and see what is really happening. Look at the plot of the growth rate against time in Figure 15-1. The growth rate plots as a straight horizontal line because the growth rate stays constant in a Steady-State Model. That makes the plot a rectangle. The height of the rectangle is the growth rate; the width is the investment period. You found the steady-state growth multiplier by multiplying the growth rate (in decimal form) by the investment period on your hand calculator. Then you tapped the e^x key. What happens when you multiply the growth rate by the investment period? That is the same as multiplying the height of the rectangle in Figure 15-1 by its width. You have done that many times. That is how you find the area of a rectangle. That is the key. The area under the growth rate curve is the "x" in e^x. It is the area under the growth rate curve that you enter into your calculator just before you tap the e^x key to find the growth multiplier.

> **The area under the growth rate forecast is the "x" in e^x. Enter that area into your calculator and tap the e^x key to find the growth multiplier.**

Finding the growth multiplier is easy in the Steady-State Model because the growth rate stays constant throughout the investment period. That makes the top boundary of the area in Figure 15-1 a straight horizontal line. It makes the figure a rectangle. And it is easy to find the area of a rectangle.

What happens when the growth rate does not stay constant? The basic idea is exactly the same. The only difference is that the top side of the rectangle is no longer a straight line. You have replaced that straight line by your forecast curve. The shape is not

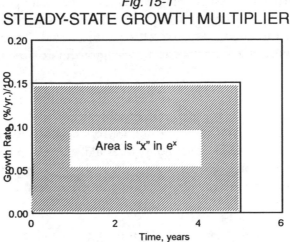

Fig. 15-1
STEADY-STATE GROWTH MULTIPLIER

a rectangle any more. You have changed the rectangle to some other shape. But the area under the new growth rate curve is still the "x" in e^x. It is still the number you enter in your calculator before you tap the e^x key.

Suppose an investor makes the growth rate forecast in Figure 15-2. Look at the forecast curve. It is anything but a straight line. Growth starts at 100 percent per year and gradually slows to 20 percent per year in five years. That is OK. No problem. The growth multiplier still depends on the area under that growth rate curve. Measure the area under the curve for the time period you are considering. Enter that area into your calculator and

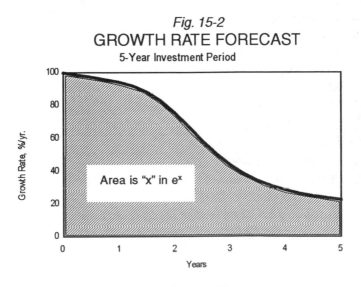

Fig. 15-2
GROWTH RATE FORECAST
5-Year Investment Period

tap the e^x key. Presto! You have the growth multiplier that corresponds to that growth rate forecast! How do you find the area under a curve? Gauss showed us how. We used his method to find the area under the curve when we discounted dividends in Chapter 13. We can use the same method to find the area under growth rate curves.

Some readers may go psychedelic when they draw their growth rate forecast curve. They may be carried away. They may let their curve swing wildly. Let's accommodate them by adding a fourth point to Gauss's method for finding areas. Four points will make the estimate of the area a little more accurate. We could add even more points to make estimating the area even more accurate. But that effort would be wasted. After all, the forecast is only an estimate. The underlying uncertainty in the growth forecast does not justify a more elaborate calculation.

Table 15-1 is the worksheet for translating your free-hand growth rate forecast into a growth multiplier. Enter the number of years you plan to hold the stock in line 1. You will need to read growth rates from your free-hand forecast curve at the four times Gauss specifies during the investment period. Line 2 shows those four times as fractions of the investment period. Multiply each time fraction in line 2 by the investment period in line 1 to find actual times in Line 3. Now read growth rates from your free-hand growth rate forecast curves at those four times and enter them in line 4. Lines 5 through 7 work

Table 15-1
GROWTH MULTIPLIER WORKSHEET

1. Investment period, years				———
2. Time, fraction of investment period	0.0694	0.33	0.67	0.9306
3. Time, Years. Multiply Line 1 by Line 2	———	———	———	———
4. Growth Rates, %/yr. (from freehand forecast curve)	———	———	———	———
5. Add the first and last entries in Line 4 and Multiply the result by 0.001739				———
6. Add the middle two entries in Line 4 and Multiply the result by 0.003261				———
7. Add Lines 5 and 6. Multiply the result by Line 1				———
8. Growth Multiplier: Enter Line 9 in your calculator and tap the e^x key				———

out the area under the growth rate curve by the Gauss averaging process. Enter that area in your calculator and tap the e^x key in line 8 and you have the growth multiplier. It is that easy.

Example 15-1 The investor who drew the growth rate forecast in Figure 15-2 plans to hold the stock for a five-year investment period. What is the five-year growth multiplier that corresponds to his growth rate forecast? Follow his computations in Table 15-2. He finds in line 3 that he needs to read growth rates from his free-hand forecast curve at 0.35, 1.65, 3.35, and 4.65 years. He reads the growth rates at those four times from his forecast curve and enters those rates in line 4. Line 7 gives the area under his growth rate forecast curve as 3.0505. He enters that number in his calculator, taps the e^x key, and finds a growth multiplier of 21.13 in line 8. If the firm follows his growth forecast, it will be 21.13 times larger in five years.

Table 15-2
GROWTH MULTIPLIER - EXAMPLE 15-1

1. Investment period, years				5
2. Time, fraction of investment period	**0.0694**	**0.33**	**0.67**	**0.9306**
3. Time, Years. Multiply Line 1 by Line 2	0.35	1.65	3.35	4.65
4. Growth Rates, %/yr. (from freehand forecast curve)	98.1	85.1	36.7	24.3
5. Add the first and last entries in Line 4 and Multiply the result by 0.001739				0.2129
6. Add the middle two entries in Line 4 and Multiply the result by 0.003261				0.3972
7. Add Lines 5 and 6. Multiply the result by Line 1				3.0505
8. Growth Multiplier: Enter Line 7 in your calculator and tap the e^x key				21.13

Forecasting the P/B Ratio

You only need to forecast what the P/B ratio will be when you finally sell the stock. Draw a free-hand forecast the same way you did for the growth rate forecast. Be realistic. Do not forecast that investors will continue to pay a high P/B ratio for the stock even after growth has slowed and profitability has fallen. You can avoid that mistake by making the P/B ratio decay faster than the return on equity decays. Keep an eye on your return on equity and growth forecasts as you forecast the P/B ratio. Remember that investors will lower the P/B ratio they are willing to pay in advance of any permanent drop in growth and profitability. Allow for the way investors anticipate decay by making your P/B ratio forecast fall faster than your return on equity forecast. Then read the P/B ratio from that curve at the end of the investment period.

What Is the Stock Worth?

Now that you have the growth multiplier and the P/B ratio, you have all the information you need to complete the worksheet for stocks that do not pay dividends. Enter your forecasts in the worksheet in Table 12-5 and find what the stock is worth.

Scenario II - Stocks That Pay Dividends

Finding what a stock is worth is still easy if the stock pays dividends. You still use the worksheet for growth stocks that pay dividends in Table 13-3. That worksheet applies to both the Half-Life Decay Model and the Unlimited Flexibility Model. The primary difference is in the way you develop the data the worksheet needs.

If the stock pays dividends you will have to include the discounted value of the dividends in the valuation. Use the same three-point averaging process to discount dividends you used for Half-Life Decay Models in Chapter 13. That means you will have to estimate dividends at those three intermediate times. How do you forecast those dividends? Multiply equity per share by return on equity to find earnings at those three times, and then by the payout fraction to find dividends. Both equity per share and the dividend payout fraction are fixed by your forecasts of the growth rate and the return on equity. Once you forecast the firm's return on equity and the growth rate of equity per share you have all the elements you need to complete the calculation. The growth rate forecast determines what equity per share will be at the three Gauss times. The growth rate and return on equity forecasts together determine what the dividend payout fraction will be at the three Gauss times. Don't worry about the details. They are all taken care of in the SmartValue worksheets.

Forecasting Growth Rates and the Return on Equity

We used the worksheet in Table 13-1 to forecast what growth rates and the return on equity would be at the three intermediate times when the key factors decayed along a path the Half-Life Decay Model describes. Life is much simpler when you forecast by drawing free-hand curves. You will not need that worksheet. How do you find the growth rates and the returns on equity? Easy. Simply read them from your forecast curves at the three intermediate times.

Translating Growth Rate Forecasts Into Equity/Share

The worksheet for translating a growth rate forecast into the equivalent forecasts of equity per share in Table 13-1 does not work in the Unlimited Flexibility Model. We will need a new worksheet for the growth multiplier in the Unlimited Flexibility Model.

The growth rate forecast carries with it an implied forecast of how large equity per share will be at any future time. We need to translate the growth rate forecast into forecasts of equity per share at the three intermediate times and at the end of the investment period. That means we need to work out growth multipliers for each of those times. You can find growth multipliers by the same method used in Scenario I. Instead of just one growth multiplier at the end of the investment period, however, you will also need growth multipliers for each of the three intermediate times. No problem. Just divide the area under the growth rate forecast into four sections, as shown in Figure 15-3. Make each of the first three sections end at one of the three intermediate times, and make the last section end at the end of the investment period. The growth multiplier for each section depends on the

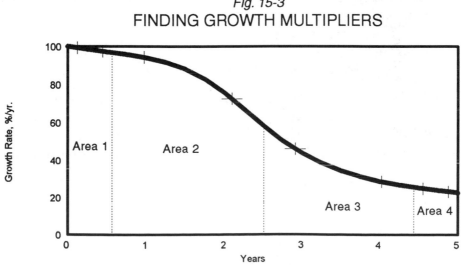

Fig. 15-3
FINDING GROWTH MULTIPLIERS

area of that section. Use Gauss's method to find that area. Measure the area of each section, enter that area in your calculator, and tap the e^x key. That is all there is to finding growth multipliers.

Figure 15-3 illustrates the process. The three vertical dashed lines in Figure 15-3 divide the total area under the growth rate curve into four smaller areas. Each of the first three areas ends at one of the three intermediate Gauss times. The last area ends at the end of the investment period. Let's keep the process simple. In place of the four-point averaging process of Scenario I, let's use a two-point averaging process to find the area of each section. Four sections with growth rates read at two points in each section gives a total of eight points. Eight points are enough. We could go overboard and use more points to measure those areas more accurately. But the underlying uncertainty in the growth rate forecast does not justify the effort.

The process is straightforward. Read growth rates from your forecast curve at the two Gauss times in each section. Use those two points to measure the area of the section. Then find the growth multiplier for each section by entering each area in your calculator and tapping the e^x key. Multiply the starting equity per share by the first growth multiplier. That gives equity per share at the first intermediate time. Proceed in the same way, section by section. Multiply the equity per share at the start of each section by the growth multiplier for that section, and find equity per share at the end of each section. That is how you find equity per share at the three intermediate times and at the end of the investment period.

The worksheet in Table 15-3 simplifies the process. Part A of the worksheet divides your growth rate forecast into the four time periods. It develops key time elements and the width of the sections under your forecast curve. Those are the sections whose areas you need to find. Use those times in Part B to locate the specific times where you are to read growth rates from your forecast curve. Calculate those times as directed, and enter them in the first column in lines 6 through 13. Then read the growth rates at those times from your forecast curve. Enter the growth rates in the last column of lines 6 through 13.

Part C of the worksheet finds the areas of each section under the forecast curve, and converts those areas to equity per share. Enter the starting equity per share in line 14. Lines 15 through 18 develop the required values of equity per share. Line "a" works out the area of each section. Line "b" translates the area into a growth multiplier. Line "c" applies the growth multiplier to the equity per share at the beginning of each section to find equity per share at the end. You will need these forecasts of equity per share for the worksheet in Table 13-3 to find what the stock is worth.

Example 15-2 Our investor from Example 15-1 decides that the stock will pay dividends after all. He keeps the same growth rate forecast, but now he has to translate that forecast into the corresponding forecast of equity per share at the three intermediate times and at the end of the five-year investment period. He uses the worksheet in Table 15-3; Table 15-4 shows his results. Part B of the worksheet develops the times where he needs to read growth rates from his forecast curve. The crosses on the curve in Figure 15-3 locate those times. He finds in line 18c that equity grows from $1 per share to $20.71 per share in five years. That makes the overall growth multiplier 20.71.

The growth multiplier of 20.71 in Example 15-2 agrees within 2 percent with the growth multiplier of 21.13 in Example 15-1. That close agreement is a tribute to Gauss's simple method for finding areas under curves. Do not worry about 2 percent errors. The primary errors in finding what a stock is worth are the errors you make in forecasting return on equity, equity growth rates, and P/B ratios. Those errors are much larger than the errors you make measuring areas under curves. If you want to make better valuations, look for ways to make better forecasts. Do not waste your time worrying about 2 percent errors in areas under curves.

What Is the Stock Worth?

Now you have all the forecasts you need to find what the stock is worth. Use the worksheet in Table 13-3. That worksheet requires forecasts of the return on equity and the equity growth rate at the three intermediate times. You also need the P/B ratio when you sell the stock. Read all those forecasts from your free-hand forecast curves. Then use the worksheet in Table 15-3 to translate your growth forecast into the corresponding forecast of equity per share at the three intermediate times and at the end of the investment period. Enter those forecasts in the same worksheet (Table 13-3) you used with the Half-Life Decay Model for stocks that pay dividends and find what the stock is worth. We will demonstrate the process by finding what Microsoft is worth in the next chapter.

Table 15-3
WORKSHEET FOR TRANSLATING GROWTH RATES INTO EQUITY/SHARE

Part A - Time Elements

1. Investment Period, years .... ————
2. Multiply Line 1 by 0.113 .... ————
3. Multiply Line 1 by 0.5 .... ————
4. Multiply Line 1 by 0.887 .... ————
5. Subtract Line 2 from Line 3 .... ————

Part B - Averaging Growth Rates

Compute times as directed and enter them in the column headed "Time, years". Then read growth rates (%/yr.) from your forecast curve at those times. Enter the growth rates in the column headed "Growth Rate, %/yr.".

	Time, years	Growth Rate, %/yr.
6. Multiply Line 2 by 0.211	————	————
7. Multiply Line 2 by 0.789	————	————
8. Multiply Line 5 by 0.211, then Add Line 2	————	————
9. Multiply Line 5 by 0.789, then Add Line 2	————	————
10. Multiply Line 5 by 0.211, then Add Line 3	————	————
11. Multiply Line 5 by 0.789, then Add Line 3	————	————
12. Add Lines 4 and 6	————	————
13. Add Lines 4 and 7	————	————
	————	————

Table 15-3 (Cont'd)
WORKSHEET FOR TRANSLATING GROWTH RATES INTO EQUITY/SHARE

Part C - Equity/Share

14. Initial Equity, $/Share .... _____
15. a. Add growth rates in Lines 6 and 7.
    Multiply by Line 2, then Divide by 200 .... _____
    b. Enter Line 15a in your calculator and tap the e^x key . _____
    c. Equity, $/Share: Multiply Line 15b by Line 14 .... _____
16. a. Add growth rates in Lines 8 and 9.
    Multiply by Line 5, then Divide by 200 .... _____
    b. Enter Line 16a in your calculator and tap the e^x key . _____
    c. Equity, $/Share: Multiply Line 16b by Line 15c .... _____
17. a. Add growth rates in Lines 10 and 11.
    Multiply by Line 5, then Divide by 200 .... _____
    b. Enter Line 17a in your calculator and tap the e^x key . _____
    c. Equity, $/Share: Multiply Line 17b by Line 16c .... _____
18. a. Add growth rates in Lines 12 and 13.
    Multiply by Line 2, then Divide by 200 .... _____
    b. Enter Line 18a in your calculator and tap the e^x key . _____
    c. Equity, $/Share: Multiply Line 18b by Line 17c .... _____

Fig. 15-4
EQUITY/SHARE - EXAMPLE 15-2

Part A - Time Elements

1. Investment Period, years	5
2. Multiply Line 1 by 0.113	0.565
3. Multiply Line 1 by 0.5	2.5
4. Multiply Line 1 by 0.887	4.435
5. Subtract Line 2 from Line 3	1.935

Part B - Averaging Growth Rates

Compute times as directed and enter them in the column headed "Time, years". Then read growth rates (%/yr.) from your forecast curve at those times. Enter the growth rates in the column headed "Growth Rate, /yr."

	Time, years	Growth Rate, %/yr.
6. Multiply Line 2 by 0.211	0.119	99.3
7. Multiply Line 2 by 0.789	0.446	97.5
8. Multiply Line 5 by 0.211, then Add Line 2	0.973	94.4
9. Multiply Line 5 by 0.789, then Add Line 2	2.092	72.6
10. Multiply Line 5 by 0.211, then Add Line 3	2.908	46.1
11. Multiply Line 5 by 0.789, then Add Line 3	4.027	28.5
12. Add Lines 4 and 6	4.554	24.8
13. Add Lines 4 and 7	4.883	23.2

Table 15-4 (Cont'd)
EQUITY/SHARE - EXAMPLE 15-2

Part C - Equity/Share

14. Initial Equity, $/Share	1.00
15. a. Add growth rates in Lines 6 and 7.	
Multiply by Line 2, then Divide by 200	0.556
b. Enter Line 15a in your calculator and tap the e^x key .	1.744
c. Equity, $/Share: Multiply Line 15b by Line 14	1.744
16. a. Add growth rates in Lines 8 and 9.	
Multiply by Line 5, then Divide by 200	1.616
b. Enter Line 16a in your calculator and tap the e^x key .	5.033
c. Equity, $/Share: Multiply Line 16b by Line 15c	8.778
17. a. Add growth rates in Lines 10 and 11.	
Multiply by Line 5, then Divide by 200	0.722
b. Enter Line 17a in your calculator and tap the e^x key ..	2.059
c. Equity, $/Share: Multiply Line 17b by Line 16c	18.074
18. a. Add growth rates in Lines 12 and 13.	
Multiply by Line 2, then Divide by 200	0.136
b. Enter Line 18a in your calculator and tap the e^x key .	1.146
c. Equity, $/Share: Multiply Line 18b by Line 17c	20.71

Summary

Draw your forecasts of the return on equity, the growth rate of equity per share, and the P/B ratio as free-hand curves on a sheet of graph paper. Free-hand curves gives you unlimited flexibility in making those forecasts. Start your forecast at the current level of each key factor, and let each factor decay away towards an appropriate long-run limit. Draw the free-hand curve to forecast the path you expect each factor to follow as it decays towards its long-run limit.

If the stock does not pay dividends, you need only forecast the growth rate and the P/B ratio. The return on equity will be identical to the growth rate you forecast. A worksheet translates the growth forecast into a growth multiplier. Enter these forecasts in the worksheet in Table 12-5 to find what the stock is worth.

If the stock pays dividends, you need to make an independent forecast of the return on equity because it will no longer be identical with the growth rate forecast. You will need forecasts of dividends at the three intermediate times required for discounting dividends. Read returns on equity and equity per share growth rates from your forecast curves at those three times. The SmartValue formula will translate those values into the corresponding dividend payouts. Use Table 15-3 to translate the forecast of growth rates into the corresponding forecast of equity per share. Enter those forecasts in Table 13-3 and find what the stock is worth

Chapter 16

What Is Microsoft Worth?

**Adjusting Earnings and the
  Return on Equity**

**What is Microsoft Worth?
  If Microsoft Does Not Pay Dividends
  If Microsoft Pays Dividends**

Investor's Return

The Unlimited Flexibility Model gives you unlimited freedom to forecast how you expect any firm to perform in the future. Let's demonstrate that model by using it to find what our investor can afford to pay for Microsoft.

Microsoft is one of the great success stories of the computer age. Just over 20 years old, Microsoft is the largest producer of computer software in the world. Microsoft's operating systems drive most of the world's personal computers. Many computer makers include Microsoft's operating system in the computers they sell. Many include other Microsoft programs as well. Microsoft's operating systems, word processor, spreadsheet, data base, and presentation programs are extremely popular with computer users everywhere. Microsoft's growth has been phenomenal. Growth averaged 34 percent per year for the past ten years — an outstanding record. Despite Bill Gates' frequent warnings that such rapid growth cannot last forever, Microsoft continues to grow at a rapid pace.

Microsoft is a favorite among technology stocks. Investors love Microsoft. They bid the P/E ratio up to 44 in late 1997. That is the problem with popular growth stocks. Microsoft is certainly an outstanding company. No question. But is it so outstanding that it is worth paying $44 for each dollar of earnings? SmartValue will tell you what you can afford to pay. Let's use the Unlimited Flexibility Model to find what Microsoft is worth to the investor we profiled in Chapter 5.

Adjusting Earnings and the Return on Equity

As always, begin the analysis by adjusting earnings and the return on equity. Look up Microsoft's historical record in Value Line. Table 16-1 reproduces Value Line's record for Microsoft. Microsoft has reinvested every penny of earnings back into the business since day one over 20 years ago. It has never paid a dividend. That makes adjusting earnings easy. With no dividends, adjusted earnings are simply the gain in equity per share from one year to the next. Adjust earnings and the return on equity in Table 16-2 the same way you did for Coca-Cola and Cisco Systems. Copy "Book Value per Share" from the sixth line of Value Line's table into Column 1 and dividends from the fourth line into Column 3 of Table 16-2. Then follow the directions and fill out the remainder of the table. Notice that the growth rate in Column 6 and the return on equity in Column 8 are identical, as they must be for a firm that does not pay dividends.

Table 16-1
MICROSOFT'S HISTORICAL PERFORMANCE

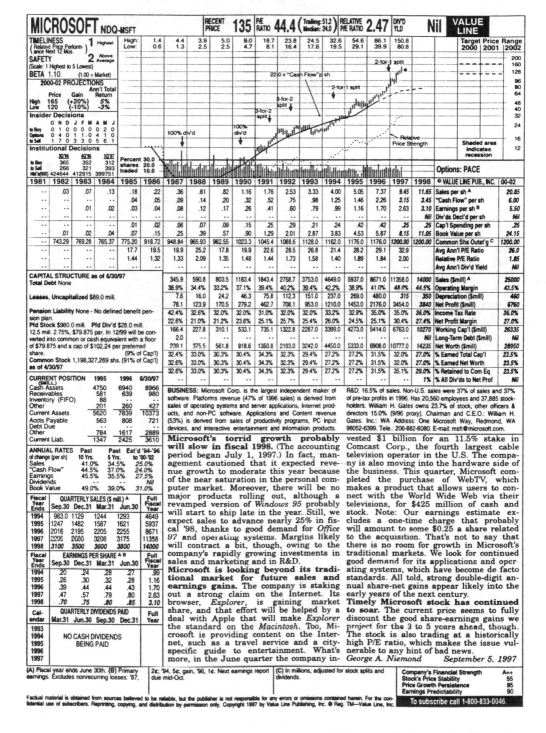

Courtesy of Value Line Publishing, Inc.

Table 16-2
ADJUSTING MICROSOFT'S EARNINGS AND RETURN ON EQUITY

Year	Col. 1 Equity, $/Sh.	Col. 2 Change in Equity, $/Sh.	Col. 3 Div., $/Sh.	Col. 4 Adjusted Earnings, $/Sh.	Col. 5 ln(Col.1)	Col. 6 Growth Rate, %/yr.	Col. 7 Avg. Equity, $/Sh.	Col. 8 Adjusted Return, %
1997	8.15	2.28	0	2.28	2.098	32.8	6.95	32.8
1996	5.87	1.34	0	1.34	1.770	25.9	5.17	25.9
1995	4.53	0.70	0	0.70	1.511	16.8	4.17	16.8
1994	3.83	0.96	0	0.96	1.343	28.9	3.32	28.9
1993	2.87	0.86	0	0.86	1.054	35.6	2.42	35.5
1992	2.01	0.72	0	0.72	0.698	44.3	1.63	44.2
1991	1.29	0.392	0	0.392	0.255	36.3	1.08	36.3
1990	0.898	0.326	0	0.326	-0.108	45.1	0.723	45.1
1989	0.572	0.183	0	0.183	-0.559	38.5	0.475	38.5
1988	0.389				-0.944			

Cols. 1 and 3: Enter book value per share and dividends directly from Value Line or the Annual Report.
Col. 2: In Column 1 subtract last year's book value from this year's value and put the result in Column 2.
Col. 4: Add Columns 2 and 3.
Col. 5: Enter the number in Column 1 in your calculator and tap the ln(x) key. Put the result in Column 5.
Col. 6: Subtract last year's entry in Column 5 from this year's entry. Multiply the result by 100.
Col. 7: Divide Column 2 by Column 6, then Multiply by 100.
Col. 8: Divide Column 4 by Column 7, then Multiply by 100.

Microsoft earned an average return of 35 percent over the past ten years, as Figure 16-1 shows. The average for the most recent five years dropped to 28 percent, caused primarily by the drop to a 17 percent return in 1995. The advent of the Windows 95 and NT operating systems boosted Microsoft's profits starting in 1996. Earnings have since improved, and the return for 1997 was back to 32.8 percent. Except for 1995 and 1996, Microsoft's adjusted return has been a little higher than the return Microsoft reported.

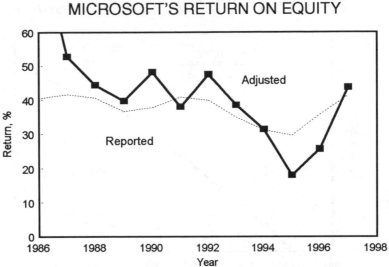

Fig. 16-1
MICROSOFT'S RETURN ON EQUITY

Equity Growth

Remember that the best way to track how fast equity per share has grown is by plotting the natural logarithm of equity per share against time. The slope of the plotted curve measures the growth rate. You already have the natural logarithm of equity per share in Column 5 of Table 16-2. Plot it on regular graph paper. Measure how fast equity has grown, and see whether growth has been stable.

Figure 16-2 shows how equity per share has grown. The curve is very nearly a straight line from 1987 to 1994. Equity per share grew at a remarkably steady rate of 39.5 percent per year during that time. The curve breaks in 1994, indicating a basic change in the nature of Microsoft's growth. Growth averaged only 25.3 percent per year since 1994.

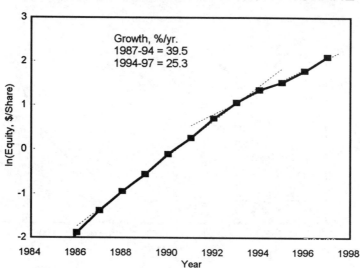

Fig. 16-2
GROWTH OF MICROSOFT'S EQUITY/SHARE

Because the growth rate of equity per share and the adjusted return on equity are identical for Microsoft, you can also read the plot of Microsoft's return on equity in Figure 16-1 as a plot of annual growth rates. Annual growth rates dropped to a low of 16.8 percent per year in 1995 but have since recovered to 32.8 percent per year in 1997.

P/B Ratio

Value Line reports a P/E ratio for Microsoft in line 8 of Table 16-1, but not a P/B ratio. That is OK. Use the worksheet in Table 7-11 to convert P/E ratios to the corresponding P/B ratios. Table 16-3 shows the conversion.

Table 16-3
MICROSOFT'S P/B RATIO

Year	Col. 1 P/E	Col. 2 Reported Earnings, $/Share	Col. 3 Average Equity, $/Share	Col. 4 P/B
1997	32.9	2.63	6.95	12.4
1996	29.1	1.70	5.17	9.57
1995	28.2	1.16	4.17	7.84
1994	21.4	0.99	3.32	6.38
1993	26.8	0.79	2.42	8.75
1992	28.5	0.60	1.63	10.5
1991	22.6	0.41	1.08	8.58
1990	19.9	0.26	0.723	7.16

Cols. 1 and 2: Copy P/E ratios and earnings per share directly from Value Line.

Col. 3: Copy the average equity per share from Col. 7 of Table 16-2.

Col. 4: Multiply column 1 by column 2, then divide by column 3.

Fig. 16-3
MICROSOFT'S P/B RATIO

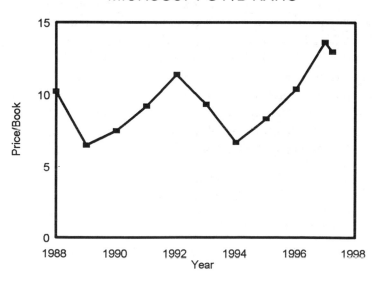

Investors have been willing to pay a high price for Microsoft. On average, investors have paid a P/B ratio of about 9 for Microsoft for the past ten years, as shown in Figure 16-3. The P/B ratio varied from a low of 6.4 in 1984 to highs of 10.5 in 1992 and 12.4 in 1997. By late 1997 investors had bid the P/B ratio up to 15. That is an extremely high price to pay even for a firm as outstanding as Microsoft. These ratios are three to seven times higher than the corresponding ratios for mature firms, which have P/B ratios closer to 2.

What Is Microsoft Worth?

Microsoft has an extraordinary record of profitability and growth. But how long can Microsoft maintain such outstanding performance? The larger Microsoft becomes, the more it has to invest to maintain rapid growth. In 1990 Microsoft only had to find profitable opportunities to invest about 320 million dollars to grow 35 percent per year. In 1997, however, Microsoft will have to find investment opportunities for nearly 4 billion dollars. That is not easy in the software business. Microsoft is brains and labor-intensive, not capital intensive. It is not like the oil business or the steel business, where a new refinery or a new steel mill can soak up capital investment by the ton. Where will Microsoft find places to invest money on that scale? Windows 95 and the NT operating systems promise a profitable future. How much capital can these software projects absorb?

Where will Microsoft find opportunities to invest dollars by the billion in the future? If it does not find opportunities on this scale, what will it do with the excess earnings? Will Microsoft begin to pay dividends? Or will it do what other firms with money piling up in their treasuries often do, and go on an acquisition binge? Acquisitions may be great for the CEO's ego, but they are frequently disasters for shareholders. Why? Because firms often pay too much for the firms they acquire. They justify the high acquisition cost by the new opportunities and the cost savings open to the combined firms. "Synergism" is the cry. But new opportunities and cost savings are much easier to predict than they are to achieve in practice. Too often the combined firm does not meet the rosy forecast. The result? Paying too much lowers the combined firm's return on equity. If Microsoft goes on an acquisition binge and pays too much, its future returns will drop, too.

The critical element in forecasting the future for a firm growing as fast as Microsoft is forecasting how long the current fast growth, high profitability, and the high P/B ratio will last. How soon will these key factors begin to fall? Once they begin falling, how fast will they fall? Bill Gates is right. Microsoft cannot maintain rapid growth and high returns on equity forever. And investors will not pay high P/B ratios forever. As growth slows, as eventually it must, Microsoft will find it increasingly difficult to find profitable places to reinvest all of its earnings. Growth will then drop below the return on equity, and Microsoft will begin to pay dividends. How do you forecast dividends? Don't worry about them. Worry instead about making reasonable forecasts of how fast equity per share grows and what happens to the return on equity. The SmartValue formula will provide a schedule of future dividend payments consistent with your growth and return on equity forecasts.

Let's find what Microsoft is worth under two scenarios, as we did in the Cisco Systems example in Chapter 14. In Scenario I Microsoft continues to reinvest all its earnings and pays no dividends. In Scenario II Microsoft is not able to find enough profitable opportunities to invest all its earnings, and begins to pay dividends during our investor's five-year investment period. Scenario I is the more likely scenario for Microsoft. Let's include Scenario II anyway. It will help illustrate how to use the Unlimited Flexibility Model.

Scenario I - Microsoft Pays No Dividends

Finding what Microsoft is worth is easier if we forecast that Microsoft will not pay any dividends. We only have to forecast Microsoft's future growth rate and P/B ratio. Forget about forecasting the return on equity. If you forecast that dividends will be zero while you hold the stock, the SmartValue formula makes the return on equity forecast identical to the growth forecast.

Growth of Equity per Share

We saw how Microsoft's equity per share has grown in Figure 16-2. Growth was steady at about 40 percent per year until 1993. Growth then slowed, and averaged only 28 percent per year since 1993. Rapid growth is something only small firms can do easily. By the time a firm becomes a behemoth like Microsoft, continuing to grow rapidly is a Herculean task. It is only natural that growth slows. As Microsoft becomes even larger, we can expect that growth will slow even more.

Our investor decides to use the Unlimited Flexibility Model to find what Microsoft is worth. He takes out a sheet of graph paper from his desk drawer and draws the free-hand forecast of Microsoft's future growth shown in Figure 16-4. First, he plots how fast Microsoft grew in the past. He has already found Microsoft's annual growth rates in Column 6 of Table 16-2. He plots those growth rates against time.

Investors are often warned that past performance is no guarantee of future performance. True enough. But those numbers did not come out of nowhere. They are Microsoft's track record. They are the best measure of how well Microsoft's management has done its job. They are management's report card. They are the only hard numbers we have to work with. Use them, by all means. They provide perspective. Your forecast must be a reasonable extension of the historical record, or it will not be credible.

Next, our investor establishes the long-run boundary for his forecast. He expects growth to line out at a current-dollar GDP growth rate of 7 percent per year when Microsoft has fully matured. To keep that limit in mind, he adds a dashed horizontal line at a long-run growth rate of 7 percent per year to his plot.

Then he ponders how Microsoft's growth is likely to slow. He knows the general shape the forecast curve must have. It must begin at Microsoft's current growth rate and then gradually approach the long-run 7 percent per year limit. Microsoft's growth has been slowing, but not along a smooth curve. Annual growth rates are high in some years and low in others. Growth dropped to a low of 17 percent per year in 1995, then jumped to 33 percent per year in 1997. He regards growth that high to be unsustainable for a firm as large as Microsoft. He shapes his forecast curve to make growth drop from the 1997 high fairly quickly, then fall more slowly as growth begins to approach the long-run limit. He sketches in his growth forecast, then steps back to see how it looks. After several erasures and redrawings, he finally settles on the forecast in Figure 16-4.

Fig. 16-4
FORECASTING MICROSOFT'S GROWTH RATE

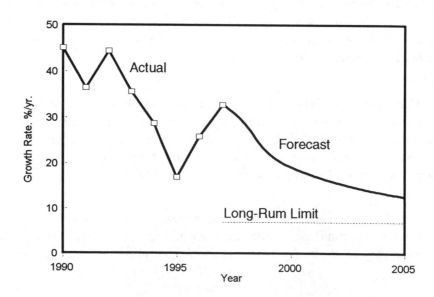

Don't worry about making a separate forecast of the return on equity. The forecast of return on equity will be identical to this growth forecast because our investor forecasts that Microsoft will not pay dividends while he holds the stock.

Translating Growth Rates into Growth Multipliers

Forecasting that Microsoft will not pay dividends simplifies the analysis. The only cash that will roll into our investor's pocket is the net proceeds he receives when he finally sells the stock. Our investor cares only about what the price of Microsoft stock will be when he sells in five years. He can ignore dividends. He uses the worksheet in Table 15-1 to translate his growth forecast into the growth multiplier for a five-year investment period. Table 16-4 shows his calculations. He reads the growth rates from his forecast curve at the times listed in line 3 of the worksheet and enters those growth rates in line 4. Lines 5 through 8 work out the area under the growth rate curve by the Gauss method.

Table 16-4
TRANSLATING THE GROWTH FORECAST INTO A FORECAST OF EQUITY PER SHARE

1. Investment period, years				5
2. Time, fraction of investment period	0.0694	0.33	0.67	0.9306
3. Time, Years. Multiply Line 1 by Line 2	0.35	1.65	3.35	4.65
4. Growth Rates, %/yr. (from freehand forecast curve)	31.6	24.2	18.4	16.2
5. Add the first and last entries in Line 4 and Multiply the result by 0.001739				0.0831
6. Add the middle two entries in Line 4 and Multiply the result by 0.003261				0.1389
7. Add Lines 5 and 6. Multiply the result by Line 1				1.110
8. Growth Multiplier: Enter Line 7 in your calculator and tap the e^ key				3.034

His growth forecast leads to a growth multiplier of 3.034 for the five-year investment period. That will make Microsoft's equity per share three times larger when he sells in five years.

Forecasting the P/B Ratio

If Microsoft's return on equity drops and growth slows as forecast, investors will certainly adjust the P/B ratio they will pay for Microsoft stock. The P/B ratio should fall as these two key factors fall. Investors will anticipate that Microsoft is slowing, and try to sell out before growth slows and the return drops. That will make the P/B forecast curve have roughly the same shape as the growth and return-on-equity forecast curves. But the changes will take place sooner.

Our investor proceeds the same way he did when he made his growth forecast. He plots the historical P/B ratios in Figure 16-5, and adds a dashed line to establish a long-run limit. He sets the long-run limit at a P/B ratio of 2.1, which corresponds to a mature firm growing at the GDP rate of 7 percent per year, paying half of its earnings out as

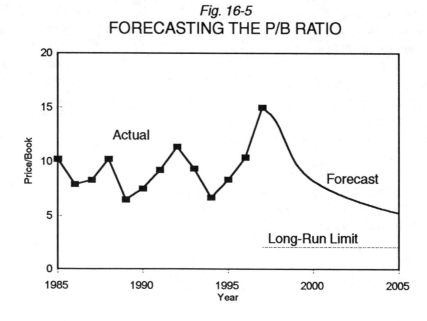

Fig. 16-5
FORECASTING THE P/B RATIO

dividends, and selling at a P/E ratio of 15. He begins his forecast curve at the current P/B ratio of 15, but has it fall off faster than his growth rate forecast. After several erasures and redrawings, he is satisfied with the forecast in Figure 16-5. His final forecast has Microsoft's P/B ratio falling from the current ratio of 15 to a ratio of 6.7 when he sells in five years.

Current Equity per Share

Microsoft reported $8.15 of equity per share at the close of fiscal 1997 which ended June 30th of 1997. This analysis is being made five months after Microsoft reported that value. With equity per share currently growing about 33 percent per year it is worth adjusting for that five month's growth. Our investor uses Table 7-7 to adjust equity per share for the growth that has occurred since equity was last reported. Table 16-5 shows the adjustment. Growth in the five months since the last annual report raises the starting equity from $8.15 to $9.35 per share.

Table 16-5
CURRENT EQUITY PER SHARE

1. Last Reported Equity, $/Share	8.15
2. Time since last report, months	5
3. Divide Current growth rate, %/year by 100	0.33
4. Multiply Line 2 by Line 3, then Divide by 12	0.1375
5. Growth Multiplier: Enter Line 4 in your calculator and tap the e^x key	1.1474
6. Current Equity/Share: Multiply Line 1 by Line 5	9.35

What Is Microsoft Worth?

Our investor now has all the information he needs to find what Microsoft is worth if Microsoft reinvests all its earnings and pays no dividends. He uses the worksheet in Table 12-5 for growth stocks that do not pay dividends. He decides that Microsoft has about the same degree of risk as Cisco Systems, and so sets his minimum acceptable return at 14 percent, the same minimum return he used for Cisco. His calculations are shown in Table 16-6.

Section I - The Investor

Nothing in our investor's financial situation has changed since he found what Cisco Systems was worth in Chapter 14. Section I of the worksheet is therefore identical to Section I of the worksheet for Cisco Systems.

Section II - The Firm

He enters his estimate of $9.35 for Microsoft's current equity per share in line 7. He worked out a growth multiplier of 3.034 for the five-year investment period in Table 16-4. He enters that growth multiplier in line 8. He reads a P/B ratio of 6.7 when he sells the stock in five years from his P/B forecast curve and enters that ratio in line 9. His growth and P/B forecasts, together with his estimate of Microsoft's current equity per share, lead to a stock price of $190.06 when he sells in five years.

Section III - What is Microsoft Worth?

The $190.06 he expects to receive when he sells, less capital gains taxes and his broker's commission, make up all the cash that will roll into his pocket if he invests in Microsoft for five years and Microsoft performs as he forecast. What is that future sum worth to him now? How much can he afford to pay for Microsoft and still earn his minimum after-tax return of 14 percent? Section III of the worksheet provides the answer. The discount factor in line 12 is the same as the factor for Cisco Systems because his minimum acceptable return and the investment period are identical for both stocks. After discounting, the $190.06 expects to receive in five years is worth only $93.44 now, as shown in line 13. Capital gains taxes reduce the stock's value even further. Line 17 shows that Microsoft stock is worth only $79.35 to this investor.

Should he buy? Certainly not! Why spend $135 for a stock that is only worth $79.35? He might want to go back and review his forecasts. But it would take a major change in those forecasts to make Microsoft an attractive investment. If he buys Microsoft anyway and Microsoft performs as he forecast, he will earn a return of only 5.1 percent, well below the 14 percent return he specified as the minimum he would accept.

Scenario II - Microsoft Begins Paying Dividends

At some point Microsoft will not find enough investment opportunities to soak up all of its earnings. After investing in every reasonable opportunity it sees, it will still have some of its earnings left over. That is when Microsoft may begin to pay dividends. Suppose our investor decides that Microsoft is reaching that point. He expects that Microsoft will begin to pay dividends during the five years he plans to hold the stock. How does that change his evaluation of Microsoft?

Table 16-6
WHAT IS MICROSOFT WORTH?
Scenario I - No Dividends

Section I - The Investor

1. Investment Period, years 5
2. Divide Incremental Tax Rate on Ordinary Income (%)
   by 100; Subtract the Result from 1.0 .... 0.6768
3. Divide Capital Gains Tax Rate (%) by 100 .... 0.248
4. Divide Minimum Acceptable Return (%) by 100 .... 0.14
5. Divide Broker's Commission (%) by 100;
   Add the Result to 1.0 .... 1.01
6. Divide Broker's Commission (%) by 100;
   Subtract the Result from 1.0 .... 0.99

Section II - The Firm

7. Initial Equity, $/Share 9.35
8. Growth Multiplier (from Table 11-2) 3.034
9. Final P/B Ratio (from Table 11-4) 6.7
10. Final Stock Price: Multiply Line 7 by Lines 8 and 9 .... 190.06

Table 16-6 (Cont'd)
WHAT IS MICROSOFT WORTH?
Scenario I - No Dividends

Section III - What the Stock Is Worth

11. Multiply Line 1 by Line 4	0.7
12. Discount Factor: Enter Line 11 in your calculator, tap the change sign (+/-) key, then tap the e^x key	0.4966
13. Present Value of Final Stock Price: Multiply Line 6 by Lines 10 and 12	93.44
14. Multiply Line 3 by Line 13	23.17
15. Subtract Line 14 from Line 13	70.27
16. Multiply Line 3 by Line 12 and Subtract the result from 1.0	0.8768
17. What the Stock is Worth: Divide Line 15 by Line 5 and by Line 16	79.35

He decides to keep the same forecasts for Microsoft's growth rate and P/B ratio that he used in Scenario I. But if Microsoft pays dividends, the return on equity forecast will no longer be identical to the growth forecast. He therefore needs to develop a separate forecast for the return on equity.

Forecasting the Return on Equity

Our investor recognizes that he must forecast a return on equity at least as high as Microsoft's growth rate, or he will be paying dividends to Microsoft instead of the other way around. He decides to draw his forecast curve on the same graph paper he used for the growth forecast. That way he can insure that his forecast of the return on equity is always equal to or higher than his growth rate forecast. He also decides on a long-run limit of 14 percent return on equity. That limit, combined with a long-run limit of 7 percent per year on growth, leads to a target dividend payout of 50 percent of earnings when Microsoft is fully mature.

He does not expect dividends to begin immediately. To make dividends zero for the initial year or two, he draws the forecast curve for the return on equity right on top of the forecast curve for Microsoft's growth rate. Making the return on equity forecast identical to the growth rate forecast insures zero dividends during the period when the two forecasts are identical. Then he makes the return on equity fall off more slowly than his growth forecast. As the two forecasts diverge, the SmartValue formula will lead to gradually increasing dividends. Dividends will be nil at first, and become significant only towards the end of the five-year investment period.

He sketches in a forecast curve and studies it. Then he erases and redraws parts of it. He continues erasing and redrawing until he is satisfied that the curve reflects his judgment about the return Microsoft will earn in the future. He finally settles on the forecast in Figure 16-6. The growth rate and return on equity forecasts both begin at a rate of 33 percent per year, and remain identical for about two years. After five years the growth forecast has dropped to 16 percent per year and the return on equity forecast to 21 percent. Those forecasts lead to a dividend payout of 24 percent of earnings after five years.

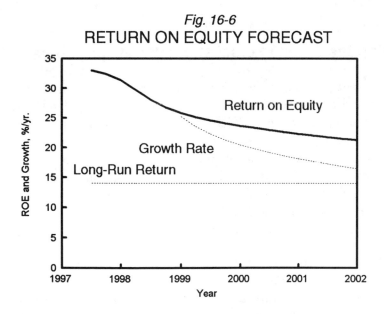

Fig. 16-6
RETURN ON EQUITY FORECAST

What Is Microsoft Worth?

We now have the basic forecasts we need to find what Microsoft stock is worth. The worksheet in Table 13-3 is the one to use for growth stocks that pay dividends. That worksheet requires forecasts of the return on equity and the growth rate of equity per share at the three intermediate times needed to discount dividends. The worksheet also requires the P/B ratio at the end of the five-year investment period. Finding these values is easy in the Unlimited Flexibility Model. Simply read the required values off of your forecast curves. You do not need a worksheet to calculate them. Table 16-7 lists the values our investor reads from his forecast curves:

Table 16-7
FORECAST VALUES FOR MICROSOFT
(Read from Forecast Curves)

	Forecast Values			
Time Fraction	**0.113**	**0.5**	**0.887**	**1.0**
Time. years	0.565	2.5	4.435	5
Growth Rate, %/yr.	30.7	20.5	16.5	
Return on Equity, %	31.0	23.7	21.3	
P/B Ratio	-	-	-	6.7

Translating the Growth Forecast into Equity per Share

The worksheet for finding what Microsoft is worth also requires forecasts of equity per share at the three intermediate times needed for discounting dividends, as well as at the end of the investment period. We have already made that forecast. It is implicit in the forecast of how fast equity per share grows. Before we can use the worksheet to find what Microsoft is worth, we have to translate the growth forecast into the corresponding forecast of equity per share. That is what Part B of the worksheet in Table 15-3 does. The process involves dividing the area under the growth rate forecast curve into four sections. The first three sections end at one of the three intermediate times required in the Stock Valuation Worksheet. The fourth ends at the end of the investment period.

Table 16-8 shows how to translate the growth forecast for Microsoft into the corresponding forecast of equity per share. Lines 6 through 13 work out the times where our investor needs to read growth rates from his forecast curve. He reads the growth rates at those times and enters the growth rates in the last column in lines 6 through 13. Lines 15a through 18a work out the area under each section of the growth forecast curve. Lines 15b through 18b convert these areas into growth multipliers. Lines 15c through 18c apply these growth multipliers to the equity per share at the beginning of each section. The resulting values for equity per share in lines 15c through 18c are the values to enter in line 9 of the Stock Valuation Worksheet.

The worksheet shows that equity per share should grow from $9.35 initially to $28.55 at the end of the five-year investment period. This result is in excellent agreement with the value of $28.37 forecast in Scenario I. The two values differ by only 0.7 percent.

Worksheet for Valuing Microsoft

We now have all the forecasts we need to find what Microsoft is worth. We need forecasts of the return on equity and the growth rate of equity per share at the three intermediate times. We also need a forecast of the P/B ratio at the end of the investment period. Our investor read all those values from his forecast curves and listed them in Table 16-7. We also need forecasts of equity per share that result from the growth rate forecast. Our investor calculated those values from his growth forecast in Table 16-8. Now it is time to go to the worksheet in Table 13-3 and find what Microsoft is worth. Our investor works out Microsoft's value in Table 16-9.

Section I - The Investor

There is no change in our investor's financial situation from Scenario I. Section I of the Stock Valuation Worksheet is therefore identical to Section I of the worksheet for Scenario I.

Section II - The Firm

Line 8 of the worksheet sets out the times where forecasts are to be read from the forecast curves. Enter the forecast of equity per share developed in Table 16-8 in line 9 of the Stock Valuation worksheet. Read the three returns on equity from the forecast curve and enter those returns in line 10. Read the three growth rates from the forecast curve and enter the growth rates in line 11. SmartValue develops the dividend payout fraction that is consistent with the growth and return on equity forecasts in line 12. The forecasts of return on equity and the equity growth rate lead to a dividend payout starting at zero and growing only to about 23 percent of earnings after five years. Line 13 applies the Smart-Value formula for dividends, and shows that dividends after taxes grow to about $0.85 per share in five year's time. Read a P/B ratio of 6.7 from the P/B forecast curve when our investor plans to sell in five years, and enter that forecast in line 14. The SmartValue stock price formula leads to a stock price of $191.29 per share in five years in line 15. The stock price comes from multiplying a final equity of $25.55 per share by a final P/B ratio of 6.7.

Section III - What is Microsoft Worth?

The discount factors used for discounting dividends and the net proceeds when the stock is sold are worked out in line 17. Lines 18 through 21 use the Gauss averaging process to find what dividends are worth after taxes and discounting. Discounted dividends in line 21 are worth $1.28 per share. Line 26 shows what Microsoft is worth to our investor. Given his forecasts of the return Microsoft will earn in the future, how fast it will grow, and the P/B ratio investors will pay for the stock, Microsoft is worth $82.11 per share.

Table 16-8
CONVERTING THE GROWTH FORECAST INTO EQUITY/SHARE

Part A - Time Elements

1. Investment Period, years 5
2. Multiply Line 1 by 0.113 .... 0.565
3. Multiply Line 1 by 0.5 .... 2.5
4. Multiply Line 1 by 0.887 .... 4.435
5. Subtract Line 2 from Line 3 .... 1.935

Part B - Averaging Growth Rates

Compute times as directed and enter them in the column headed "Tiime, years". Then read growth rates (%/yr.) from your forecast curves at those times. Enter the growth rates in the column headed "Growth Rate, %/yr."

	Time, years	Growth Rate, %/yr.
6. Multiply Line 2 by 0.211	0.119	32.5
7. Multiply Line 2 by 0.789	0.446	31.2
8. Multiply Line 5 by 0.211, then Add Line 2	0.973	28.8
9. Multiply Line 5 by 0.789, then Add Line 2	2.092	21.9
10. Multiply Line 5 by 0.211, then Add Line 3	2.908	19.4
11. Multiply Line 5 by 0.789, then Add Line 3	4.027	17.2
12. Add Lines 4 and 6	4.554	16.4
13. Add Lines 4 and 7	4.883	15.9

Table 16-8 (Cont'd)

CONVERTING THE GROWTH FORECAST INTO EQUITY/SHARE

14. Initial Equity, $/Share 9.35
15. a. Add growth rates in Lines 6 and 7.
     Multiply by Line 2, then Divide by 200 .... 0.180
     b. Enter Line 15a in your calculator and tap the e^x key . 1.197
     c. Equity, $/Share: Multiply Line 15b by Line 14 .... 11.19
16. a. Add growth rates in Lines 8 and 9.
     Multiply by Line 5, then Divide by 200 .... 0.491
     b. Enter Line 16a in your calculator and tap the e^x key . 1.634
     c. Equity, $/Share: Multiply Line 16b by Line 15c 18.28
17. a. Add growth rates in Lines 10 and 11.
     Multiply by Line 5, then Divide by 200 .... 0.354
     b. Enter Line 17a in your calculator and tap the e^x key . 1.425
     c. Equity, $/Share: Multiply Line 17b by Line 16c 26.05
18. a. Add growth rates in Lines 12 and 13.
     Multiply by Line 2, then Divide by 200 .... 0.0912
     b. Enter Line 18a in your calculator and tap the e^x key . 1.096
     c. Equity, $/Share: Multiply Line 18b by Line 17c 28.55

Table 16-9
WHAT IS MICROSOFT WORTH?
Scenario II - Microsoft Pays Dividends

Section I - The Investor

1. Investment Period, years	5
2. Divide Incremental Tax Rate on Ordinary Income (%) by 100; Subtract the Result from 1.0	0.6768
3. Divide Capital Gains Tax Rate (%) by 100	0.248
4. Divide Minimum Acceptable Return (%) by 100	0.14
5. Divide Broker's Commission (%) by 100; Add the Result to 1.0	1.01
6. Divide Broker's Commission (%) by 100; Subtract the Result from 1.0	0.99

Section II - The Firm

	0.113	0.5	0.887	1.0
7. Time, fraction of investment period				
8. Time, Years. Multiply Line 1 by Line 7	0.565	2.5	4.435	5
9. Equity, $/Share*	11.19	18.28	26.05	28.55
10. Return on Equity, %*	31.0	23.7	21.3	
11. Growth Rate, %/yr.*	30.7	20.5	16.5	
12. Payout Fraction: Divide Line 11 by Line 10. Subtract the result from 1.0	0.010	0.135	0.225	
13. Dividends, $/Share: Multiply Line 2 by Lines 9, 10, and 12, then Divide by 100	0.023	0.396	0.845	
14. Final P/B Ratio*				6.7
15. Final Stock Price: Multiply Line 9 by Line 14				191.29

* Read from forecast curves.

Table 16-9 (Cont'd)
WHAT IS MICROSOFT WORTH?
Scenario II - Microsoft Pays Dividends

Section III - What the Stock Is Worth

16. Multiply Line 8 by Line 4	0.0791	0.35	0.6209	0.7
17. Discount Factor: Enter Line 16 in your calculator, tap the change sign (+/-) key, then tap the e^x key	0.9239	0.7047	0.5375	0.4966
18. Discounted Dividends: Multiply Line 13 by Line 17	0.021	0.279	0.454	
19. Add the 1st and 3rd numbers in Line 18 and Multiply the result by 0.278				0.132
20. Multiply the 2nd number in Line 18 by 0.444				0.123
21. Discounted Dividends: Add Lines 19 and 20 and Multiply the result by Line 1				1.275
22. Discounted Stock Price: Multiply Line 6 by Line 15 and by the last number in Line 17				95.00
23. Multiply Line 3 by Line 22				23.56
24. Subtract Line 23 from Line 22				71.00
25. Multiply Line 3 by the last number in Line 17 and Subtract the result from 1.0				0.8768
26. What the Stock is Worth: Add Lines 21 and 24, then Divide by Line 5 and by Line 25				82.11

The forecast that the return on equity would fall off more slowly in Scenario II makes Microsoft worth $82.11 -- just slightly more than the $79.35 found in Scenario I.

What Should Our Investor Do?

At the time of this analysis Microsoft was selling for $135 per share. SmartValue has made this investor's choice simple. Should he pay $135 for a stock that is only worth $79 to $82? Of course not! SmartValue has helped our investor avoid paying too much for a glamour stock.

Why is Microsoft selling at such a high price? There are a number of reasons. Perhaps other investors are much more optimistic about Microsoft's future. They think Microsoft's rapid growth, high returns, and high P/B ratio will last much longer than our investor does. Or perhaps they have not done their homework. They do not realize they are paying too much. Perhaps they are paying $135 per share simply because they are caught up in the euphoria that surrounds a glamor stock like Microsoft.

Investor's Return

What return might our investor expect if he buys Microsoft at $135 and Microsoft performs as he forecast? Remember that the investor's return is the discount rate that makes Microsoft's value just equal to the market price. Our investor finds his rate of return by repeating the Stock Valuation Worksheet at several minimum acceptable rates of return. He then plots Microsoft's value against the minimum acceptable return in Figure 16-7, and finds the point where the value curve crosses a horizontal line drawn at Microsoft's market price. The two curves cross at a return of 5.1 percent. A return of 5.1 percent is well below the 14 percent return he set as the minimum return he would accept.

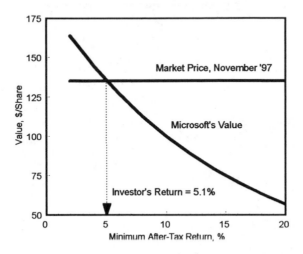

Fig. 16-7
INVESTOR'S RETURN FROM
MICROSOFT

SUMMARY

Microsoft is one of the most glamorous of hi-tech growth stocks. But its rapid growth cannot last forever. Growth will slow, and the return on equity will fall. Investors will respond by paying lower P/B ratios for the stock as Microsoft matures. The Unlimited Flexibility Model permits complete freedom in forecasting how these key factors might change in the future. Our investor drew free-hand curves on a sheet of graph paper to forecast how fast Microsoft's return on equity would fall, how the growth of equity per share would slow, and the P/B ratio investors would pay. SmartValue translated these forecast curves into a value of about $79 to $82 for this investor, well below Microsoft's current market price of $135. Microsoft costs too much for our investor.

Chapter | 17

When Do I Sell?

A Rational Selling Strategy
   Money Forgone by Not Selling
   Money Received by Selling
Sell or Hold On?
Coca-Cola Example

Up to this point we have been concerned with buying stocks. How do you tell if a stock is a buy? Now you know. Use SmartValue to find what the stock is worth. Once you know what a stock is worth, the buy/don't buy decision is easy. Buy the stock if SmartValue tells you the stock is worth more than it costs. Do not buy the stock if Smart Value tells you the stock costs more than it is worth. It is that simple. SmartValue has done its job. It has helped you find stocks that are bargains. And it has helped you avoid paying too much for stocks.

But buying low is only half the battle. Selling high is the other half. Suppose SmartValue tells you a stock is a buy. It is worth more than it costs. Acting on that analysis, you go ahead and buy the stock. What then? What do you do with a stock after you buy it? Do you hold it forever? We saw in Chapter 9 that "Buy-and-Hold" is not always a good strategy. Or do you hold it a while and then sell it? If you decide to hold it a while, how long should you hold it? How do you tell when it is time to sell? Books on investing are not very helpful when it comes to advice on when to sell. Simple rules of thumb, like "Sell when the stock drops ten percent" masquerade as sage investment advice. SmartValue can do better than that.

You will not know whether the stock was really a buy until after you finally sell. Then you know the results. You do not have to make any forecasts. All the numbers are in. You know what you paid for the stock. You know what you sold it for. And you know the dividends you collected while you held the stock. Then it is easy to tell if you earned more from the stock than the stock cost. You used SmartValue to make an intelligent buy decision. Now how do you use SmartValue to decide when it is the right time to sell? SmartValue provides a rational way to tell when it is time to sell.

A Rational Selling Strategy

You are perfectly free to call your broker at any time and order him to sell your stock. If you do so, a bundle of money will tumble into your pocket. You will receive the market price of the stock at the time you sell, less your broker's commission. And you will have to pay a capital gains tax to the federal and state governments. Now look at what happens if you do not call your broker. Every day you do not sell, you forego the use of the money you could have had in your hand if you had sold. What do you get in return for foregoing that money? You will continue to receive dividends. And you will continue to enjoy any rise in the price of the stock. You are, in effect, investing the money you could have had in your hand in order to continue enjoying the gains from owning the stock.

Should you sell the stock or keep it and forego the use of that money? Easy question. That is Economics 101. All you have to do is compare the gain from continuing to hold the stock with the money you forego by not selling. If you expect to receive more money from continuing to hold the stock than you would forego, do not sell. Hold on to the stock. Continue collecting dividends and watch the price of the stock go up. But if you forego more money by not selling now than you expect to receive by continuing to hold the stock, then sell. You will, of course, have to discount the money you expect to receive by continuing to hold the stock because that money does not roll into your pocket now. It rolls into your pocket in the future.

SmartValue formulas are flexible. You can use the same analysis you used to buy the stock to tell you when you should sell it. After all, what did the worksheets we used to find what a stock was worth tell us? The worksheets told us the discounted value of the money that rolls into your pocket from holding the stock for a given period of time. That is one part of the sell now/continue to hold decision. That is the dollar incentive for continuing to hold the stock.

When should you test whether now is the time to sell? Certainly you should test whenever there is a significant development you think will affect the firm's future. Any significant development will affect your forecast of the return the firm will earn, how fast it will grow, and the P/B ratio investors will pay. Even if there is no significant development, decide whether to sell or hold on to the stock each time the firm reports its quarterly results. Quarterly reports are important. They give you one more piece of information to add to the analysis you made when you originally bought the stock. That is when you can tell whether the firm is tracking the forecasts you made. If the firm is diverging from your forecast, it is time to revise your forecast.

How much longer should you consider holding the stock? You can choose any holding period, at least in theory. But there is a practical problem The analysis requires forecasting how the stock's price will change over the period. Forecasting price changes over extremely short periods, such as from one day to the next, is near impossible. Forecasting price changes is more reasonable over longer periods. One year is a good compromise. Look at the firm's results each quarter and ask yourself, "Should I sell now, or keep this stock one more year?" If the stock still looks promising, ask the same question when the next quarterly report comes out. That way you can make an intelligent sell or hold decision quarter by quarter, and continue holding the stock until SmartValue tells you it is time to sell.

Why would you sell? The primary reason is that you expect a downturn in the firm's business, which will be reflected by a downturn in the price of the stock. You want to get out before that happens. Perhaps investor euphoria has driven the stock's price above what SmartValue tells you the stock is worth. You expect that investors will eventually realize their mistake, and the stock will gradually drift back to what it is really worth. You want to sell before that happens. Or perhaps you have hit a streak of luck. Perhaps some other firm is trying to acquire your firm. That is often a bonanza for stockholders of the firm being acquired. Why? Because the acquiring firm often pays too much for the firm it acquires. If some other firm is trying to acquire the firm you own congratulate yourself. Then take the money and run. The shareholders of the acquired firm are the winners. The shareholders of the acquiring firm are the losers. They have acquired an asset for which they have paid too much.

Why would you hold on to a stock? The primary reason is that the firm is performing as well or better than you had projected. It is growing. It is profitable. Other investors recognize that performance and are bidding up the price of the stock. You want to hold on to the stock so you can enjoy the rise in its price.

The Sell-Or-Hold Decision

Deciding whether to sell a stock or hold on to it is a straightforward decision. The first step is to find how much money you forego by holding on to the stock instead of selling it now. The second step is to forecast how much money will roll into your pocket if you hold the stock for another year, and then sell. That forecast involves future dollars. Discount those dollars to find what they are worth today. Then compare what you expect to gain by holding on to the stock with the money you forego by not selling now. If you expect to gain more money than you forego, hold on to the stock one more year. If you expect to forego more money than you expect to gain by holding on to the stock, sell it now.

How Much Money Do You Forego?

Figuring the money you forego is easy. You know the current market price of the stock. You know your broker's commission. You know what you originally paid for the stock. That means you know your capital gains and the capital gains tax you will have to pay if you sell now. Subtract the tax from the proceeds you would receive if you sold. That is it. That is the money you forego by not selling now. You do not even have to bother with discounting. That is because the money you get if you sell the stock now rolls into your pocket immediately.

Forecasting the Gains From Holding the Stock

Figure your gains from holding on to the stock for a short holding period like one year. Using a short holding period has an important advantage. Over that short a period, even growth stocks are likely to perform at steady-state conditions. Estimating the gain from continuing to hold the stock is easier when steady-state conditions apply. You can, of course, use the worksheet for the Half-Life Decay Model or the Unlimited Flexibility Model for finding what the stock is worth if you decide that a steady-state model is not appropriate for your particular stock.

How much money will tumble into your pocket if you hold the stock another year? The biggest chunk of that money is the net proceeds when you sell one year from now. The net proceeds depends on what the price of the stock will be one year from now, the capital gains tax you will have to pay, and your broker's commission. We will use the SmartValue formula to forecast the price of the stock. That will require forecasting the growth rate so we can find equity per share one year from now. You will also have to forecast the P/B ratio so you can translate that future equity into the future stock price.

The P/B ratio is the critical forecast. That is where most of the error in the analysis comes from. How should you forecast the P/B ratio? There are a number of things to consider. Where is the ratio now compared to the historical average over the past few years? If the P/B ratio is high relative to the historical average, you should ask why it is high, and what is keeping it high. You might want to forecast that the ratio will begin moving back towards that historical average. Or the ratio might be low relative to the historical average. Ask why the ratio is low. You might want to forecast that the ratio might begin recovering back towards that historical average.

Interest rates are important, too. Remember that the general level of interest rates is one of the primary elements investors use to determine the minimum return they will insist on. What is the outlook for interest rates? If you expect interest rates to go up, investors will recognize that they can get higher returns from other investments. They will insist on a higher return from stocks, and they will discount future gains from stocks more heavily. That will make all stocks less valuable, and the P/B ratio fall. If you expect interest rates to come down, that means investors will recognize their returns from other investments will also be lower. They will accept lower returns from stocks, and will discount future gains less heavily. That will make all stocks and the P/B ratio go up. The outlook for the firm is also important, but that outlook is already reflected in the current P/B ratio. It is **changes** in the outlook that affect the P/B ratio. If you foresee any significant changes, take them into account.

Do not worry as much about dividends. Dividends are less important. They will not amount to much over a period as short as one year. They will be certainly be small relative to the net proceeds when you sell. And dividends are more predictable than the stock price one year from now. Dividends tend to stay the same from one quarter to the next quarter. Once each year management normally decides whether to increase the dividend. You can tell from the past pattern of dividend payments when dividends are likely to increase. You might forecast that dividends will grow in line with the growth you forecast for equity per share.

The analysis you made when you decided to buy the stock will also be useful in deciding when to sell. When you were thinking about buying the stock, you looked up the firm in Value Line. You sent for the firm's annual report. You analyzed the firm's performance as we did for Coca Cola, Cisco Systems, and Microsoft in earlier chapters. You plotted the adjusted return the firm earned on stockholder equity. You plotted how equity per share grew. And you plotted the P/B ratio investors were willing to pay for the stock. As a serious investor, you have not been idle in the meantime. Each time the firm issued a quarterly report you added the new data to your plots. New data are always useful. They help you see whether the firm is still on track. Is it following the forecasts you originally made when you decided to buy the stock? If actual performance is beginning to diverge from your original forecast, the new data gives you a basis for revising your forecasts.

Should You Sell or Continue Holding the Stock?

We now have a clear strategy for deciding whether to sell a stock or keep it another year. Table 17-1 is the worksheet that simplifies the analysis. Section I details the investor's financial situation. It is identical to Section I in previous worksheets for finding what stocks are worth. Use a short holding period like one year in line 1 so that you can use the steady-state model later in the worksheet.

Section II is a key part of the analysis. It develops the money you forego by not selling the stock now. The only information Section II requires is the current price of the stock, and what you originally paid for the stock when you bought it. You need the original cost to figure your capital gains tax. Be sure to include broker's commissions in the original cost. Line 9 works out your capital gains tax. Line 10 tells you how much money you forego by not selling now.

Section III works out the amount of money that will tumble into your pocket if you hold the stock one more year. Start with the current equity per share in line 11. If that value is out of date by several months, use Table 7-7 to estimate the current value. Divide your forecast of next year's growth rate of equity per share by 100 in line 12 to put the growth rate in decimal form. Find the growth multiplier that corresponds to your growth forecast in line 13. Your forecast of the P/B ratio one year from now goes in line 14. Use it to forecast the price of the stock one year from now in line 15. Lines 16 and 17 work out your capital gains tax when you sell one year from now. The net proceeds that roll into your pocket when you sell one year from now is worked out in line 18.

The money that will roll into your pocket if you hold the stock rolls in during the coming year. Section IV discounts that money to find what it is worth today. Line 21 develops the discount factor that applies to the sale one year from now. Line 22 develops the discount factor for the dividends that roll in during the year. These discount factors find what the proceeds from the sale one year from now are worth today in line 23, and what dividends are worth in line 24. What is the total gain from holding the stock for one more year after discounting? That is what line 25 shows.

How do you tell whether to sell now, or to hold the stock one more year? Compare the total gain for holding one more year in line 25 with the money you forego by not selling now in line 18. If line 18 is greater than line 25, you forego more money by not selling now than you gain from holding the stock another year. That is the signal to sell now. But if line 25 is greater than line 18, you will gain more by holding the stock one more year than you forego by not selling now. That is the signal to hold on to the stock for one more year.

Table 17-1
SELL NOW OR CONTINUE HOLDING

Section I - The Investor

1. Holding Period, years .... _____
2. Divide Incremental Tax Rate on Ordinary Income (%)
     by 100; Subtract the Result from 1.0 .... _____
3. Divide Capital Gains Tax Rate (%) by 100 .... _____
4. Divide Minimum Acceptable Return (%) by 100 .... _____
5. Divide Broker's Commission (%) by 100;
     Add the Result to 1.0 .... _____
6. Divide Broker's Commission (%) by 100;
     Subtract the Result from 1.0 .... _____

Section II - Money Foregone By Not Selling

7. Current Stock Price, $/Share .... _____
8. Original Cost, $/Share .... _____
9. Capital Gain: Multiply Line 6 by line 7,
     then Subtract Line 8 .... _____
10. Capital Gains Tax: Multiply Line 9 by Line 3 .... _____
11. Money Foregone: Multiply Line 6 by Line 7.
     Then Subtract Line 9 from the result .... _____

Table 17-1 (Cont'd)
SELL NOW OR CONTINUE HOLDING

Section III - Gain From Keeping Stock

12. Current equity, $/Share .... _____
13. Divide growth of equity per share (%/yr.) by 100 .... _____
14. Growth Multiplier: Multiply Line 1 by Line 13.
    Enter the result into your calculator and tap the e^x key . _____
15. Forecast of P/B ratio .... _____
16. Future Stock price: Multiply Line 12
    by Lines 14 and 15 .... _____
17. Capital Gain: Multiply Line 6 by Line 16.
    Subtract Line 8 from the result .... _____
18. Capital Gains Tax: Multiply Line 3 by Line 17 .... _____
19. Net Proceeds: Multiply Line 6 by Line 16.
    Subtract Line 18 from the result .... _____
20. Dividend Forecast, $/Share .... _____

Section IV - Discounting

21. Multiply Line 1 by Line 4 .... _____
22. Discount Factor 1: Enter Line 21 into your calculator,
    tap the change sign (+/-) key, then the e^x key .... _____
23. Discount Factor 2: Subtract Line 22 from 1.0.
    Divide the result by Line 21 .... _____
24. Discounted Net Proceeds: Multiply Line 19 by Line 22 . _____
25. Discounted Dividends: Multiply Line 2
    by Lines 20 and 23 .... _____
26. Discounted Gain from Keeping Stock:
    Add Lines 24 and 25 .... _____

Coca-Cola Example

Back in Chapter 8 we used SmartValue to find whether our investor should buy Coca-Cola. This time, let's assume that our investor already owns Coca-Cola. He bought it some time ago, and paid $30 per share, including his broker's commission. Now he wonders whether he should sell it now or hold on to it for one more year. He makes the same analysis he did in Chapter 7, only this time he is making a sell or hold decision, not a buy or not buy decision.

In Chapter 7 our investor found that Coca-Cola's equity per share grew at an average rate of 12.1 percent per year from 1992 through 1996. He forecast that equity per share would grow 12 percent per year in the future.

He also found that investors had bid Coca-Cola's P/B ratio up from 4 in the mid 1980's to 24 in late 1997. That worries him. A P/B ratio of 24 is extraordinarily high for a mature firm like Coca-Cola. He does not believe that investors will continue to pay such a high P/B ratio for such a mature firm. He forecasts that the P/B ratio will drop to perhaps 19 one year from now.

Coca-Cola's last annual report listed equity at $2.50 per share. In Chapter 7 our investor allowed for the growth that had taken place since that report was issued, and estimated that equity per share is currently closer to $2.79 per share.

That is the basic information our investor needs to decide whether to sell his Coca-Cola shares now, or to hold on to them for another year. He fills out the Sell or Hold worksheet; Table 17-2 shows his calculations. His financial situation is the same as described in Chapter 7, so that, except for the time horizon, Section I of the worksheet is identical to Section I of the worksheet he used in Chapter 8 to find what Coca-Cola was worth. For the sell or hold decision he changes his time horizon to one year. He continues to require a minimum return of 10.3 percent, the same minimum return he required in Chapter 9.

In Section II he enters the current market price of $64 per share in line 7 and his original cost of $30 per share in line 8. If he sells now, line 10 shows he will have to pay a capital gains tax of $8.27 per share. The money he foregoes by not selling now is $55.09 per share — the current market price less the capital gains tax and his broker's commission.

Will he gain enough by holding on to the stock another year to justify foregoing $55.09 if he does not sell now? Section III works out the gains for holding the stock one more year. Our investor enters his $2.79 estimate of the current equity per share in line 12 and his forecast of 12 percent growth in line 13. That forecast leads to a growth multiplier of 1.1275 in line 14. His forecast of a 19 P/B ratio one year from now goes in line 15. The current equity per share, together with the growth and P/B ratio forecasts lead to a stock price of $59.77 one year from now in line 16. Line 18 shows that he will have to pay a capital gains tax of $7.23. That tax and his broker's commission will leave him with net proceeds of $51.94 per share in line 19 if he sells one year from now. He examines Coca-Cola's pattern of quarterly dividend payments and concludes that he is likely to receive $0.50 in dividends in the coming year. He enters that forecast in line 20.

The money he expects to receive has to be discounted to find what it is worth today. That's what Section IV of the worksheet does. Line 22 develops the discount factor that applies to his net proceeds when he sells a year from now; line 23 develops the discount factor that applies to the dividends he expects during the coming year. Lines 24 and 25 discount the net proceeds and the dividends. The total of what he expects to receive if he holds the stock another year is worth $47.18 today, as line 26 shows.

Should he sell now, or hold on to his stock for another year? It is Economics 101 again. You do not have to be a rocket scientist to know that it does not make sense to pass up $55.09 now in order to achieve gains worth only $47.18. Our investor is better off selling now than holding his stock for another year.

What About the Holding Period?

You might wonder whether the decision to sell Coca Cola now was not due primarily to choosing one year as the holding period. Suppose our investor had chosen two years. Or three. Or four. That would have allowed those Coca Cola shares more time to grow in price. Dividends would have been higher, too. Wouldn't that change the decision? It is true that the steady-state model would lead to higher stock prices as time went on. But our investor would have received the proceeds from the eventual sale further out in time. That means those proceeds would have been discounted more heavily. It turns out that extending the holding period a few more years makes little difference in the result. The answer still is to sell those shares now.

What if extending the holding period from one year to two years does change the answer from sell now to hold on? That would imply a poor return in the first year which was more than offset by a better return in the second year. It would still be better to sell now and avoid the first year's poor return, then buy back next year and enjoy the second year's better return.

Table 17-2

SELL COCA-COLA NOW OR CONTINUE HOLDING?

Section I - The Investor

1. Holding Period, years 1
2. Divide Incremental Tax Rate on Ordinary Income (%)
   by 100; Subtract the Result from 1.0 .... 0.6768
3. Divide Capital Gains Tax Rate (%) by 100 .... 0.248
4. Divide Minimum Acceptable Return (%) by 100 .... 0.103
5. Divide Broker's Commission (%) by 100;
   Add the Result to 1.0 .... 1.01
6. Divide Broker's Commission (%) by 100;
   Subtract the Result from 1.0 .... 0.99

Section II - Money Foregone By Not Selling

7. Current Stock Price, $/Share 64
8. Original Cost, $/Share 30
9. Capital Gain: Multiply Line 6 by line 7,
   then Subtract Line 8 .... 33.36
10. Capital Gains Tax: Multiply Line 9 by Line 3 .... 8.27
11. Money Foregone: Multiply Line 6 by Line 7.
    Then Subtract Line 10 from the result 55.09

Table 17-2 (Cont'd)
SELL COCA-COLA NOW OR CONTINUE HOLDING?

Section III - Gain From Keeping Stock

12. Current equity, $/Share	2.79
13. Divide growth of equity per share (%/yr.) by 100	0.12
14. Growth Multiplier: Multiply Line 1 by Line 13. Enter the result into your calculator and tap the e^x key	1.1275
15. Forecast of P/B ratio	19
16. Future Stock price: Multiply Line 12 by Lines 14 and 15	59.77
17. Capital Gain: Multiply Line 6 by Line 16. Subtract Line 8 from the result	29.17
18. Capital Gains Tax: Multiply Line 3 by Line 17	7.23
19. Net Proceeds: Multiply Line 6 by Line 16. Subtract Line 18 from the result	51.94
20. Dividend Forecast, $/Share	0.50

Section IV - Discounting

21. Multiply Line 1 by Line 4	0.103
22. Discount Factor 1: Enter Line 21 into your calculator, tap the change sign (+/-) key, then the e^x key	0.9021
23. Discount Factor 2: Subtract Line 22 from 1.0. Divide the result by Line 21	0.9505
24. Discounted Net Proceeds: Multiply Line 19 by Line 22	46.86
25. Discounted Dividends: Multiply Line 2 by Lines 20 and 23	0.32
26. Discounted Gain from Keeping Stock: Add Lines 24 and 25	47.18

Risk

The forecast of next year's P/B ratio strongly influences the sell or hold decision. That means that errors in forecasting the P/B ratio are important. They could easily change the answer from sell now to hold on, and vice versa. That makes the analysis uncertain. How do you make a sell or hold decision when the result is so sensitive to the P/B forecast? The best way is to tackle the uncertainty in the P/B forecast directly, and allow for risk by the Monte Carlo method detailed in the next chapter.

SUMMARY

An intelligent decision to buy a stock is only half the battle. Making an intelligent decision on when to sell that stock is the other half. If you sell the stock now, you receive the market price less your broker's commission and capital gains taxes. If you hold on to the stock instead of selling now, you forego the use of that money. In return for foregoing that money, you continue to receive dividends and enjoy any price increases in the stock. Whether you should sell now or hold on depends on whether the money you receive from holding on is greater than the money you forego by not selling now. A worksheet simplifies the analysis.

Chapter 18

Risk

The Monte Carlo Method

Probability

Choosing Random Values

**Generating a Random Sample of
   Stock Values**

An Example - Cisco Systems

Tailoring to Your Tolerance for Risk

Summary

Stocks are risky. Why? Because you have to forecast how the firm will perform in the future when you invest in a stock. And forecasts are uncertain. They may be reasonable, but they are still uncertain. They are bound to be wrong. That is where risk originates. It grows from forecasting errors. Investing would be easy if the firm performed exactly as you had forecast. But the firm will not perform exactly that way. It may not do as well as you forecast. It might even do better. It might follow your return on equity forecast reasonably well, but not your forecast of the P/B ratio. But it will not follow any of your forecasts exactly. That is what makes investing in stocks risky. Inaccurate forecasts. That means your estimate of what the stock is worth is not 100 percent accurate, either. It is, after all, only an estimate. A reasonable estimate, to be sure. A useful estimate. But still an estimate. The firm may not be worth what you calculate. It might even be worth more.

Investing in a stock is not like investing in a bond or a certificate of deposit. If you buy a bond or a CD, you know exactly what the interest payments will be. You know when the bond or the CD will mature. You know how much you will be repaid when the bond or CD matures. Stocks are not like that. You do not know the return the firm will earn. You do not know how fast it will grow. You do not know what dividends the stock will pay. And you do not know what the price of the stock will be when it comes time to sell. Sure, you make forecasts you believe are reasonable. But you do not know for sure. And that is why stocks are risky.

The easy way to allow for risk is to add a risk premium to the minimum rate of return you insist on. Adding a risk premium raises the rate at which you discount the future cash you hope a stock will put in your pocket. The higher the risk premium, the more heavily you discount. And the more heavily you discount, the lower the value you place on any stock. That is what the risk premium does. It adjusts the most you should pay for any stock to stay within your tolerance for risk. The higher the risk, the less you should be willing to pay. That is how the risk premium reduces your risk of paying too much for a stock.

That is how the investor we followed in Chapter 5 allowed for risk. He judged that the money he was investing cost 9.3 percent — the return he could have earned from Vanguard's S&P 500 Index Fund. Then he added a risk premium. The risk premium depended on his tolerance for risk, and on just how risky he judged an individual stock to be. The total of what his money cost and the risk premium set the minimum rate of return he insisted on for any investment. That was the discount rate SmartValue used to discount the money he expected that stock to deliver in the future.

You can set your minimum acceptable return the same way. How much risk can you tolerate? Does risk upset you? Make it harder to sleep at night? If it does, choose a high risk premium. Is the stock risky? If it is, make the risk premium even higher. The higher the risk premium, the more heavily you discount, and the lower the price you will be willing to pay for any stock.

Setting the "right" risk premium is not easy. It is a matter of judgment. Seat-of-the-pants judgement. It depends on how much risk you are willing to accept. It depends on how risky you judge a particular stock to be. But you have to be careful when you set a risk premium. Set the premium too low and you run too high a risk of paying too much for stocks. Set the premium too high and you rule out too many stocks. You then have too small a pool of stocks to choose from. Set the premium high enough and no stocks will meet your high return standard.

Remember that you compete with all other investors. One of the dimensions of that competition is the risk premium each investor insists on. The investor willing to accept the lowest risk premium discounts the cash that stock will generate the least. He places the highest value on the stock. He is the likely buyer, and sets the price of the stock.

The Monte Carlo Method

Using a risk premium is the easy way out. But there is a better way. The better way is to tackle the uncertainty in your forecasts head-on. That is what the Monte Carlo method does. It tackles risk directly. The basic idea is to generate a random sample of possible values for a stock. Then examine that sample. The average of all the stock values in the random sample gives you the best estimate of what the stock is really worth. The range of values in the sample tells you something about how low and how high the stock's value might actually be.

That is a key step in the Monte Carlo method — thinking of your forecast as a range of possible values instead of as a single specific value. Think of your forecast as a range of possible values, such as the forecast in Figure 18-1. This kind of plot is called a probability distribution. The horizontal scale shows a range of possible returns extending from a low of zero percent return to a high of 35 percent return. The vertical scale shows the relative likelihood of actually achieving any return in this range. In this example, an investor has forecast that the most likely return is 20 percent — that is where the distribution curve peaks. That is where the likelihood is the greatest. Returns near 20 percent, say, from 18 to 22 percent, are near the peak of the curve. They are less likely to happen than the value at the peak, but they still have a good chance of happening. Returns further from the 20 percent peak, say 15 percent on the low side or 25 percent on the high side, are about halfway down from the peak of the curve. They are about half as likely, but they

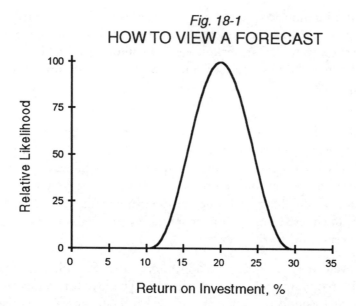

Fig. 18-1
HOW TO VIEW A FORECAST

still could happen. Returns much lower or much higher than the 20 percent peak, such as a return of 10 percent on the low side or 30 percent on the high side, are very unlikely. The distribution curve has dropped to a likelihood of nearly zero at those extreme returns.

That is the way to think of your forecasts. Think of them as probability distributions like the one in Figure 18-1, and not as a forecast of a single return. That is the way to recognize the source of risk in your evaluation. Recognize that the actual outcome may well turn out different than the outcome you had forecast. Different, but, hopefully, still somewhere near your forecast of the most-likely outcome.

The Monte Carlo approach is straightforward:

1. Estimate the likely range of values you expect for key factors like the rate of return the you expect the firm to earn, how fast you expect it to grow, and the P/B ratio you expect investors will pay for its stock. Estimate the most-likely values, then estimate the range in which you think the actual outcome might lie.

2. Forecast the firm's future by choosing at random a forecast for each key factor from within the range of possible values developed in Step 1. The set of forecasts chosen this way represents one possible forecast of the firm's future.

3. Feed the forecasts developed in Step 2 into the appropriate SmartValue worksheet and find what the stock is worth. The value you calculate is one possible value for the stock.

4. Repeat this process a number of times. Each time you repeat this process you generate another possible value for the stock. By repeating this process a number of times, you generate a random sample of possible values for the stock.

5. Analyze the random sample of possible stock values. The average of all the stock values in the sample is the best estimate of what the stock is really worth. The proportion of values that lie in any given range tells you the probability that the stock's actual value lies in that range.

Ideally, Monte Carlo studies are done on a computer, where you can easily generate random samples of possible stock values by the thousand. That is great if you have a computer and the appropriate software. But you do not need a computer. You can do it by hand. Not a thousand random outcomes, of course. But you do not need a thousand outcomes. You can learn a lot about risk by working out just a few random stock values.

Probability

Each key factor is not going to turn out to have the precise value you forecast. That means you have to change the way you think about your forecast. Suppose you forecast that a firm will earn a 20 percent return on equity. That does not mean you really expect the firm will earn exactly a 20 percent return and no other. Not even a 19.9 percent return; not even a 20.1 percent return. Rather, you expect the firm will earn a return somewhere in the neighborhood of 20 percent. It could be lower than 20 percent. It could be higher. But it will lie in some range around the 20 percent you forecast as the most-likely return.

Establishing A Probability Distribution

Estimating the range of values each key factor might have and the likelihood of each possible value, such as the curve in Figure 18-1, is easier than you might think. You obviously have to forecast the most-likely value you expect each factor might have. You have to make that forecast in any case. You can define the whole distribution curve by making just two additional estimates. One estimate is how low you think the actual outcome might be. The second estimate is how high you think that outcome might be. These three estimates — the low, the most likely, and the high outcomes — give Smart-

Value all the information it needs to define the complete probability distribution. Those three estimates tell SmartValue just how likely any value of that factor might be. And SmartValue knows that any value chosen at random is more likely to be nearer your most-likely estimate than either the low or the high end of the range.

Do not try to estimate the absolute low or the absolute high value for any factor. Those extreme values are hard to estimate. It is easier to come in a way from the extremes of the possible range of values. Instead of trying to estimate the absolute low, estimate a low value such that you judge there is only a five percent chance — one chance in twenty — that the actual value might be even lower. Choose the high value the same way. Choose a value you judge has only a five percent chance of being exceeded. SmartValue can tell from those estimates what the extreme low value is and what the extreme high value is.

> **Just three estimates — the most-likely value, and how low and how high that value might be — are enough to establish a probability distribution completely.**

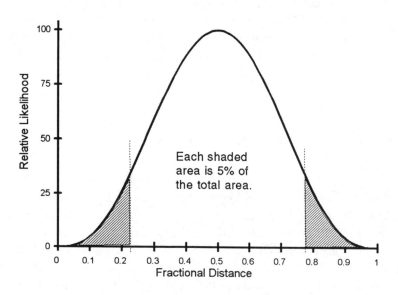

Fig. 18-2
CHOOSING LOW AND HIGH VALUES

How Likely Is Any Value?

How do you find the probability that a key factor like return on equity will fall within any given range? The probability that a factor will lie in any given range depends on the area under the distribution curve, as shown in Figure 18-2. This plot is just like Figure 18-1, except that the horizontal scale has been generalized to make it fit any factor. The horizontal scale now measures the factor's value as a fraction of the distance from the factor's extreme low value to that factor's extreme high value. The fractional distance begins at zero at the extreme low value and increases to 1.0 at the extreme high value. It the distribution were symmetrical, for example, the most likely value would be at the midpoint of the distribution, and would have a fractional distance of 0.5. The factor's value would be halfway between the extreme low value and the extreme high value.

The total area under the curve represents 100 percent probability — it is certain that the factor will turn out to be somewhere between the extreme low value and the extreme high value. What about the probability that the factor will lie within any given range? The percentage of the total area that lies within that range measures that probability. For example, the shaded area under the curve and to the left of the left-most dashed vertical line in Figure 18-2 is five percent of the total area. That means there is only a five percent chance that the actual value will be lower than that dashed line. That dashed line is where you should make your low estimate. In the same way, the shaded area under the curve and to the right of the right-most dashed vertical line is five percent of the total area. There is only a five percent chance that the actual value will be higher than that dashed line. That is where you should make your high estimate. Estimating the low and high values at the five percent probability levels lets you control the shape of the distribution curve

Symmetry

The distribution curves in Figures 18-1 and 18-2 are symmetrical. That part of the curve above the peak value is a mirror image of the part below the peak. That makes the area under the curve above the peak value the same as the area below the peak. It is just as likely that the actual value will turn out to be higher than your most-likely forecast than lower. But you may not always want symmetrical distributions. That is particularly true with hot growth stocks. You may not think there is much chance a growth stock will grow much faster than the torrid pace it is growing now. It is much more likely that growth will turn out to be slower than you had forecast. You need a distribution that assigns a higher probability to slower growth than to faster growth. You need an asymmetrical distribution to reflect that kind of forecast.

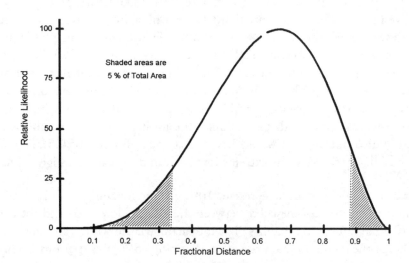

Fig. 18-3
ASYMMETRICAL DISTRIBUTION

That is easy with SmartValue. Your forecast does not have to be symmetrical. The low estimate does not have to be the same distance from the most-likely estimate as the high estimate. Suppose you think a low outcome is more likely. Simply forecast a wider range of possible values below the most likely estimate and a narrower range above. Figure 18-3 shows an asymmetric distribution. This forecaster has judged that low outcomes are more likely than high outcomes. He therefore made his low estimate well below the most-likely forecast. At the same time, he made his high estimate only a little higher than the most-likely forecast. That puts more of the area under the curve, and therefore more of the probability, below the most-likely forecast at the peak of the curve.

SmartValue needs an index to describe how asymmetrical any distribution is. That is what the asymmetry ratio does. It measures how asymmetrical your forecast is. The ratio is simply the distance above your most-likely forecast divided by the distance below:

Asymmetry Ratio = (High Estimate - Most Likely)/(Most Likely - Low Estimate)

Suppose you forecast that a firm is most likely to earn a return on equity of 20 percent. You believe that lower returns are more likely than higher returns. You therefore forecast a five percent chance the return might be as low as 15 percent, or 5 percentage points below your most-likely forecast. But you also forecast a five percent chance the return might only be as high as 22 percent, or 2 percentage points higher than your most-likely forecast. Your forecast has an asymmetry ratio of 0.4:

$$\text{Asymmetry Ratio} = (22 - 20)/(20 - 15) = 2/5 = 0.4$$

A symmetrical forecast has the same area above the most-likely forecast as below. It has an asymmetry ratio of 1.0. A forecast like Figure 18-3 has a greater likelihood of low than of high outcomes. More of its area lies below the most-likely forecast than above. That makes the asymmetry ratio somewhere between zero and one. A forecast with a greater likelihood of high outcomes would have an asymmetry ratio greater than one.

Choosing Random Values

Probability distributions are a key element in the Monte Carlo method. They are the tool you use to generate random values for any factor. They insure that the random values you generate conform to your expectations of how likely various outcomes are.

Begin risk analysis by examining all the forecasts you must make to find what a stock is worth. Which forecasts are the critical ones? Which of those are the most uncertain? Those are the forecasts you need to develop probability distributions for. Those are the factors you need to generate random values for. Keep the process simple. Don't bother making probability distributions for factors that are less important, or that you can forecast with reasonable certainty. Just forecast those factors at their most-likely values.

After you have decided which factors are the most important and the most uncertain, the next step is to develop probability distributions for those factors, then use those probability distributions to choose random values for those factors. Although you will choose those values randomly, they must conform to the shape of the distribution. There must be a greater likelihood of choosing a value near the most-likely forecast than of choosing a value near either extreme.

Distribution curves like those in Figures 18-1 through 18-3 are ideal for picturing the probability of various possible outcomes. But they are not very useful as working tools. That is because it is difficult to read areas, and therefore probabilities, from these plots. We need instead a plot that is graduated directly in probability. Choosing random values will be much easier if we replot the distribution in Figure 18-2. Begin at the extreme low end of Figure 18-2. Measure the area under the curve as a percentage of the total area at a number of points as you proceed from zero percent of the area at the extreme low end of the distribution (a fractional distance of zero) to 100 percent of the area at the extreme high end (a fractional distance of 1.0). Then plot the percentage of the total area

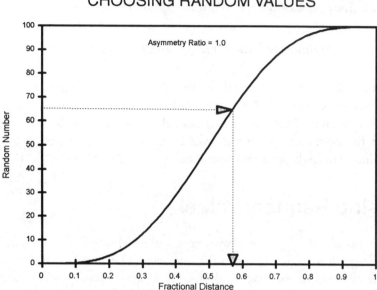

Fig. 18-4
CHOOSING RANDOM VALUES

against the fractional distance. Figure 18-4 is the resulting plot; it shows how the cumulative area under the distribution curve increases as you move from that factor's extreme low value towards its extreme high value. The vertical scale begins with zero percent of the total area, or zero probability, at the factor's extreme low value and gradually increases to 100 percent of the total area, or 100 percent probability, as you move along the horizontal scale and approach that factor's extreme high value.

How do you pick a random value for any factor whose distribution you have established? Figure 18-4 makes choosing random values easy. Pick a number at random from zero to 100. Suppose you happen to pick 65 as the random number. Enter 65 on the vertical scale of Figure 18-4 and read across horizontally to the distribution curve. When you reach the curve, read down vertically to find the fractional distance for that factor. In the example shown in Figure 18-4 a random number of 65 leads to a random value for the key factor 57 percent of the way from the extreme low to the extreme high value for that factor. Don't worry about the details. A worksheet will make the process easy.

Where do you find random numbers? Appendix Table A1 lists a thousand of them. They range from a low of zero to a high of 100. When you use the Monte Carlo method, decide on how many random outcomes you plan to develop, and on how many key factors you need to develop probability distributions for. Suppose you decide to compute five random values for a stock, and there are four factors important enough and uncertain enough to deserve probability distributions. Picking four sets of five random values each will require 4 times 5, or 20 random numbers. Enter the table of random numbers at any location, and read off 20 consecutive numbers. Then use those numbers to generate random values for each key factor.

The shape of the curve in Figure 18-4 is worth a little study. The middle 70 percent of the probability range is nearly a straight line, which covers only about 35 percent of the possible range of values for the factor. That means that 70 percent of the random values you choose will lie in a relatively narrow band centered on the most-likely forecast and will include only about 35 percent of the possible range of values. What about extreme values? They lie near the top and the bottom of the plot. You are likely to pick a high random value only about 15 percent of the time. That is because only the upper 15 percent of the vertical scale leads to high random values for the factor. In the same way, there is only about a 15 percent chance of picking a low random value.

Random Value Worksheet

So much for the basic idea of how to choose random values. Let's get down to cases. Suppose you want to do a risk analysis. You have identified a key factor that is uncertain. You have estimated the most-likely value for that factor, and how low and how high you think that value might actually be. Based on those estimates, how do you go about setting up a probability distribution for that factor and then using the distribution to choose random values for that factor?

The worksheet in Table 18-1 does the job. The worksheet begins with your estimates of the low, most-likely, and high values for any uncertain factor and develops the appropriate probability distribution from those estimates. You can then feed random numbers into that distribution and the worksheet will convert them into random values for the uncertain factor.

At certain points in the worksheet you are asked to pick a random value using the process illustrated in Figure 18-4. Appendix Table A2 simplifies that process. That is where to go to choose random values. Appendix Table A2 is simply Figure 18-4 recast as a table to make it easier to read. The table has also been extended to include a range of asymmetry ratios. The left-most column of Appendix Table A2 lists the value of an uncertain factor in terms of the fractional distance from the extreme low estimate of that factor (a fractional distance of zero) to the extreme high estimate (a fractional distance of 1.0). It corresponds to the horizontal scale of Figure 18-4. The body of the table contains a number of columns for asymmetry ratios ranging from zero to one in steps of a tenth. Each asymmetry ratio column corresponds to a distribution curve like the one in Figure 18-4. Each column shows the percentage of the area under the distribution curve from a factor's extreme low value up to the fractional distance shown in the left-most column.

When you need to choose a random number and use it to read a value from a probability distribution, here is what to do. Start with the first number on your list of random numbers. Then go to Appendix Table A2 and follow these simple instructions:

1. Go to the column with the asymmetry ratio closest to the ratio developed in line 7 of the worksheet.

2. Run your finger down that column until you come to the number closest to the random number you have chosen.

3. Read across horizontally to the fractional distance in the left-most column. Enter that fractional distance in line 14 of the worksheet and continue with the worksheet.

Appendix Table A2 only gives values for asymmetry ratios of 1.0 or less. What do you do if the asymmetry ratio is greater than 1.0? You can still use the table. But you need to make three adjustments:

1. Use the reciprocal of the asymmetry ratio (1.0 divided by the ratio). Suppose you have an asymmetry ratio of 2.5. The reciprocal is 1 divided by 2.5, or 0.4. Use the asymmetry ratio column headed "0.4". The worksheet will tell you when you need to use the reciprocal.

2. Subtract the random number you have picked from Appendix Table A1 from 100 before you enter Appendix Table A2. If you choose a random number of 75, for example, subtract 75 from 100 and look for a random number of 25 as you read down an asymmetry ratio column in Appendix Table A2.

3. Subtract the value you read for the fractional distance in the left-most column of Appendix Table A2 from 1.0, and use that difference in the worksheet in Table 18-1.

Suppose the asymmetry ratio is 1.4. The worksheet will tell you to take the reciprocal, which is 1 divided by 1.4, or 0.714. Round the reciprocal to 0.7, and use that column in Appendix Table A2. That takes care of Step 1. Suppose you choose 53.8 as a random number. Subtract 53.8 from 100 and use 46.2 as a new random number. That takes care of Step 2. Go down the column for an asymmetry ratio of 0.7 and look for the random number closest to 46.2. The closest random number is 47.1, which occurs at a fractional distance of 0.59. Subtract 0.59 from 1.0. That takes care of Step 3. Go back to the worksheet and use 1.0 minus 0.59, or 0.41 as the fractional distance.

Don't worry about asymmetry ratios above 1.0. When you analyze how risky stocks are, you will usually forecast that an actual outcome is more likely to fall below rather than above the most-likely forecast, which makes the asymmetry ratio less than 1.0. That means you will normally be able to read fractional distances directly from Appendix Table A2. You will not have to bother with taking reciprocals and subtracting random numbers from 100 and fractional distances from 1.0.

Back to the worksheet. The worksheet is divided into three sections. Section I works out the asymmetry ratio that corresponds to your low, most-likely, and high estimates. Section II develops the appropriate probability distribution. Section III uses that probability distribution to choose random values for the uncertain factor.

Section I - Asymmetry Ratio

Enter your estimates of the most-likely value and how low and how high you think the value might actually be in lines 1 through 3. Make your low and high estimates such that there is only a five percent chance they will be exceeded. Line 7 develops the asymmetry ratio. The asymmetry ratio must be 1.0 or less. If the ratio in line 6 is greater than 1.0 line 7 instructs you to take its reciprocal. If the ratio in line 6 is 1.0 or less, simply copy that ratio into line 7.

Section II - Probability Distribution

Go to the column in Appendix Table A2 that corresponds to the asymmetry ratio in line 7 and read a fractional distance using 95 as the "random" number in line 8. That establishes your high estimate at the 95 percent probability level, i.e., there is only a 5 percent chance of exceeding your high estimate. In the same way, read a fractional distance using 5 as the "random" number in line 9. That establishes your low estimate at the 5 percent probability level, i.e., there is only a 5 percent chance the actual value will be less than your low estimate. The rest of Section II develops information SmartValue needs to convert the fractional distances you read from Appendix Table A2 into actual values for the uncertain factor.

If the asymmetry ratio in line 7 is 1.0 or less, you are all set. But if the asymmetry ratio in line 6 is greater than 1.0, remember that you have to make some adjustments. You will have to subtract the 95 in line 8 from 100, and enter Appendix Table A2 at 100 minus 95, or 5. When you read the fractional distance from the table, you will have to subtract that reading from 1.0 and enter the result in line 8. Make the same adjustments in line 9.

Table 18-1

WORKSHEET FOR CHOOSING RANDOM VALUES

I. Asymmetry Ratio

1. Most-likely estimate .... _____
2. Low estimate (5% probability level) .... _____
3. High estimate (5% probability level) .... _____
4. Subtract line 1 from Line 3 .... _____
5. Subtract Line 2 from Line 1 .... _____
6. Divide Line 4 by Line 5 .... _____
7. Asymmetry Ratio: If Line 6 is greater than 1.0, Divide
   1.0 by Line 6. If Line 6 is less than 1.0, copy Line 6. .... _____

II. Probability Distribution

8. Use the ratio in Line 7 and read a fractional distance
   in Appendix Table A2 at a random number of 95* .... _____
9. Use the ratio in Line 7 and read a fractional distance
   in Appendix Table A2 at a random number of 5* .... _____
10. Subtract Line 2 from Line 3 .... _____
11. Subtract Line 9 from Line 8 .... _____
12. Divide Line 10 by Line 11 .... _____
13. Multiply Line 8 by Line 12.
    Subtract the result from Line 3 .... _____

* If line 6 is greater than 1.0, subtract the random number from 100 before using Appendix table A2, and subtract the fractional distance read from the table from 1.0.

Table 18-1 (Cont'd)
WORKSHEET FOR CHOOSING RANDOM VALUES

III Choosing Random Values

14. Enter a random number from Appendix Table A1 .... _____
15. Locate that random number in Appendix Table A2
    and read across to a fractional distance. .... _____
16. Multiply Line 12 by Line 15 .... _____
17. Random Value: Add Lines 13 and 16 .... _____

Section III - Choosing Random Values

Now you are ready to generate random values. Start at any location in Appendix Table A1 and read consecutively as many random numbers as you will need. Begin with the first random number on your list and enter it in line 14. Go to Appendix Table A2 and find the fractional distance that corresponds to that random number at the asymmetry ratio in line 7. Enter that fractional distance in line 15. Remember that you have to make some adjustments if the asymmetry ratio in line 6 is greater than 1.0. Lines 16 and 17 convert the fractional distance to the random value for that factor.

Once you have found the asymmetry ratio and set up the probability distribution in Sections I and II, generating more random values is easy. Simply enter the next random number in line 14 and repeat Section III. You do not have to redo Sections I and II until you move on to a new uncertain factor with different low, most-likely, and high estimates.

Some Practical Considerations

Picking random values is not a complicated process. It only looks that way. Here is how to streamline the process. You do not have to locate a random value precisely on the distribution curve. Getting reasonably close to the exact location on the curve is good enough. Keep the process simple. Suppose you calculate an asymmetry ratio of 0.4368 in the worksheet, for example. You do not need it that precise. Round it off to the nearest tenth. Round it to 0.4. Then you can read a number from the column for an asymmetry ratio of 0.4. You will not have to bother interpolating between the columns for asymmetry ratios of 0.4 and 0.5. Keep the random number entry simple, too. The random number you choose is not likely to correspond exactly to any entry in the asymmetry ratio column of Appendix Table A2. That is OK. Don't fret. Settle for the entry closest to the random number. Then read across to the fractional distance. That fractional distance will be more than adequate for risk analysis, even though it may differ slightly from the distance you would calculate from a more careful interpolation. Suppose you have rounded the asymmetry ratio to 0.4, and choose a random number of 37.6. That number does not appear in the column for an asymmetry ratio of 0.4. The nearest number is 37.2 at a fractional distance of 0.65. That number is good enough. Use it.

Parallel Movement

The random values you choose for the key factors are not likely to vary independently of one another. Suppose you choose a random return on equity that happens to fall well below your most-likely forecast. That means the firm will earn less and have less money to reinvest to make the firm grow. If the amount of money to reinvest is low, the firm's growth rate will be low as well. How do you think investors will react to a lower return and slower growth? They will be disappointed, of course. They will show their disappointment by lowering the P/B ratio they are willing to pay for the stock. What does this mean for risk analysis? It means that return on equity, growth rate, and the P/B ratio are all likely to move up and down together. They do not fluctuate independently. Their half lives, too, are likely to move up and down together.

There is an easy way to make these key factors move up and down together. Simply use the same random number to choose random values for each set of factors that move together. Each factor can have its own distribution curve. That is no problem. But use the same random number when you use Appendix Table A2. Suppose you are choosing a random return on equity and pick a random number of 86. That number is far down an asymmetry ratio column in Appendix Table A2. It will likely cause you to choose a random return above your most-likely forecast. Now use the same random number of 86 when you choose a random growth rate and a random P/B ratio. That will make the random values for those factors above their most-likely estimates as well. Using the same random number insures that all three factors move up and down together.

Generating a Random Value for a Stock

Examine all the forecasts you must make to find what a stock is worth. Identify the factors that are the most important and the most uncertain. The P/B ratio, the return on equity, and the growth rate are always important. If you are using a half life to describe how those factors decay with time, those half lives are important, too. Those are the factors you need to describe by probability distributions. You may know the other factors that determine a stock's value well enough, or they may not be important enough, to justify all that work. If you are fairly confident about your forecast of any factor, use the most-likely estimate as your forecast for that factor. Do not bother generating random values for those factors. The complete set of forecasts -- factors you have generated randomly and factors you have forecast at their most-likely values -- represent one possible forecast of the firm's future. The firm might actually perform that way.

What Discount Rate?

The next step is to feed that random forecast into the appropriate SmartValue worksheet and find what the stock is worth if the firm follows that forecast. What discount rate should you use to find what the stock is worth? One choice is to remove the risk premium from the minimum rate of return you insist on earning. Set the risk premium at zero. Discount only at the cost of the money you are investing. You are still allowing for risk. The possibility of random forecasts below your most-likely forecast allows for risk. The Monte Carlo analysis will then tell you your chance of losing money, i.e., of earning a return below the return you could have earned on the alternative investment.

You may not be comfortable removing the risk premium completely for a risky stock. You may want to insist on some return above the cost of the money you are investing. Go ahead and include a risk premium if it makes you feel more comfortable. The Monte Carlo analysis will then tell you your chance of earning a return below whatever minimum return you specify as being acceptable.

Generating a Random Sample

You now have a forecast of how the firm might perform. Enter that forecast into the appropriate SmartValue worksheet and find what the stock is worth if the firm follows that forecast. The value you find for the stock is just one possible estimate of what the stock is worth. You cannot tell much from a sample with just one outcome. You need a bigger sample. Getting a bigger sample is easy. Enter the next random number in the worksheet for random values and make a new random forecast. The process is easier now. Nothing in Sections I and II of the worksheet for random values has changed. You only need to rework lines 14 through 17 for each new random value. When you develop a new random forecast, enter that forecast in the stock valuation worksheet, and develop another possible value for the stock. The more random stock values you generate, the larger is your random sample, and the more reliable is your analysis. Try to generate at least five random stock values. They will tell you almost as much as a sample of several hundred random values.

A Practical Example - Cisco Systems

Doing risk analysis by the Monte Carlo method is easier than you might think. Let's go back to our investor who analyzed Cisco System's stock back in Chapter 14. We will follow him as he extends his study of Cisco to include risk analysis.

If Cisco reinvests all its earnings over the next five years and does not pay any dividends, our investor concluded in Chapter 14 that Cisco's stock was worth $59.14 per share. At that price, Cisco is a buy. But his estimate is valid only if Cisco performs exactly as he had forecast. He knows that Cisco is not going to perform exactly as he had forecast. He recognizes that his forecasts are only estimates. They are subject to error. What to do? He decides to use the Monte Carlo method to get a better feel for how risky an investment in Cisco's stock might be.

Principal Sources of Risk

Our investor recognizes that his most uncertain forecasts are how fast Cisco's return on equity, growth rate, and P/B ratio decay from their high current levels towards their lower long-run limits as Cisco matures. He used a half life to describe how fast this decay proceeds. Those half lives are the most uncertain factors in the analysis. They are the factors that need probability distributions. He decides to set up a probability distribution for each half life. He recognizes that if the return on equity decays faster than his most-likely forecast, the growth rate and the P/B ratio will decay faster, too. That means these half lives are linked — they will all fluctuate up and down together. Because they all fluctuate up and down together he can use a single random number to generate a random half life for each key factor. He still does not expect Cisco to pay any dividends during the five years he plans to hold the stock. That simplifies the analysis. With zero dividends he only has to worry about the half lives for the growth rate and the P/B ratio. The return on equity forecast will be identical to the growth rate forecast, which means that both will have identical half lives.

He decides against setting up distribution curves for the initial return on equity, growth rate, and P/B ratio. Their forecasts begin at the current levels of those factors; he believes he knows those values reasonably well. He is less certain about setting up distribution curves for the long-run limits of these factors. They are obviously less certain than the current values. But they are so far out in time that they have only a small influence on what happens during the five years he expects to hold the stock. After thinking it over, he decides to keep the analysis simple, and develop random values only for the half lives of the growth rate and the P/B ratio.

Those choices set the scale of the risk analysis. He will only have to develop two probability distributions — one for the half life of the growth rate, and one for the half life of the P/B ratio. Each random value he calculates for Cisco's stock will require only a single random number because the half lives are linked — they move up and down together.

Estimating the Range of Possible Half Lives

The greatest concern is how fast Cisco's growth rate and P/B ratio might decay from their current levels towards their long-run limits. Cisco's equity per share is growing about 50 percent per year, an extraordinary growth rate. In Chapter 14 our investor forecast that Cisco's growth would begin at 40 percent per year and decay towards a long-run limit of 7 percent per year with a five-year half life. A five-year half life means Cisco would still be growing 23.5 percent per year five years from now, and 15 percent per year ten years from now. He believes that shorter half lives are more likely than longer half lives. After some thought, he decides there is a five percent chance that the half life could be as short as two years, which is three years shorter than his most-likely estimate. But he makes his high estimate only two years longer than his most-likely estimate, or seven years.

Cisco's stock currently sells at an 11.9 P/B ratio. In Chapter 14 our investor forecast that the P/B ratio would gradually decay towards a long-run limit of 2.1 with a 3.5-year half life. He made the half life for the P/B ratio only 70 percent of the half life for the growth rate to recognize that investors would anticipate the slowing of Cisco's growth. They will lower the price they would be willing to pay for the stock faster than growth slowed. He decides to keep the half life for the P/B ratio at 70 percent of the half life for the growth rate. He therefore forecasts that the half life for the P/B ratio might be as short as 0.7 times 2, or 1.4 years, or as long as 0.7 times 7, or 4.9 years.

Selecting Random Half Lives

He begins the Monte Carlo risk analysis by deciding how many random stock values to compute. Each stock value he computes requires only one random number. He therefore picks a random starting point in Appendix Table A1 and reads one random number for each random stock value he intends to calculate.

Our investor sets up two worksheets for choosing random values. The first worksheet develops random values for the growth rate half life; the second develops random values for the P/B ratio half life. Because he is going to use the same random number in both worksheets, he fills both out simultaneously. Let's follow him as he fills out the worksheet for the growth rate half life in Table 18-2. The first step is to establish the

Table 18-2
WORKSHEET FOR CHOOSING RANDOM HALF LIVES FOR CISCO'S GROWTH RATE

I. Asymmetry Ratio

1.	Most-likely estimate	5
2.	Low estimate (5% probability level)	2
3.	High estimate (5% probability level)	7
4.	Subtract line 1 from Line 3	2
5.	Subtract Line 2 from Line 1	3
6.	Divide Line 4 by Line 5	0.67
7.	Asymmetry Ratio: If Line 6 is greater than 1.0, Divide 1.0 by Line 6. If Line 6 is less than 1.0, copy Line 6.	0.67

II. Probability Distribution

8.	Use the ratio in Line 7 and read a fractional distance in Appendix Table A2 at a random number of 95*	0.85
9.	Use the ratio in Line 7 and read a fractional distance in Appendix Table A2 at a random number of 5*	0.31
10.	Subtract Line 2 from Line 3	5
11.	Subtract Line 9 from Line 8	0.54
12.	Divide Line 10 by Line 11	9.26
13.	Multiply Line 8 by Line 12. Subtract the result from Line 3	-0.87

* If line 6 is greater than 1.0, subtract the random number from 100 before using Appendix table A2, and subtract the fractional distance read from the table from 1.0.

Table 18-2 (Cont'd)
WORKSHEET FOR CHOOSING RANDOM HALF LIVES FOR CISCO'S GROWTH RATE

III Choosing Random Values

14. Enter a random number from Appendix Table A1	23.5
15. Locate that random number in Appendix Table A2 and read across to a fractional distance.	0.47
16. Multiply Line 12 by Line 15	4.35
17. Random Value: Add Lines 13 and 16	3.48

asymmetry ratio in Section I of the worksheet. He enters the most-likely, low, and high estimates for the half lives in lines 1 through 3. The asymmetry ratio that corresponds to this forecast is 0.67. That ratio is less than 1.0. That means he will not have to worry about taking reciprocals and subtracting random numbers from 100 and fractional distances from 1.0.

The next step is to establish the probability distribution, and the procedure for translating fractional distances into half lives. That is what Section II of the worksheet does. Line 8 asks for a fractional distance from Appendix Table A2 at a random number of 95. The 95 corresponds to the 95 percent probability level. He rounds off the asymmetry ratio to 0.7, runs his finger down the 0.7 column in Appendix Table A2, and looks for the number closest to 95. The closest number is 94.6 at a fractional distance of 0.85. He enters that distance in line 8 of the worksheet. Line 9 asks for the same information using 5 as the random number. The closest number to 5 in that column is 5.3 at a fractional distance of 0.31. That is the value that goes in line 9. Lines 10 through 13 develop values he will need to convert fractional distances to half lives in Section III of the worksheet.

He has now established the distribution curve. He is now ready to generate random half lives. That is what Section III of the worksheet does. Our investor goes to Appendix Table A1 and reads as many random numbers as he needs. His first random number is 23.5. He enters that number in line 14 of both worksheets, and reads down the column for an asymmetry ratio of 0.7 to the entry closest to 23.5, then reads across to a fractional distance of 0.47. That is the entry that goes in line 15. Line 17 shows that the corresponding half life is 3.48 years — a little below his most likely forecast of 5 years. The same procedure in the second worksheet yields a half life of 2.43 years for the P/B ratio.

Developing additional random returns is much easier. He has already established the distribution curve. He does not have to repeat lines 1 through 13 again. He just enters the next random number in line 14, and repeats lines 15 through 17. He continues cycling through lines 14 through 17 until he generates as many random half lives as he needs.

A Random Value for Cisco's Stock

With random half lives available, our investor can now feed his forecasts into the worksheet for finding what growth stocks are worth and find the corresponding value for Cisco's stock. In Chapter 14 he discounted the future cash he expected from Cisco at his minimum acceptable return of 14 percent. His minimum return was based on his estimate that he could have earned a 9.3 percent return by investing in an S&P 500 Index Fund plus a 5 percent risk premium. He decides to omit the 5 percent risk premium, and discount the cash he expects Cisco to put in his pocket at a 9.3 percent discount rate. He decides to use risk analysis to find the chance he will lose money, i.e., that he will earn some return below the return he could have earned from the S&P 500 Index Fund.

He enters his forecasts in the worksheet for finding what stocks are worth, discounts at the rate of 9.3 percent in Section III of that worksheet, and finds that Cisco stock is worth $51.41 per share. That is one possible value for Cisco. It is the first value in the random sample of stock values he plans to develop. To complete risk analysis, he returns to the worksheets for generating random half lives. He picks a new random number, and generates a new random set of half lives. He then feeds the new set of half lives into the worksheet for finding what growth stocks are worth and develops another random value for Cisco's stock. He now has a sample of two possible values for Cisco's stock. He continues through this cycle in order to build a larger sample of random stock values. The larger the sample he develops, the more reliable is the analysis. He should develop a sample of at least five possible stock values.

Results of Risk Analysis

If the key factors follow our investor's most-likely forecasts, he estimated that $59.14 was the most he could pay for Cisco and still earn a 14 percent return -- the 9.3 percent return he expected from the S&P 500 Index Fund plus a 5 percent risk premium.

When he excludes the risk premium and repeats the analysis with all factors forecast at their most-likely values he finds that he can afford to pay $79 and still earn the 9.3 percent that his money costs. Notice that lowering the minimum return he is willing to accept from 14 percent to 9.3 percent raises the amount he can afford to pay from $59 to $79 per share.

Risk analysis provides a much better feel for what a stock is worth than a single evaluation with all factors forecast at their most-likely values. Equally important, it tells you your chances of losing money if you buy the stock.

What Cisco's Stock Is Worth

The best estimate of what Cisco's stock is really worth is the average of all the random stock values the Monte Carlo process develops. This average value is far more reliable than any single estimate. As our investor builds up a sample of random values for the stock, the result he tracks most carefully is the average of his random sample of stock values. He pays less attention to individual results; it is the average of all the random values that is important. Figure 18-5 shows how the average of all the random stock values changes as he increases the size of the random sample from 1 to 100 stock values. The average of the random stock values bounces at first because there are only a few random

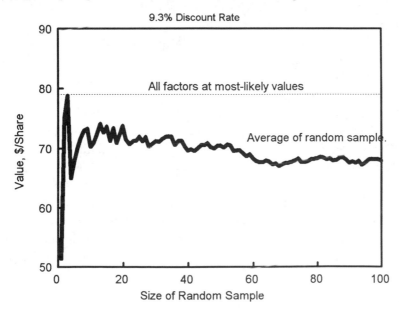

Fig. 18-5
AVERAGE OF RANDOM VALUES FOR CISCO SYSTEMS

values in the average. Adding one more result can change the average by a significant amount. As the number of random values in the average grows, adding one more result has a smaller and smaller effect, and the average stabilizes.

By chance, his first random trial yields an estimate of only $51.41 per share, well below the $79 he found with all factors at their most-likely values. His second random value is $98.72 per share, which raises the average to $75.07 per share. His fifth random value brings the average to $67.64 per share. Ten random values brings the average to $70.28 per share. A much larger sample of 100 random values yields an average value of $67.88 per share. Note that the average stock value from the random samples is well below the $79 he found if all key factors followed his most-likely forecasts. That is because he forecast a greater likelihood that the half lives would be shorter, which means that the growth rate and the P/B ratio would decay faster than the most-likely forecast.

Ten random valuations is not an unreasonable number to do by hand, particularly if you are a serious investor, or if you are investing a large sum. It gives this investor some assurance that Cisco's stock is worth something close to $70 per share. Not absolute assurance, of course. But much more assurance than the average investor has working from hunches.

Uncertainty in Estimated Stock Value

Your estimate of what a stock is worth is obviously an uncertain estimate. You should think of your estimate as a probability distribution just like the one in Figure 18-2. The wider the distribution spreads, the more uncertain is your estimate of what the stock is worth. The wider the distribution spreads, the greater is the chance the stock is worth less than it costs. There is a way to measure how wide a probability distribution spreads. That measure is called the standard deviation. The wider the distribution, the greater the standard deviation. If you knew the stock's value with complete certainty, the distribution curve would collapse to a vertical line at the stock's known value. There would be zero likelihood of any other value. With zero uncertainty the standard deviation would also collapse to zero. As the uncertainty of the stock's value increases, the distribution curve widens, the standard deviation increases, and your estimate becomes more uncertain.

The average of all the stock values in your random sample, which is the best measure of what the stock is worth, has its own probability distribution. One of the advantages of risk analysis is that the probability distribution for the average of all the stock values tightens as you add more stock values to your random sample. The distribution becomes narrower. The standard deviation shrinks. Your estimate becomes more certain.

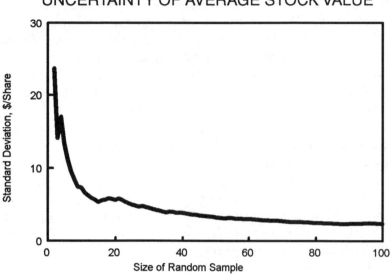

Fig. 18-6
UNCERTAINTY OF AVERAGE STOCK VALUE

How does our investor's valuation of Cisco become more certain as he adds more stock values to his random sample? Figure 18-6 shows how the standard deviation of the average of all the stock values in his random sample shrinks as he adds more random values to the sample. He needs at least two random values to calculate a standard deviation. With only two random values the standard deviation is $24 per share. Five random values brings the standard deviation down to $13.45 per share. By ten random values the standard deviation is down to $7.31 per share; by twenty it is down to $5.63 per share.

The standard deviation is an important measure of uncertainty because it tells you the likely range of values for the stock. For a random sample of ten stock values, for example, there is an 80 percent chance that the stock's value will lie in a band extending 1.37 standard deviations on either side of the average value. In the Cisco example a sample of ten random stock values yielded an average value of $70.28 per share with a standard deviation of $7.31 per share. The 80 percent probability band therefore extends 1.37 times $7.31, or $10.01 on either side of the $70.28 average. Our investor can therefore feel 80 percent certain that Cisco is worth somewhere between $61 and $81 per share. For more information on how the standard deviation is related to probability read the section on Student's t test in any statistics book.

Your hand calculator knows how to find both averages and standard deviations for any sample. Check the instruction book to find how to enter the sample values, and which key to tap for the average and which key for the standard deviation.

Your Chances of Losing Money

One of the prime reasons for doing risk analysis is to estimate your chances of losing money. You need to think of losing money in a new way. You can buy a stock, hold it a while, then sell it at a higher price than you paid for it, and still lose money. How can that be? Remember that back in Chapter 5 you decided on the minimum rate of return you would accept based on the return you could earn on the next best use of your money. Our investor estimated he could earn a 9.3 percent return by investing in an S&P 500 Index Fund. That was his next best use for his money. Suppose he takes that 9.3 percent money and invests it instead in a stock that earns only 5 percent. He could have earned 9.3 percent. Instead, he earns only 5 percent. He has lost money. He has lost money, even though he earned a 5 percent return on the stock.

SmartValue helps you avoid losing money this way by having you discount future cash flows at the minimum rate of return you will accept when you use a worksheet to find what a stock is worth. The value you calculate is the most you can pay for a stock and still earn at least the minimum return you specified.

Most investors worry that they could lose money if they buy a stock. They are right to worry. The firm may not perform as they had forecast. The stock might not really be worth what they paid for it. The stock's price might go down, not up. What to do? How do you alleviate that worry? Risk analysis helps. Suppose you use risk analysis and generate ten random values for a stock. Three of the random values are less than the stock's market price, the other seven are higher. That means you have a 30 percent chance of losing money, that is, of earning some return below the return you specified.

There is a special kind of graph paper that is especially useful for analyzing the results of risk analysis, and the way the individual results scatter around the average result. The paper is called probability paper. This paper features a special horizontal scale so graduated that any distribution which has the expected scatter (such as Figure 18-2) plots as a straight line. The stock values our investor found for Cisco after generating random samples of five and ten stock values is shown in Figure 18-7. The dashed curve is the distribution curve drawn through a random sample of 100 stock values. Notice how close a sample as small as five random stock values comes to the much larger sample of 100 random values. This example demonstrates that you do not need a computer to generate random samples by the thousand. A small sample done on a hand calculator yields results that are almost as useful. An appendix to this chapter shows how to plot stock values on probability paper.

The distribution curves for Cisco in Figure 18-7 are not quite straight lines. That is due to the probability distributions for the half lives. Those random values at the left side of the plot are from forecasts with very short half lives. The P/B ratio falls quickly in those

Fig. 18-7
RISK ANALYSIS OF CISCO SYSTEMS
5 RANDOM STOCK VALUES

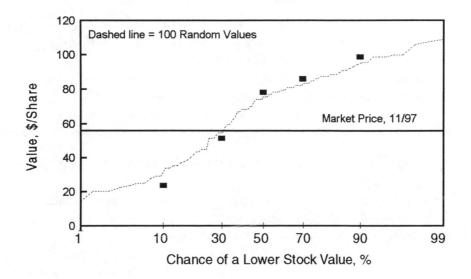

10 RANDOM STOCK VALUES

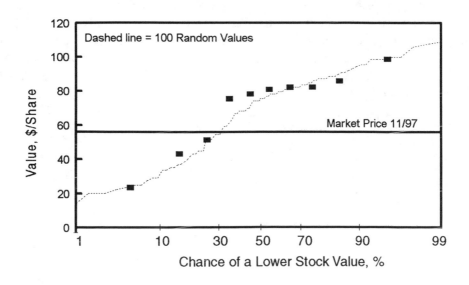

cases. That means the price of the stock is much lower than the most-likely estimate when the investor sells. The same is not true for values at the extreme right side of the plot. Those values are from forecasts with longer half lives. Longer half lives cause only a small rise in the price of the stock when the investor sells. Longer half lives therefore have a much smaller effect on the stock's value than shorter half lives do.

How can you use a plot like Figure 18-7 to estimate your chances of losing money? Draw a horizontal line on the plot at the current market price. Now find the place where the distribution curve crosses the market price line, and read the corresponding probability on the horizontal scale. That reading is the probability that the stock's value is below the market price. The distribution curve you would draw through the sample of five, ten, and a hundred points in the Cisco example all show about a 30 percent chance of losing money, i.e., a 30 percent chance that the stock is worth less than the $56 market price.

Tailoring the Analysis to Your Tolerance for Risk

You can also use the distribution curve in Figure 18-7 to tailor risk analysis to your individual tolerance for risk. How great a risk of losing money are you willing to accept? How great a risk of paying too much for a stock? Are you conservative and willing to accept only a 10 percent chance of losing money? A little more daring, perhaps, and willing to accept a 20 percent chance? Or would you damn the torpedoes and take anything up to a 50 percent chance?

That is a basic decision. It determines what kind of an investor you are. Decide what risk of losing money you can accept. Then locate that risk on the horizontal scale of Figure 18-7, read up to the distribution curve, then read across to the maximum price you should pay on the vertical scale. If our investor would only accept a 10 percent chance of losing money, he would read a maximum price of about $29 per share from Figure 18-7, and conclude that Cisco was too risky. If he were willing to accept a 20 percent chance of losing money, he would be willing to pay as much as $43 for Cisco. Cisco would still be too risky. And if he would accept a 50 percent chance of losing money, he would be willing to pay up to $74 per share. At that tolerance for risk, Cisco is a buy.

Risk analysis can be a sobering experience. The results may surprise you. If you have a low tolerance for risk, you might find that all stocks cost too much. You might have to increase your tolerance for risk substantially before you find any stocks you feel comfortable with. Or you might have to switch to bonds, money market funds, or certificates of deposit. You might even have to rethink what kind of an investor you are.

Summary

The Monte Carlo method is the best way to analyze the risk of investing in a stock. The basic idea is to generate a random sample of possible values for the stock. Then analyze that sample. The average of all the stock values in the sample is the best estimate of what the stock is worth. The way stock values in the sample scatter around the average value provides information on the likely range of stock values, and your chances of losing money if you invest in the stock.

Think about the key forecasts that determine what a stock is worth. Think about your forecast of the return on equity you expect the firm to earn, how fast you expect equity per share to grow, the P/B ratio you expect investors to pay for its stock, and how fast each of these key factors might decay with time. Then decide which factors are the most important and the most uncertain. Estimate the most-likely value for those factors, and also how low and how high you think the actual values might be. Then use the worksheet in Table 18-1 to generate a random set of values for those factors. Feed that random set of forecasts into the appropriate SmartValue worksheet and find what a stock is worth. You now have one possible value for the stock. Repeat the process. Each time you repeat the process you add another possible stock value to your random sample of stock values. Generate at least five random stock values, and preferably more.

Examine that random sample. The average of all the stock values in that sample is the best estimate of what the stock is worth. Plot the sample values on probability paper, along with the curent market price. Read from the plot the probability that you will lose money, i.e., that the stock costs more than it is worth.

How to Use Probability Paper

List the stock values in your random sample in the following worksheet. The example shows the first ten random values our investor found for Cisco Systems.

Table 18-3

RISK ANALYSIS - CISCO SYSTEMS

Result Number	Horizontal Scale[1]	Vertical Scale $/Share
1	5	51.41
2	15	98.77
3	25	86.06
4	35	23.65
5	45	78.29
6	55	80.95
7	65	82.25
8	75	82.39
9	85	75.56
10	95	43.29

1. Subtract 0.5 from the number in Col. 1. Then divide by the number of random values and multiply by 100

Calculate the horizontal scale value in Column 2, and place a tick mark on the horizontal scale of the probability plot for each result. Place a tick mark on the vertical scale for each entry in Column 3. Match the lowest tick mark on the horizontal scale with the lowest tick mark on the vertical scale, and plot a point at that combination. Proceed in the same manner, tick mark by tick mark, until all results have been plotted.

Chapter 19

Worksheets for Every Day Use

Analyzing Historical Performance

Forecasts

What is the Stock Worth?

Investor's Rate of Return

Sell or Hold?

Risk Analysis

This chapter is the place to come after you are comfortable with using the Smart-Value worksheets to value stocks. All the worksheets you will use frequently are collected in this chapter for your convenience. The worksheets retain their original numbering. That will make it easier to refer back to the instructions on how to fill out the worksheet should you need to refresh your memory.

Analyzing Historical Performance

Begin the process of finding what any stock is worth by analyzing that firm's past performance. The first step in that analysis is to adjust the earnings and return on equity the firm reports to the earnings and return on equity that SmartValue needs. Use the worksheet in Table 7-2 to make the adjustment.

Table 7-2
ADJUSTING EARNINGS AND THE RETURN ON EQUITY

Year	Col. 1 Equity, $/Sh.	Col. 2 Change in Equity, $/Sh.	Col. 3 Div., $/Sh.	Col. 4 Adjusted Earnings $/Sh.	Col. 5 ln(Col 1)	Col. 6 Growth Rate, %/yr.	Col. 7 Average Equity, $/Sh.	Col. 8 Adjusted Return, %

Cols. 1 and 3: Enter book value per share and dividends directly from Value Line or the Annual Report.
Col. 2: In Column 1 subtract last year's book value from this year's value and put the result in Column 2.
Col. 4: Add Columns 2 and 3.
Col. 5: Enter the number in Column 1 in your calculator and tap the ln(x) key.
Col. 6: Subtract last year's entry in Column 5 from this year's entry. Then multiply the result by 100.
Col. 7: Divide Column 2 by Column 6, then Multiply by 100.
Col. 8: Divide Column 4 by Column 7, then Multiply by 100.

Return on Equity

After you have adjusted the firm's reported results, see how the adjusted return on equity has varied with time. Plot the returns. Do they tend to fluctuate around some stable average value? If they do, and the return is not unusually high the firm is mature. It is reasonable to forecast that the firm's returns will continue to fluctuate around that same average value. You can use the worksheet for mature firms to find what the stock is worth. But if the firm's return is high, or has been decaying, you may not want to forecast that the return will suddenly stabilize. It is more reasonable to forecast that the return will continue to decay towards some long-run limit typical of a mature firm. You should then use either the Half-Life Decay Model or the Unlimited Flexibility Model to find what the stock is worth. If the firm is earning a high return, it is risky to forecast that that high return will continue unchanged. Forecast that the return will eventually decay towards an appropriate long-run limit, and use the Half-Life Decay Model or the Unlimited Flexibility Model to find what the stock is worth.

Growth Rate

Column 6 of Table 7-2 lists annual growth rates. Annual growth rates normally scatter around some average growth rate. The best way to average these annual growth rates is to plot equity per share against time on semi-log graph paper, or the natural logarithm of equity per share on normal graph paper. Draw the best straight line you can through the data. The growth rate is the slope of that line. Use the worksheet in Table 7-4 to find the growth rate. Use Part A of the worksheet if you plotted the data on semi-log graph paper, and Part B if you plotted the natural logarithm on normal graph paper. If growth is slowing, the data will plot on a curved line instead of a straight line.

Table 7-4

WORKSHEET FOR FINDING GROWTH RATES

Part A - From Semi-Log Plot

1. Equity at right-hand end of the straight line, $/Sh. .... _____
2. Time corresponding to Line 1, years .... _____
3. Equity at left-hand end of the straight line, $/Sh. .... _____
4. Time corresponding to Line 3, years .... _____
5. Divide Line 1 by Line 3 .... _____
6. Enter Line 5 in your calculator and tap the ln(x) key ..... _____
7. Subtract Line 4 from Line 2 .... _____
8. Growth Rate, %/yr.: Divide Line 6 by Line 7,
   then Multiply by 100 .... _____

Part B - From ln(Equity/Share) Plot

1. ln(Equity/Sh.) at right-hand end of the straight line .... _____
2. Time corresponding to Line 1, years .... _____
3. ln(Equity/Sh.) at left-hand end of the straight line .... _____
4. Time corresponding to Line 3, years .... _____
5. Subtract Line 3 from Line 1 .... _____
7. Subtract Line 4 from Line 2 .... _____
8. Growth Rate, %/yr.: Divide Line 5 by Line 6,
   then Multiply by 100 .... _____

P/B Ratio

Value Line reports P/E ratios, not P/B ratios. Use the worksheet in Table 7-6 to convert P/E ratios into the equivalent P/B ratios.

Table 7-6
FINDING THE P/B RATIO

Year	Col. 1 P/E Ratio	Col. 2 Reported Earnings, $/Share	Col. 3 Average Equity, $/Share	Col. 4 Average P/B Ratio
____	____	____	____	____
____	____	____	____	____
____	____	____	____	____
____	____	____	____	____

Cols. 1 and 2: Copy P/E ratios and reported earnings per share directly from Value Line.
Col. 3: Copy the average equity per share from Col. 7 of Table 7-2.
Col. 4: Multiply Column 1 by Column 2, then Divide by Column 3.

Adjust Equity per Share for Growth Since Last Report

The equity per share the firm last reported may be several months old at the time you analyze the stock. Use the worksheet in Table 7-7 to estimate the current equity per share.

Table 7-7
ADJUSTING FOR RECENT GROWTH IN EQUITY/SHARE

1. Initial Equity, $/Share .... _____
2. Divide the Growth Rate (%/yr.) by 100 .... _____
3. Length of growth period, months .... _____
4. Multiply Line 2 by Line 3, then Divide by 12 .... _____
5. Growth Multiplier: Enter Line 3 in your calculator and tap the e^x key .... _____
6. Current Equity, $/Share: Multiply Line 1 by Line 5 .... _____

Forecasts

If the firm is mature you can reasonably forecast that the firm's return on equity and the growth rate of equity per share will stay constant at their current levels. The P/B ratio need not stay constant; you only have to forecast what that ratio will be when the time comes to sell the stock.

If the firm is a growth firm the return on equity and the growth rate are not likely to stay constant. It is more realistic to forecast that the return on equity and the growth rate will both decay from their current levels towards some long-run value appropriate for a mature firm. Reasonable long-run values for a mature firm which grows at the current-dollar GDP growth rate of about 7 percent per year and pays half of its earnings out as dividends is a growth rate of about 7 percent per year and a return on equity of about 14 percent. If that firm's stock sold at a P/E ratio of about 15, the corresponding P/B ratio would be about 2.1.

You can use a half life to describe how fast the return on equity, growth rate, and P/B ratio decay towards their respective long-run limits. You can also forecast by drawing free-hand forecast curves on a sheet of graph paper.

Scenario I - No Dividends

If you expect that the growth firm will reinvest all its earnings in the business and pay no dividends, you need only forecast the growth rate of equity per share and what the P/B ratio will be when you eventually sell the stock. You also have to translate your growth rate forecast into the corresponding forecast of equity per share.

If you use a half life to describe how fast the return on equity falls, growth slows, and the P/B ratio drops, use Table 12-1 to translate your growth forecast into the equity per share when you sell. If you forecast by drawing free-hand forecast curves, use Table 15-1. Use Table 12-3 to forecast the P/B ratio at the end of the investment period.

Scenario II - The Stock Pays Dividends

You need to make additional forecasts if you expect the growth firm to pay dividends while you hold its stock. You need to forecast the return on equity and the growth rate of equity per share at the three intermediate times required for discounting dividends. You also need to translate your growth rate forecast into the corresponding forecast of equity per share at those same three tines.

Table 12-1

GROWTH MULTIPLIER FOR HALF-LIFE DECAY MODEL

1. Investment period, years .... _____
2. Initial Growth Rate, (%/yr.)/100 (decimal form) .... _____
3. Long-Run Growth Rate, (%/yr.)/100 (decimal form) ...... _____
4. Initial Margin: Subtract Line 3 from Line 2 .... _____
5. Half Life, years .... _____
6. Divide 0.6931 by Line 5, then Multiply by Line 1 .... _____
7. Enter Line 6 in your calculator, tap the
   change sign (+/-) key, and then the e^x key .... _____
8. Subtract Line 7 from 1.0 .... _____
9. Multiply Line 4 by Line 8, then Divide by Line 6 .... _____
10. Add Lines 3 and 9. Multiply the result by Line 1. .... _____
11. Growth Multiplier: Enter Line 10 in your
    calculator and tap the e^x key .... _____

Table 15-1

GROWTH MULTIPLIER FOR FREE-HAND FORECASTS

1. Investment period, years					_____
2. Time, fraction of investment period	0.0694	0.33	0.67	0.9306	
3. Time, Years. Multiply Line 1 by Line 7	_____	_____	_____	_____	
4. Growth Rates, %/yr. (from freehand forecast curve)	_____	_____	_____	_____	
5. Add the first and last entries in Line 4 and Multiply the result by 0.001739					_____
6. Add the middle two entries in Line 4 and Multiply the result by 0.003261					_____
7. Add Lines 5 and 6. Multiply the result by Line 1					_____
8. Growth Multiplier: Enter Line 9 in your calculator and tap the e^x key					_____

Table 13-1
WORKSHEET FOR FORECASTING RETURN ON EQUITY, GROWTH RATE, AND EQUITY/SHARE

A. Forecasting Growth Rate and Return on Equity

		0.113	0.5	0.887	1.0
1.	Investment period, years				____
2.	Initial Value				____
3.	Long-Run Limit				____
4.	Initial Margin: Subtract Line 3 from Line 2				____
5.	Half Life, years				____
6.	Divide 0.6931 by Line 5				____
7.	Time, fraction of investment period	0.113	0.5	0.887	1.0
8.	Time, Years. Multiply Line 1 by Line 7	____	____	____	____
9.	Multiply Line 8 by Line 6	____	____	____	____
10.	Decay Factor: Enter Line 9 in your calculator, tap the change sign (+/-) key, then tap the e^x key	____	____	____	____
11.	Future Values: Multiply Line 4 by Line 10, then Add line 3	____	____	____	____

B. Translate Growth Forecast into Equity/Share

12.	Initial Equity, $/Share				____
13.	Subtract Line 10 from 1.0, then Divide by Line 9	____	____	____	____
14.	Multiply Line 4 by Line 13, then Add Line 3	____	____	____	____
15.	Multiply Line 14 by Line 8, then Divide by 100	____	____	____	____
16.	Growth Multiple: Enter Line 15 in your calculator and tap the e^x key	____	____	____	____
17.	Equity, $/Share: Multiply Line 12 by Line 16	____	____	____	____

Table 15-3
WORKSHEET FOR TRANSLATING GROWTH RATES INTO EQUITY/SHARE

Part A - Time Elements

1. Investment Period, years .... _____
2. Multiply Line 1 by 0.113 .... _____
3. Multiply Line 1 by 0.5 .... _____
4. Multiply Line 1 by 0.887 .... _____
5. Subtract Line 2 from Line 3 .... _____

Part B - Averaging Growth Rates

Compute times as directed and enter them in the column headed "Time, yrs." Then read growth rates (%/yr.) from your forecast curve at those times. Enter the growth rates in the column headed "Growth Rates, %/yr.

	Time, years	Growth Rate, %/yr.
6. Multiply Line 2 by 0.211	_____	_____
7. Multiply Line 2 by 0.789	_____	_____
8. Multiply Line 5 by 0.211, then Add Line 2	_____	_____
9. Multiply Line 5 by 0.789, then Add Line 2	_____	_____
10. Multiply Line 5 by 0.211, then Add Line 3	_____	_____
11. Multiply Line 5 by 0.789, then Add Line 3	_____	_____
12. Add Lines 4 and 6	_____	_____
13. Add Lines 4 and 7	_____	_____

Table 15-3 (Cont'd)

WORKSHEET FOR TRANSLATING GROWTH RATES
INTO EQUITY/SHARE

14. Initial Equity, $/Share .... _____

15. a. Add growth rates in Lines 6 and 7.
     Multiply by Line 2, then Divide by 200 .... _____
    b. Enter Line 15a in your calculator and tap the e^x key . _____
    c. Equity, $/Share: Multiply Line 15b by Line 14 .... _____

16. a. Add growth rates in Lines 8 and 9.
     Multiply by Line 5, then Divide by 200 .... _____
    b. Enter Line 16a in your calculator and tap the e^x key . _____
    c. Equity, $/Share: Multiply Line 16b by Line 15c .... _____

17. a. Add growth rates in Lines 10 and 11.
     Multiply by Line 5, then Divide by 200 .... _____
    b. Enter Line 17a in your calculator and tap the e^x key . _____
    c. Equity, $/Share: Multiply Line 17b by Line 16c .... _____

18. a. Add growth rates in Lines 12 and 13.
     Multiply by Line 2, then Divide by 200 .... _____
    b. Enter Line 18a in your calculator and tap the e^x key . _____
    c. Equity, $/Share: Multiply Line 18b by Line 17c .... _____

Table 12-3
WORKSHEET FOR FORECASTING THE P/B RATIO

1. Investment period, years .... _____
2. Initial P/B Ratio .... _____
3. Long-Run P/B Ratio... _____
4. Initial Margin: Subtract Line 3 from Line 2 .... _____
5. Half Life, years .... _____
6. Divide 0.6931 by Line 5, then Multiply by Line 1 .... _____
7. Enter Line 6 in your calculator, tap the
   change sign (+/-) key, and then the e^x key .... _____
8. Final P/B Ratio: Multiply Line 4 by Line 7,
   then Add Line 3 .... _____

If you use a half life to describe how fast the return on equity, the growth rate, and the P/B ratio decay, use part A of Table 13-1 to forecast the return on equity and the growth rate of equity per share at the three intermediate times. Then use Part B of Table 13-1 to translate the growth rate forecast into the corresponding forecast of equity per share. Use Table 12-3 to forecast the P/B ratio at the end of the investment period.

If you forecast the return on equity, the growth rate and the P/B ratio by drawing free-hand curves on a sheet of graph paper, read the return on equity and the growth rate from your forecast curves at the three intermediate times. Then use the worksheet in Table 15-3 to translate the growth rate forecast into the corresponding forecast of equity per share at the three intermediate times and at the end of the investment period. Read the P/B ratio at the end of the investment period from your forecast curve.

What Is the Stock Worth?

SmartValue employs a set of three worksheets to find what any stock is worth. One worksheet is for mature firms you expect to follow steady-state conditions. Two worksheets find what growth stocks are worth. One of these worksheets is for growth stocks that do not pay dividends. The other is for growth stocks that do pay dividends.

All three worksheets are similar. Section I describes the investor and is identical for all three worksheets. Section II incorporates your forecasts of how the firm will perform. Section III discounts the money the stock will put into your pocket and tells you what the stock is worth.

Mature Firms.

Use the worksheet in Table 6-1 if you forecast that the firm's return on equity and growth rate will stay constant during the period you hold the stock.

Growth Firms That Do Not Pay Dividends

If you do not expect a growth firm to pay dividends while you hold the stock you only need to forecast the growth rate of equity per share and the P/B ratio when you sell the stock. The forecast of return on equity will be identical to the growth rate forecast.

Forecast the initial value and the long-run value you expect when the firm is fully mature. Forecast how the value moves from the initial towards the long-run value either by forecasting the half life (the time you expect it will take to go halfway from the initial to the long-run value), or by drawing a free-hand forecast on a sheet of graph paper.

Use the worksheet in Table 12-1 to find the growth multiplier for the investment period if you used a half-life to forecast the decay pattern. Use the worksheet in Table 15-1 if you drew a free-hand forecast curve. Use the worksheet in Table 12-3 to find the P/B ratio at the end of the investment period. Then use the worksheet in table 12-5 to find what the stock is worth.

Growth Firms That Pay Dividends

If you do expect the firm to pay dividends, the firm's return on equity will no longer be identical to the firm's growth rate. You will need an independent forecast of the return on equity. You will also need to forecast the return on equity and the growth rate at three intermediate times during the investment period.

If you use a half life to describe how fast the return on equity decays and growth slows, use Part A of the worksheet in Table 13-1 to forecast returns on equity and growth rates at the three intermediate times. Then use Part B of that worksheet to translate your growth rate forecast into forecasts of equity per share at the three intermediate times.

If you made your forecast by drawing free-hand curves, read the return on equity and the growth rate from your forecast curves at the three intermediate times. The use the worksheet in Table 15-3 to translate the growth forecast into a forecast of equity per share.

Finally, use the worksheet in Table 13-3 to find what the stock is worth.

Table 6-1
WHAT ARE MATURE FIRMS WORTH?

I - The Investor

1. Investment Period, years .... _____
2. Divide Incremental Tax Rate on Ordinary Income (%)
   by 100; Subtract the Result from 1.0 .... _____
3. Divide Capital Gains Tax Rate (%) by 100 .... _____
4. Divide Minimum Acceptable Return (%) by 100 .... _____
5. Divide Broker's Commission (%) by 100;
   Add the Result to 1.0 .... _____
6. Divide Broker's Commission (%) by 100;
   Subtract the Result from 1.0 .... _____

II - The Firm

7. Initial Equity, $/Share .... _____
8. Projected Return on Equity, % .... _____
9. Projected Growth Rate, %/yr. .... _____
10. Dividend Payout Fraction: Divide Line 9 by Line 8,
    then Subtract the Result from 1.0 .... _____
11. Initial Dividend, $/Share: Multiply Line 7
    by Lines 8 and 10, then Divide by 100 .... _____
12. Multiply Line 1 by Line 9, then Divide by 100 .... _____
13. Growth Multiplier: Enter Line 12 in your calculator
    and tap the e^x key .... _____
14. Final Equity, $/Share: Multiply Line 7 by Line 13 .... _____
15. Projected Price/Book Ratio .... _____
16. Final Stock Price: Multiply Line 14 by Line 15 .... _____

Table 6-1 (Cont'd)
WHAT ARE MATURE FIRMS WORTH?

III - What is the Stock Worth?

17. Multiply Line 1 by Line 4 .... _____

18. Enter Line 17 in your calculator, tap the change
sign (+/-) key, then tap the e^x key .... _____

19. Multiply Line 13 by Line 18 .... _____

20. If Line 19 is less than 1.0:

   20a. Subtract Line 19 from 1.0 .... _____

   20b. Divide Line 9 by 100 and Subtract the Result
from Line 4

   20c. Divide Line 20a by Line 20b .... _____

   If Line 19 is greater than 1.0:

   20a. Subtract 1.0 from Line 19 .... _____

   20b. Divide Line 9 by 100, then
Subtract Line 4 from the Result .... _____

   20c. Divide Line 20a by Line 20b .... _____

   If Line 19 is equal to 1.0:

   20c. Copy Line 1 .... _____

21. Present Value of Dividends: Multiply Line 2 by
Lines 11 and 20c .... _____

22. Present Value of Final Stock Price: Multiply Line 6
by Lines 16 and 18 .... _____

23. Multiply Line 3 by Line 22 .... _____

24. Subtract Line 23 from Line 22 .... _____

25. Multiply Line 3 by Line 18 and
Subtract the Result from 1.0 .... _____

26. Value of Stock: Add Lines 21 and 24, then
Divide the Result by Line 5 and by Line 25 .... _____

Table 12-5
WHAT ARE NON-DIVIDEND PAYING GROWTH STOCKS WORTH?

I - The Investor

1. Investment Period, years .... _____
2. Divide Incremental Tax Rate on Ordinary Income (%)
   by 100; Subtract the Result from 1.0 .... _____
3. Divide Capital Gains Tax Rate (%) by 100 .... _____
4. Divide Minimum Acceptable Return (%) by 100 .... _____
5. Divide Broker's Commission (%) by 100;
   Add the Result to 1.0 .... _____
6. Divide Broker's Commission (%) by 100;
   Subtract the Result from 1.0 .... _____

II - The Firm

7. Initial Equity, $/Share .... _____
8. Growth Multiplier (from Table 12-1) .... _____
9. Final P/B Ratio (from Table 12-3) .... _____
10. Final Stock Price: Multiply Line 7 by Lines 8 and 9 .... _____

III - What is the Stock Worth?

11. Multiply Line 1 by Line 4 .... _____
12. Discount Factor: Enter Line 11 in your calculator,
    tap the change sign (+/-) key, then tap the e^x key .... _____
13. Present Value of Final Stock Price: Multiply Line 6
    by Lines 10 and 12 .... _____
14. Multiply Line 3 by Line 13 .... _____
15. Subtract Line 14 from Line 13 .... _____
16. Multiply Line 3 by Line 12 and
    Subtract the result from 1.0 .... _____
17. What the Stock is Worth: Divide Line 15 by Line 5
    and by Line 16 .... _____

Table 13-3
WHAT ARE DIVIDEND-PAYING
GROWTH STOCKS WORTH?

I - The Investor

1. Investment Period, years .... _____
2. Divide Incremental Tax Rate on Ordinary Income (%)
     by 100; Subtract the Result from 1.0 .... _____
3. Divide Capital Gains Tax Rate (%) by 100 .... _____
4. Divide Minimum Acceptable Return (%) by 100 .... _____
5. Divide Broker's Commission (%) by 100;
     Add the Result to 1.0 .... _____
6. Divide Broker's Commission (%) by 100;
     Subtract the Result from 1.0 .... _____

II. The Firm

	0.113	0.5	0.887	1.0
7. Time, fraction of investment period				
8. Time, Years. Multiply Line 1 by Line 7				
9. Equity, $/Share*				
10. Return on Equity, %*				
11. Growth Rate, %/yr.*				
12. Payout Fraction: Divide Line 11 by Line 10. Subtract the result from 1.0				
13. Dividends, $/Share: Multiply Line 2 by Lines 9, 10, and 12, then Divide by 100				
14. Final P/B Ratio*				
15. Final Stock Price: Multiply Line 9 by Line 14				

* From Table 13-1.

Table 13-3 (Cont'd)
WHAT ARE DIVIDEND-PAYING GROWTH STOCKS WORTH?

III - What is the Stock Worth?

16. Multiply Line 8 by Line 4
17. Discount Factor: Enter Line 16 in your calculator, tap the change sign (+/-) key, then tap the e^x key
18. Discounted Dividends: Multiply Line 13 by Line 17
19. Add the 1st and 3rd numbers in Line 18 and Multiply the result by 0.278
20. Multiply the 2nd number in Line 18 by 0.444
21. Discounted Dividends: Add Lines 19 and 20 and Multiply the result by Line 1
22. Discounted Stock Price: Multiply Line 6 by Line 15 and by the last number in Line 17
23. Multiply Line 3 by Line 22
24. Subtract Line 23 from Line 22
25. Multiply Line 3 by the last number in Line 17 and Subtract the result from 1.0
26. What the Stock is Worth: Add Lines 21 and 24, then Divide by Line 5 and by Line 25

Investor's Rate of Return

You need to find what the stock is worth at two different discount rates to find your rate of return. Find what the stock is worth when you discount future cash flows at your minimum acceptable rate of return. That is one of the values you need. If the stock is worth more than it costs, find what the stock is worth at a second discount rate about five percentage points above your minimum acceptable rate of return. If the stock costs more than it is worth, find what the stock is worth at a second discount rate about five percentage points below your minimum acceptable rate of return. The value five percentage points away from your minimum acceptable return is the second value. Enter the stock values at the two discount rates in the worksheet in Table 9-3 and find your rate of return.

You can refine your estimated return by making a second pass through the worksheet. Find what the stock is worth when you discount future cash flows at your estimated rate of return from the first pass, and use that as one of the two required values. Use whichever of the two original values is closest to your estimated return as the other value. Enter both values in the worksheet and calculate a new rate of return. Two passes through the worksheet should provide a rate of return good enough for all practical purposes.

Sell or Hold

Use the worksheet in Table 17-1 to decide whether you should sell your stock or keep it for another year. Hold on to the stock if the value in line 26 is greater than the value in line 11. Otherwise, sell. The sell or hold on calculation is subject to considerable error because it requires an estimate of how much the stock price will change in the coming year. This calculation is a good candidate for risk analysis.

Table 9-3

ESTIMATING THE INVESTOR'S RATE OF RETURN

1. Market Price, $/Share .... _____
2. Stock Value at low discount rate, $/Share .... _____
3. Low discount rate, % .... _____
4. Stock Value at high discount rate, $/Share .... _____
5. High discount rate, % .... _____
6. Subtract Line 4 from Line 2 .... _____
7. Subtract Line 3 from Line 5 .... _____

Investor's Return - At Least One Value Above Market Price

8a. Subtract Line 1 from Line 2 .... _____
8b. Multiply Line 8a by Line 7, then Divide by Line 6 .... _____
8c. Investor's Return, %: Add Lines 3 and 8b .... _____

Investor's Return - Both Values Below Market Price

9a. Subtract Line 2 from Line 1 .... _____
9b. Multiply Line 9a by Line 7, then Divide by Line 6 .... _____
9c. Investor's Return, %: Subtract Line 9b from Line 3 .... _____

Table 17-1
SELL NOW OR CONTINUE HOLDING

I - The Investor

1. Holding Period, years .... _____
2. Divide Incremental Tax Rate on Ordinary Income (%)
   by 100; Subtract the Result from 1.0 .... _____
3. Divide Capital Gains Tax Rate (%) by 100 .... _____
4. Divide Minimum Acceptable Return (%) by 100 .... _____
5. Divide Broker's Commission (%) by 100;
   Add the Result to 1.0 .... _____
6. Divide Broker's Commission (%) by 100;
   Subtract the Result from 1.0 .... _____

II - Money Foregone by Not Selling

7. Current Stock Price, $/Share .... _____
8. Original Cost, $/Share .... _____
9. Capital Gain: Multiply Line 6 by line 7,
   then Subtract Line 8 .... _____
10. Capital Gains Tax: Multiply Line 9 by Line 3 .... _____
11. Money Foregone: Multiply Line 6 by Line 7.
   Then Subtract Line 10 from the result .... _____

Table 17-1 (Cont'd)
SELL NOW OR CONTINUE HOLDING

III - Gain from Keeping Stock

12. Current equity, $/Share .... _____
13. Divide growth of equity per share (%/yr.) by 100 .... _____
14. Growth Multiplier: Multiply Line 1 by Line 13.
Enter the result into your calculator and tap the e^x key . _____
15. Forecast of P/B ratio .... _____
16. Future Stock price: Multiply Line 12
by Lines 14 and 15 .... _____
17. Capital Gain: Multiply Line 6 by Line 16.
Subtract Line 8 from the result .... _____
18. Capital Gains Tax: Multiply Line 3 by Line 17 .... _____
19. Net Proceeds: Multiply Line 6 by Line 16.
Subtract Line 18 from the result .... _____
20. Dividend Forecast, $/Share .... _____

IV - Discounting

21. Multiply Line 1 by Line 4 .... _____
22. Discount Factor 1: Enter Line 21 into your calculator,
tap the change sign (+/-) key, then the e^x key .... _____
23. Discount Factor 2: Subtract Line 22 from 1.0.
Divide the result by Line 1 and by Line 4 .... _____
24. Discounted Net Proceeds: Multiply Line 19 by Line 22 .
25. Discounted Dividends: Multiply Line 2
by Lines 20 and 23 .... _____
26. Discounted Gain from Keeping Stock:
Add Lines 24 and 25 .... _____

Risk Analysis

The basic idea of risk analysis is to generate a random sample of possible values for the stock. The best estimate of what the stock is worth is the average of the random sample of stock values. The standard deviation of the random sample provides a way to estimate the probability that the actual value of the stock lies within any given range.

Use the worksheet in Table 18-1 to generate random forecasts of the uncertain factors in the analysis. The major uncertain factors are the return on equity, the growth rate, the P/B ratio, and their half lives. Sections I and II of the worksheet develop a probability distribution from estimates of the most-likely value of any factor, coupled with estimates of how low and how high the value might actually be. Section III develops random values for that factor.

Once you have a set of random forecasts for the return on equity, the growth rate of equity per share, the P/B ratio, and their half lives, use the appropriate SmartValue worksheet to find what the stock is worth if the firm follows those forecasts. Then repeat the process a number of times to generate a random sample of stock values.

Table 18-1
WORKSHEET FOR CHOOSING RANDOM VALUES

I - Asymmetry Ratio

1. Most-likely estimate .... _____
2. Low estimate (5% probability level) .... _____
3. High estimate (5% probability level) .... _____
4. Subtract line 1 from Line 3 .... _____
5. Subtract Line 2 from Line 1 .... _____
6. Divide Line 4 by Line 5 .... _____
7. Asymmetry Ratio: If Line 6 is greater than 1.0, Divide
   1.0 by Line 6. If Line 6 is less than 1.0, copy Line 6. .... _____

Table 18-1 (Cont'd)
WORKSHEET FOR CHOOSING RANDOM VALUES

II - Probability Distribution

8. Use the ratio in Line 7 and read a fractional distance
    in Appendix Table A2 at a random number of 95* .... _____
9. Use the ratio in Line 7 and read a fractional distance
    in Appendix Table A2 at a random number of 5* .... _____
10. Subtract Line 2 from Line 3 .... _____
11. Subtract Line 9 from Line 8 .... _____
12. Divide Line 10 by Line 11 .... _____
13. Multiply Line 8 by Line 12.
    Subtract the result from Line 3 .... _____

* If line 6 is greater than 1.0, subtract the random number from 100 before using
Appendix table A2, and subtract the fractional distance read from the table from
1.0.

III - Choosing Random Values

14. Enter a random number from Appendix Table A1 .... _____
15. Locate that random number in Appendix Table A2
    and read across to a fractional distance. .... _____
16. Multiply Line 12 by Line 15 .... _____
17. Random Value: Add Lines 13 and 16 .... _____

Appendix

1,000 Random Numbers
Choosing Random Values

Table A1

A THOUSAND RANDOM NUMBERS

5.1	63.8	44.5	51.2	41.4	79.8	92.1	9.0	42.5	83.3
38.6	2.1	51.7	23.0	97.2	2.9	19.1	2.9	25.8	41.7
81.1	55.1	65.9	16.2	51.7	65.5	6.0	1.5	67.3	12.1
19.0	56.1	39.0	79.6	25.3	5.7	73.7	93.4	80.7	46.8
79.0	29.7	53.5	3.2	34.6	80.1	38.0	19.3	40.6	4.9
17.2	58.5	15.3	13.4	40.2	85.3	34.4	92.9	68.7	92.6
79.4	34.4	43.3	23.6	0.0	93.3	53.4	99.8	85.2	48.9
19.9	37.0	82.0	66.7	8.8	24.6	94.3	2.7	10.8	57.5
92.4	37.9	59.9	77.6	15.1	36.2	61.2	54.8	28.0	42.4
16.3	59.8	9.4	93.0	56.0	19.2	91.8	67.7	85.4	75.7
0.7	17.9	64.0	48.2	30.5	61.6	56.3	15.1	60.7	3.4
88.8	29.1	81.5	90.0	35.3	76.5	93.7	85.3	22.3	12.6
19.8	19.3	65.4	58.9	26.8	8.6	40.3	75.7	36.6	31.5
35.6	86.6	16.3	71.0	13.3	25.6	20.2	37.5	59.1	13.2
27.5	93.1	69.9	23.3	83.8	52.7	82.5	95.2	56.2	69.1
84.0	33.0	94.3	13.5	92.0	30.6	54.2	16.1	40.5	1.1
17.4	32.6	1.2	10.8	30.4	89.7	20.5	52.9	3.0	48.0
61.9	31.0	85.7	38.1	13.1	73.5	56.1	50.1	91.1	2.6
84.7	28.3	30.7	80.6	57.9	70.5	56.4	65.1	84.7	30.4
25.5	57.5	7.8	83.5	32.0	92.3	51.5	63.0	27.2	90.0
92.4	60.2	67.7	23.5	73.7	63.5	78.3	2.6	89.8	80.2
23.0	71.0	80.5	88.7	40.1	63.7	12.5	48.9	99.6	60.5
89.8	64.4	16.0	94.1	65.9	1.7	64.2	67.5	24.1	42.8
5.7	7.5	84.4	56.4	65.0	81.7	2.4	30.3	99.9	46.0
81.9	54.8	12.8	41.1	33.3	78.0	88.2	65.8	40.8	76.9
13.7	93.3	1.9	98.9	98.5	75.4	38.3	98.8	15.6	41.4
89.7	57.2	36.3	58.2	41.6	90.8	87.9	96.6	43.4	90.0
42.4	18.6	3.1	28.2	0.5	71.9	23.7	17.7	16.5	27.4
7.7	51.7	19.0	87.1	95.5	45.6	60.8	45.7	37.1	86.4
94.6	18.6	93.6	14.1	33.6	26.3	70.9	33.3	78.0	83.3

Table A1 (Cont'd)
A THOUSAND RANDOM NUMBERS

74.0	13.1	40.2	39.4	85.5	69.6	60.8	69.9	29.4	58.5
0.7	12.2	28.6	42.5	75.1	61.5	29.1	69.2	56.8	22.2
21.2	12.4	10.1	52.2	89.0	37.7	62.9	72.3	69.1	51.8
19.9	34.0	80.3	47.7	95.8	52.0	34.5	26.3	80.6	84.8
5.8	7.9	11.7	91.7	89.4	33.0	84.1	25.1	57.2	20.0
64.2	3.4	82.9	6.1	38.3	10.5	43.2	42.8	74.5	63.8
4.7	15.6	47.9	60.5	37.6	88.6	89.6	6.2	88.6	78.1
95.5	82.1	43.8	44.9	44.2	56.0	89.2	41.1	76.1	65.2
60.5	28.5	56.2	77.2	32.6	1.0	94.0	86.0	92.5	62.4
80.5	37.2	49.9	89.5	28.7	18.4	59.4	77.7	52.1	99.9
45.0	60.2	30.6	79.6	46.8	74.6	1.0	50.3	59.9	37.5
20.0	13.4	87.8	14.8	50.0	34.8	80.5	60.1	87.7	12.2
12.4	28.9	16.0	82.2	89.0	56.1	22.9	84.9	68.2	60.3
62.0	82.1	90.8	41.4	15.1	71.2	21.7	87.3	33.6	43.9
45.0	97.7	61.0	90.2	91.2	84.9	92.0	81.6	72.3	27.7
14.1	54.0	97.2	84.4	97.1	29.8	96.5	48.4	32.9	69.2
62.7	42.1	7.0	69.3	34.9	99.8	42.9	84.9	24.9	25.3
68.7	58.8	96.6	94.7	33.3	37.2	56.7	56.6	65.3	86.7
88.2	57.3	99.1	81.1	16.9	46.9	6.4	73.0	31.2	49.0
88.8	89.8	42.6	75.6	35.9	10.5	82.7	54.6	13.0	65.6
44.6	36.2	16.2	56.7	0.9	15.8	32.2	90.5	57.1	26.7
50.8	33.0	58.4	91.7	95.3	38.0	34.7	71.8	21.4	97.0
21.9	82.1	64.2	84.9	26.4	25.9	67.2	16.4	93.4	16.4
57.2	23.9	35.3	61.2	93.2	41.0	19.1	0.9	69.9	44.0
1.3	57.6	51.0	64.3	55.8	83.1	56.7	88.9	53.4	23.4
80.2	48.9	82.6	7.9	100.0	74.3	88.9	59.9	43.3	87.6
76.0	38.7	4.2	19.9	59.6	60.9	31.8	16.5	61.4	71.9
43.1	7.3	83.8	1.0	89.9	33.8	12.7	67.4	64.2	86.5
73.9	50.5	80.6	17.9	63.6	26.6	6.5	10.7	74.4	97.6
48.9	33.3	27.4	1.4	22.2	32.6	68.6	67.1	70.7	77.8

Table A1 (Cont'd)
A THOUSAND RANDOM NUMBERS

80.7	18.9	95.3	55.1	38.1	54.0	44.1	67.6	3.9	11.5
87.9	97.3	56.3	11.1	71.6	43.4	6.9	21.1	78.8	93.3
90.9	93.8	60.8	52.7	6.2	49.5	77.3	53.4	56.1	30.5
61.4	47.1	92.3	66.2	9.9	54.6	57.0	54.1	91.6	26.9
0.8	97.9	88.4	61.0	87.7	79.4	93.7	81.4	16.2	95.8
11.0	46.7	2.4	71.2	3.9	2.9	64.1	96.6	98.7	17.2
0.9	46.0	82.8	4.8	10.2	34.9	38.0	54.7	81.8	12.0
0.4	12.7	34.5	18.0	65.9	92.4	30.1	35.2	91.3	70.3
51.8	63.1	69.8	65.6	4.2	26.2	52.0	80.8	87.2	55.3
25.8	77.0	36.6	20.7	35.3	57.7	20.5	76.7	72.2	7.2
38.0	39.1	34.7	34.2	68.8	59.0	76.1	59.8	11.1	23.0
94.0	96.0	45.1	90.8	43.3	31.8	85.8	41.1	26.9	33.4
11.5	82.9	48.8	78.4	80.4	42.1	98.8	24.7	88.6	60.2
63.6	37.8	36.0	49.8	82.5	97.4	71.0	81.2	5.9	63.4
60.2	11.2	20.1	66.8	0.1	5.9	58.6	70.9	8.0	82.2
60.1	69.7	58.2	70.5	32.7	11.1	19.5	32.6	5.4	53.6
96.7	26.4	39.6	99.0	56.1	92.1	4.1	80.2	52.1	67.5
10.3	7.4	57.5	34.3	38.8	41.0	82.0	12.5	96.5	57.0
53.2	19.7	20.3	98.3	33.2	25.3	3.0	20.3	58.3	98.0
61.0	38.0	25.1	46.9	69.4	10.2	77.9	42.8	94.7	87.2
15.5	4.1	53.1	76.3	10.8	99.3	84.1	6.8	49.7	12.5
8.5	35.4	25.0	22.7	61.5	78.1	90.4	64.6	51.7	19.2
37.8	23.7	43.6	49.9	60.0	22.1	95.2	58.3	16.3	15.9
40.3	49.3	29.3	9.6	37.5	43.4	64.3	77.0	44.5	30.0
66.1	42.0	63.3	33.1	62.0	82.4	92.9	70.4	42.4	59.6
25.9	81.8	92.3	23.1	38.5	17.9	87.6	45.3	6.7	50.7
74.4	79.3	51.1	16.1	46.1	21.2	47.6	95.5	72.9	2.3
75.5	75.3	71.5	66.5	1.0	29.5	28.9	47.9	46.2	29.7
93.2	55.8	65.3	22.5	85.2	56.6	68.6	49.1	14.5	78.7
47.4	56.4	32.0	98.1	90.1	51.1	45.5	19.1	84.2	55.7

Table A1 (Cont'd)
A THOUSAND RANDOM NUMBERS

1.5	35.2	0.1	95.8	39.9	94.8	37.0	90.5	84.2	54.2
20.8	85.0	2.5	13.0	38.5	70.1	17.0	74.6	8.8	17.0
70.6	41.6	89.1	30.8	22.7	11.5	98.4	50.7	57.1	61.6
89.7	10.0	56.9	16.6	6.0	75.6	83.4	19.2	5.2	53.4
3.4	71.6	95.2	46.2	71.6	96.1	12.8	24.3	51.7	76.6
71.1	92.0	32.0	32.1	10.0	12.3	7.1	22.2	80.3	36.0
24.7	48.0	85.8	94.0	94.7	34.5	17.4	4.3	18.0	46.4
94.6	81.1	23.4	69.3	74.6	92.0	33.2	34.7	3.2	70.7
43.3	71.5	87.9	52.7	80.6	87.7	16.2	51.4	96.1	19.0
21.6	1.7	91.7	49.5	34.5	26.5	15.1	12.3	90.6	99.8

Table A2
CHOOSING RANDOM VALUES

Fractional Distance	Asymmetry Ratio: 1	0.9	0.8	0.7	0.6	0.5	0.4	0.3	0.2	0.1	0
0	0.0	0.0	0.0	0.0	0.0	0.0	0.0	0.0	0.0	0.0	0.0
0.01	0.0	0.0	0.0	0.0	0.0	0.0	0.0	0.0	0.0	0.0	0.0
0.02	0.0	0.0	0.0	0.0	0.0	0.0	0.0	0.0	0.0	0.0	0.0
0.03	0.0	0.0	0.0	0.0	0.0	0.0	0.0	0.0	0.0	0.0	0.0
0.04	0.0	0.0	0.0	0.0	0.0	0.0	0.0	0.0	0.0	0.0	0.0
0.05	0.0	0.0	0.0	0.0	0.0	0.0	0.0	0.0	0.0	0.0	0.0
0.06	0.0	0.0	0.0	0.0	0.0	0.0	0.0	0.0	0.0	0.0	0.0
0.07	0.1	0.0	0.0	0.0	0.0	0.0	0.0	0.0	0.0	0.0	0.0
0.08	0.1	0.1	0.0	0.0	0.0	0.0	0.0	0.0	0.0	0.0	0.0
0.09	0.2	0.1	0.1	0.0	0.0	0.0	0.0	0.0	0.0	0.0	0.0
0.1	0.3	0.2	0.1	0.0	0.0	0.0	0.0	0.0	0.0	0.0	0.0
0.11	0.4	0.2	0.1	0.1	0.0	0.0	0.0	0.0	0.0	0.0	0.0
0.12	0.5	0.3	0.2	0.1	0.1	0.0	0.0	0.0	0.0	0.0	0.0
0.13	0.7	0.4	0.2	0.1	0.1	0.1	0.0	0.0	0.0	0.0	0.0
0.14	0.9	0.6	0.3	0.2	0.1	0.1	0.1	0.1	0.0	0.0	0.0
0.15	1.2	0.7	0.4	0.3	0.2	0.1	0.1	0.1	0.1	0.1	0.1
0.16	1.5	1.0	0.6	0.4	0.2	0.2	0.1	0.1	0.1	0.1	0.1
0.17	1.9	1.2	0.7	0.5	0.3	0.2	0.1	0.1	0.1	0.1	0.1
0.18	2.3	1.5	0.9	0.6	0.4	0.3	0.2	0.2	0.1	0.1	0.1
0.19	2.8	1.8	1.2	0.7	0.5	0.3	0.2	0.2	0.2	0.2	0.2
0.2	3.3	2.2	1.4	0.9	0.6	0.4	0.3	0.2	0.2	0.2	0.2
0.21	3.9	2.6	1.7	1.1	0.7	0.5	0.4	0.3	0.3	0.2	0.2
0.22	4.6	3.1	2.1	1.3	0.9	0.6	0.5	0.4	0.3	0.3	0.3
0.23	5.4	3.7	2.4	1.6	1.1	0.7	0.6	0.4	0.4	0.3	0.3
0.24	6.2	4.3	2.9	1.9	1.3	0.9	0.7	0.5	0.5	0.4	0.4
0.25	7.1	5.0	3.4	2.2	1.5	1.1	0.8	0.6	0.5	0.5	0.5
0.26	8.0	5.7	3.9	2.6	1.8	1.3	0.9	0.7	0.6	0.6	0.5
0.27	9.1	6.5	4.5	3.1	2.1	1.5	1.1	0.9	0.7	0.7	0.6
0.28	10.2	7.4	5.2	3.5	2.4	1.7	1.3	1.0	0.9	0.8	0.7
0.29	11.3	8.3	5.9	4.1	2.8	2.0	1.5	1.2	1.0	0.9	0.8
0.3	12.6	9.3	6.6	4.6	3.2	2.3	1.7	1.4	1.2	1.0	0.9
0.31	13.9	10.4	7.5	5.3	3.7	2.7	2.0	1.6	1.3	1.2	1.1
0.32	15.3	11.6	8.4	5.9	4.2	3.1	2.3	1.8	1.5	1.3	1.2
0.33	16.8	12.8	9.4	6.7	4.8	3.5	2.6	2.1	1.7	1.5	1.4
0.34	18.4	14.1	10.4	7.5	5.4	3.9	3.0	2.3	2.0	1.7	1.5
0.35	20.0	15.4	11.5	8.3	6.0	4.4	3.3	2.6	2.2	1.9	1.7

Table A2 (Cont'd)
CHOOSING RANDOM VALUES

Fractional Distance	Asymmetry Ratio:										
	1	0.9	0.8	0.7	0.6	0.5	0.4	0.3	0.2	0.1	0.0
0.36	21.7	16.9	12.7	9.3	6.7	5.0	3.8	3.0	2.5	2.1	1.9
0.37	23.4	18.4	13.9	10.2	7.5	5.5	4.2	3.3	2.8	2.4	2.1
0.38	25.2	20.0	15.2	11.3	8.3	6.2	4.7	3.7	3.1	2.7	2.4
0.39	27.1	21.6	16.6	12.4	9.2	6.9	5.2	4.2	3.4	3.0	2.6
0.4	29.0	23.3	18.0	13.6	10.1	7.6	5.8	4.6	3.8	3.3	2.9
0.41	30.9	25.0	19.6	14.8	11.1	8.4	6.4	5.1	4.2	3.6	3.2
0.42	32.9	26.9	21.1	16.1	12.2	9.2	7.1	5.7	4.7	4.0	3.5
0.43	35.0	28.7	22.8	17.5	13.3	10.1	7.8	6.2	5.1	4.4	3.8
0.44	37.1	30.7	24.5	18.9	14.5	11.1	8.6	6.8	5.7	4.8	4.2
0.45	39.2	32.6	26.2	20.4	15.7	12.1	9.4	7.5	6.2	5.3	4.5
0.46	41.3	34.6	28.0	22.0	17.0	13.1	10.2	8.2	6.8	5.8	4.9
0.47	43.5	36.7	29.9	23.6	18.4	14.2	11.1	8.9	7.4	6.3	5.4
0.48	45.6	38.8	31.8	25.3	19.8	15.4	12.1	9.7	8.0	6.8	5.8
0.49	47.8	40.9	33.8	27.1	21.3	16.7	13.1	10.6	8.7	7.4	6.3
0.5	50.0	43.0	35.8	28.9	22.9	18.0	14.2	11.5	9.5	8.0	6.8
0.51	52.2	45.2	37.8	30.7	24.5	19.3	15.3	12.4	10.3	8.7	7.4
0.52	54.4	47.3	39.9	32.6	26.1	20.8	16.5	13.4	11.1	9.4	7.9
0.53	56.5	49.5	42.0	34.6	27.9	22.2	17.7	14.4	12.0	10.1	8.6
0.54	58.7	51.7	44.1	36.6	29.6	23.8	19.0	15.5	12.9	10.9	9.2
0.55	60.8	53.9	46.3	38.6	31.5	25.4	20.4	16.7	13.8	11.7	9.9
0.56	62.9	56.1	48.5	40.7	33.4	27.0	21.8	17.9	14.9	12.6	10.6
0.57	65.0	58.3	50.7	42.8	35.3	28.8	23.3	19.1	15.9	13.5	11.3
0.58	67.1	60.4	52.9	44.9	37.3	30.5	24.8	20.4	17.1	14.5	12.1
0.59	69.1	62.5	55.1	47.1	39.3	32.3	26.4	21.8	18.2	15.5	13.0
0.6	71.0	64.7	57.2	49.2	41.4	34.2	28.1	23.2	19.5	16.5	13.8
0.61	72.9	66.7	59.4	51.4	43.5	36.2	29.8	24.7	20.7	17.6	14.7
0.62	74.8	68.8	61.6	53.6	45.6	38.1	31.6	26.3	22.1	18.8	15.7
0.63	76.6	70.8	63.7	55.8	47.8	40.1	33.4	27.9	23.5	20.0	16.7
0.64	78.3	72.7	65.9	58.0	49.9	42.2	35.3	29.5	24.9	21.2	17.8
0.65	80.0	74.6	67.9	60.2	52.1	44.3	37.2	31.3	26.4	22.5	18.9
0.66	81.6	76.5	70.0	62.4	54.4	46.4	39.2	33.0	28.0	23.9	20.0
0.67	83.2	78.3	72.0	64.6	56.6	48.6	41.2	34.9	29.6	25.3	21.2
0.68	84.7	80.0	74.0	66.7	58.8	50.8	43.2	36.7	31.3	26.8	22.5
0.69	86.1	81.7	75.9	68.8	61.0	53.0	45.3	38.7	33.0	28.3	23.8
0.7	87.4	83.2	77.7	70.9	63.2	55.2	47.5	40.7	34.8	29.9	25.1

Table A2 (Cont'd)
CHOOSING RANDOM VALUES

Fractional Distance	Asymmetry Ratio:										
	1	0.9	0.8	0.7	0.6	0.5	0.4	0.3	0.2	0.1	0.0
0.71	88.7	84.8	79.5	73.0	65.4	57.5	49.7	42.7	36.7	31.6	26.5
0.72	89.8	86.2	81.3	75.0	67.6	59.7	51.9	44.8	38.6	33.3	28.0
0.73	90.9	87.6	83.0	76.9	69.8	62.0	54.1	46.9	40.6	35.1	29.6
0.74	92.0	88.9	84.5	78.8	71.9	64.2	56.4	49.1	42.6	36.9	31.2
0.75	92.9	90.1	86.1	80.6	74.0	66.5	58.7	51.3	44.7	38.8	32.8
0.76	93.8	91.3	87.5	82.4	76.0	68.7	61.0	53.6	46.8	40.8	34.6
0.77	94.6	92.3	88.9	84.1	78.0	70.9	63.3	55.9	49.0	42.8	36.3
0.78	95.4	93.3	90.2	85.7	79.9	73.1	65.6	58.2	51.2	44.9	38.2
0.79	96.1	94.2	91.4	87.2	81.8	75.2	67.9	60.5	53.5	47.0	40.1
0.8	96.7	95.0	92.5	88.7	83.6	77.3	70.2	62.9	55.9	49.3	42.1
0.81	97.2	95.8	93.5	90.1	85.3	79.4	72.4	65.3	58.2	51.5	44.2
0.82	97.7	96.4	94.4	91.3	87.0	81.4	74.7	67.6	60.6	53.9	46.4
0.83	98.1	97.0	95.3	92.5	88.5	83.3	76.9	70.0	63.1	56.2	48.6
0.84	98.5	97.6	96.1	93.6	90.0	85.1	79.1	72.4	65.5	58.7	50.9
0.85	98.8	98.0	96.8	94.6	91.4	86.9	81.2	74.8	68.0	61.2	53.3
0.86	99.1	98.4	97.4	95.5	92.7	88.6	83.3	77.1	70.5	63.7	55.8
0.87	99.3	98.8	97.9	96.3	93.8	90.2	85.3	79.4	73.0	66.3	58.3
0.88	99.5	99.1	98.4	97.1	94.9	91.7	87.2	81.7	75.6	69.0	61.0
0.89	99.6	99.3	98.7	97.7	95.9	93.0	89.0	83.9	78.1	71.7	63.7
0.9	99.7	99.5	99.1	98.2	96.7	94.3	90.7	86.1	80.6	74.4	66.5
0.91	99.8	99.7	99.3	98.7	97.5	95.5	92.3	88.2	83.0	77.1	69.4
0.92	99.9	99.8	99.5	99.1	98.1	96.5	93.8	90.2	85.5	79.9	72.4
0.93	99.9	99.9	99.7	99.4	98.7	97.4	95.2	92.0	87.8	82.7	75.5
0.94	100.0	99.9	99.8	99.6	99.1	98.1	96.4	93.8	90.1	85.4	78.7
0.95	100.0	100.0	99.9	99.8	99.4	98.8	97.5	95.4	92.3	88.2	82.0
0.96	100.0	100.0	100.0	99.9	99.7	99.3	98.4	96.8	94.4	90.9	85.4
0.97	100.0	100.0	100.0	99.9	99.9	99.6	99.1	98.0	96.3	93.5	88.9
0.98	100.0	100.0	100.0	100.0	100.0	99.9	99.6	99.0	97.9	96.0	92.5
0.99	100.0	100.0	100.0	100.0	100.0	100.0	99.9	99.7	99.2	98.3	96.2
1	100.0	100.0	100.0	100.0	100.0	100.0	100.0	100.0	100.0	100.0	100.0

Index